JACINDA ARDERN

A NEW KIND OF LEADER

MADELEINE CHAPMAN

The History Press

For Uncle Fata, who would have been the first to read this and the first to brag about it. Sooole.

Contents

Prologue

19 October 2017

Jacinda Ardern did not want to be prime minister. 'I've seen how hard it is to raise a family in that role,' she explained in 2014. A year later, she stated it more bluntly: 'I don't want to be prime minister.' Whether this was simply a party line or a more firmly held personal one, it sounded convincing.

So perhaps it surprised Ardern, more than anyone else, that on a bright, spring afternoon in 2017 she was waiting to find out if she would become Prime Minister of New Zealand.

Her political ascent had been steady then rapid. First elected in 2008, she was at the time the youngest sitting MP. Just nine years later she was the leader of the opposition. At the start of 2017 Ardern had still seemed like a team player with a long career ahead of her. Then a fellow MP resigned and she took over his seat. Two weeks later the deputy leader stepped down and she took over from her. A mere five months after that, when the party leader resigned, Ardern stepped up and took the job – one she claimed she'd never wanted.

At that point she had just seven weeks to turn around Labour's terrible polling and win the election. Her debut speech as leader led to a surge in support for the party – and with a campaign featuring an open commitment to action on climate change and a lot of Facebook Live videos, Ardern lifted the Labour Party from their worst polling in decades to winning enough votes to potentially form a government.

But to do so they had to form a coalition – and that meant negotiating with New Zealand First, who held nine seats. Winston Peters, the leader of New Zealand First, in the role of kingmaker for the third time in his political career, had spent several weeks in negotiations with both Labour and National (who had won more votes but still needed his party in order to govern). If he chose to go with Labour and their fellow left Green Party, they'd form a coalition minority government. But when he stepped up to the microphone Labour still had no idea which way his vote would go. Peters had played his cards close to his chest.

Surrounded by staff in her office, Ardern watched her television like everyone else as Peters addressed the nation, describing his difficulty in making the decision. He was the political Bachelor, idly twirling his final rose.

When he finally announced that he'd chosen Labour, Ardern's office erupted. A bottle of whisky was opened and Ardern poured for everyone except herself.

Her morning sickness hadn't kicked in yet, but it would. Just six days earlier, three weeks after the election – and in the middle of negotiations with New Zealand First – Ardern had found out she was pregnant with her first child.

She'd be combining parenthood with political high office after all.

After nine years of saying she didn't want to be in charge and seven weeks of saying she did, 37-year-old Jacinda Ardern became the fortieth Prime Minister of New Zealand.

From Murupara to Morrinsville

The photograph from 1985 shows two smiling girls in a trailer with a dozen other neighbourhood kids. One of the girls has light blonde hair, the other brown. They sport impressive mullets and are the only white faces in the group.

Jacinda Ardern and her older sister, Louise, grew up in Murupara, a small forestry town in the middle of New Zealand's North Island. The population of 2000 was over-whelmingly indigenous, so the girls' schoolmates were predominantly Māori.

Jacinda Kate Laurell Ardern was born on 26 July 1980 in Hamilton, but her first memories were formed here, in Murupara, where the family moved when Jacinda was five. Her father, Ross, was posted there as a police officer. Murupara was a tough area. The Tribesmen – a newly formed motorcycle gang – ran the town, and the privatisa-tion of the forestry industry had seen many locals end up on the dole. The Arderns lived in front of the police station, and Jacinda witnessed no shortage of poverty and violence in her time there. Jacinda has said her early childhood shaped her as a politician. 'If it's possible to begin building your social conscience when you are a small child,' she said, 'then that is what happened to me.'

Of course, as a five-year-old, Jacinda didn't see kids without shoes and think of the privatisation of primary industries and the collapse of central government. She just saw kids without shoes and thought it was unfair. 'I never viewed the world through the lens of politics then, and in many ways still don't,' she would later say. 'Instead, I try to view it through the lens of children, people, and the most basic concept of fairness.'

As a child, Jacinda was relatively insulated from the injustice around her in Murupara. Her family were financially better off than most of their neighbours. But as Ross was a police officer, some of the locals weren't fans of the family. Bottles were thrown at the Arderns' house, and altercations occurred outside the station.

One day, Jacinda ventured out the back gate to walk to the shops and stumbled upon her dad surrounded by a group of men who clearly weren't happy. Ross was talking to them calmly, trying to deescalate the situation. He spotted Jacinda, frozen on the spot. 'Run along, Jacinda. It's all right,' he told her, before turning his attention back to the men. It was just a moment, but his approach to conflict stayed with her. Years later, as an MP, Jacinda would be known for her diplomacy when dealing with colleagues and opponents alike.

Although Jacinda's family moved away from Murupara when she was eight, she has strong memories of her time there. The many, many jobs lost. The neighbour who died and who she later learned had committed suicide. The babysitter who turned yellow one day from hepatitis and didn't babysit anymore. It wasn't political, it was just unfair.

***

In 1987, Jacinda's parents announced the family was moving. To the big city? No, to Morrinsville.

Morrinsville wasn't a metropolis, but it was bigger and broader than Murupara – more of a microcosm of the country as a whole, with wealth and poverty close neighbours. Families that owned large, successful dairy farms lived around the corner from recently arrived refugees. The largest, fanciest establishment was the Morrinsville Golf Club, which shared a border with the Ardern family home. The house – a Lockwood design, constructed without nails – had been built by Jacinda's grandfather.

To earn pocket money, Jacinda kept the family fruit stall stocked. Golfers heading down the fairway over the back fence could buy an apple for 20 cents, slotting their coins into the honesty box. Beyond the green, Mount Te Aroha sat in the distance, snow on its peak.

In Morrinsville, there was poverty, but it was not so explicit as it had been in Murupara. Still, Jacinda had developed a keen eye for unfairness and at Morrinsville Intermediate she found a way to channel her energy: the Student Council.

At meetings held in the staffroom, young council members, aged between eleven and thirteen, aired their concerns about the inflating price of juicies, a frozen drink snack, or their scepticism over safety concerns that prohibited them from riding their bikes the last 50 metres to school. The issues were presented seriously enough, but the earnestness of the young council members' delivery masked the fact that most students applied to the council for one reason and one reason only: to get out of class for a period.

Except, that is, for the council president, Jacinda Ardern. Jacinda genuinely saw herself as the voice of her peers, representing them in a democratic system, a concept that had almost certainly never crossed her peers' minds. Once the half-hearted juicie complaints had been voiced, Jacinda got down to business. Having done some independent research into local charities and their funding situations, she proposed (read: decided) which one to support with the funds raised from the school's next mufti day. Her fellow council members nodded along to her proposal in solemn agreement. Jacinda was very good at being in charge.

Jacinda's interest in student politics from a young age didn't appear to be the work of overzealous parents, and the sentiments she conveyed weren't parroted: they were genuine. Even as a twelve-year-old, Jacinda had a spontaneous and genuine interest in advocacy.

At Morrinsville College, four years later, the issues were somewhat more substantial. The Board of Trustees had to weigh up the matter of shorts: for girls, that is. Jacinda, now seventeen and the sole student representative on the Board, argued passionately for girls to have the option of wearing shorts. As it stood, the uniform was skirts for the girls, shorts or pants for the boys, and collared shirts for everyone. Jacinda seemed to be on a mission to overhaul the uniform entirely, having successfully argued the previous year for a redesign of the shirts. Staff wanted students to tuck their shirts in and the students didn't want to. So Jacinda had put a proposal to the Board for new shirts to be introduced that were designed to be worn untucked. She convinced them and oversaw the change.

The Board, mostly men, were used to having a student representative present at meetings, but never before had that student been so vocal or so effective. It was strange. Jacinda would come to the meetings, held outside school hours, with notes prepared, and argue at length about numerous issues. She was animated and engaged the entire time. It was almost like she *wanted* to be there. That wasn't just unusual for a girl from Morrinsville in the '90s, it was weird for any kid, anywhere.

Beyond her success in Board meetings, Jacinda excelled in a year group that was particularly high-achieving. She wasn't Head Girl; that was Virginia Dawson, who, after stints at Oxfam and UNICEF, is now the Head of Development Co-operation at the New Zealand Embassy in Myanmar. Jacinda chose instead to focus her efforts on being the student representative. She knew that was where the power to make real change lay. Years later, we would see an echo of this, when – as a thirty-something MP – she insisted on numerous occasions that she did not want to be prime minister because she believed she could have more impact as a minister instead.

Morrinsville is a dairy farming town. It proudly claims to have the most cows per hectare in the world. At its busiest, the town's Fonterra factory processes over one million litres of milk per day. Two hours south of Auckland and a non-descript left turn off State Highway 1, the road narrows on the way to Morrinsville. Mobile phone coverage drops out but eventually returns. In her 2008 maiden speech to parliament, refuting claims that she was 'radical', Jacinda said: 'My answer to that is very simple. I'm from Morrinsville. Where I come from, a radical is someone who chooses to drive a Toyota rather than a Holden or a Ford.'

In Morrinsville, Ross Ardern was one of two local officers, before working in Hamilton as a detective.

Jacinda's mother, Laurell, worked in the Morrinsville College cafeteria. She had given up a job in office administration to raise Jacinda and Louise. According to students at Morrinsville College at the time, no culinary favours were afforded the Ardern sisters despite their connection to cafeteria staff.

The Matamata-Piāko farming district is traditionally a blue (National) area, and Morrinsville is one of many rural towns in New Zealand to reliably vote National, the country's largest conservative party, at every general election. Students of Morrinsville College in the '90s had grown up with David Lange as prime minister. A Labour man, Lange was an exceptional orator and an otherwise popular prime minister, most famous for his anti-nuclear stance and for quipping that he could 'smell the uranium' on the breath of his opponent during a debate around nuclear weapons on British television. He was a star for politically minded teenagers all over New Zealand, but in the corridors of Morrinsville College he was the enemy, because that was the talk students overheard at their family dinner tables. The Ardern dinner table was a local anomaly: Laurell Ardern came from a family of staunch Labour supporters.

Jacinda began at Morrinsville College in 1994. It was the only local choice for secondary schooling, though some of the wealthier parents sent their kids to schools in Hamilton, 30 kilometres away. At Morrinsville College, each year group had between seventy and 100 students: essentially every teenager in the town went there. The make-up of the student population mirrored that of Morrinsville as a whole: largely Pākehā, with a growing Māori population, a strong Indian community through the farming industry, a number of Cambodian refugee families who had been placed there upon arrival in New Zealand, and, according to students and staff there at the time, not a single Pacific Islander.

Everyone knew everyone in Morrinsville. And they knew who your family was. For Jacinda, that meant she and Louise were seen as a pair. Louise was considered a bit 'cooler' than Jacinda, which roughly translates as 'less earnestly enthusiastic about student politics'. Since then, Louise has managed, quite impressively, to go largely unremarked upon in the New Zealand media. Although she's the only sibling of the prime minister with the greatest name recognition around the world, Louise Ardern remains an enigma.

Jacinda might not have been cool, but she wasn't *uncool*, an important distinction that many former classmates are quick to make. She did lots of things that teenagers would deem uncool. She was the Board of Trustees student representative for not one year but two, a feat never before seen and never repeated. She participated in debating. She entered, and won, speech competitions. She didn't drink alcohol. A decade later Jacinda would be known as the cool, young politician who could engage thousands of followers on social media and was a DJ on the side, but at school, by all definitions she was a nerd. A successful and well-liked nerd, but a nerd nonetheless.

If her fellow students remember her at all, they describe her as 'nice', which is damning with faint praise. For a lot of people, being referred to as 'nice' equates to being considered boring. And maybe she was a bit. There are people who went to Morrinsville College in the same year as Jacinda who have no distinct memories of her at all. Unsurprisingly, it's the staff who remember her the most: since she was a student representative, debater and speech-giver, they heard the most from Jacinda while she was at school. And of all the staff, no one was more instrumental in Jacinda's life than Gregor Fountain.

Mr Fountain began teaching at Morrinsville College in 1995 as a 22-year-old. Fresh out of teachers' college in Christchurch, after growing up in Wellington, he took a step into the rural unknown in moving to Morrinsville. Students remember him for his interactive style as a social studies and history teacher. He often made the class re-enact historical moments instead of simply reading about them. When teaching a class about Gandhi, he dressed up as the Indian activist, an approach that perhaps wouldn't fly so well in 2020 as it did in 1995, but was nonetheless effective. He was interested in local politics and activism and was proudly liberal in an overwhelmingly conservative school. Barely older than the students he was teaching, and bringing with him his liberal 'city' sensibilities and enthusiasm, Mr Fountain was an immediate hit. And particularly with fourteen-year-old Jacinda Ardern.

Not only did Mr Fountain have similar interests to politically engaged students, he had a lot of knowledge he was willing to pass on to any students who showed an appetite for it. Speaking to Mark Sainsbury shortly before the 2017 election, Ardern recalled that Mr Fountain had taught her 'to question the basis of all my opinions. Why do you think that? Where did it come from? He was my teacher when I found out how to think.'

Mr Fountain taught general history but also made a point of teaching a fuller version of New Zealand's history. In New Zealand, as in other colonised countries, the history most often taught is that of the colonisers. In this version, adventurous Captain Cook discovered New Zealand and signed a treaty with the indigenous Māori people (The

Treaty of Waitangi/Te Tiriti o Waitangi) so that Europeans and Māori could live peacefully alongside each other. The more accurate but less commonly conveyed history is full of conflict and violence and the attempted genocide of the New Zealand Wars that were waged between Māori and Europeans for ownership of the land. Mr Fountain introduced both versions to his students, and some, like Jacinda, were hooked.

It was timely. In 1995, the Crown formally apologised to Waikato-Tainui as part of a Deed of Settlement for the lands that were unjustly confiscated during the New Zealand Wars. Jacinda was fifteen at the time and in Mr Fountain's history class: she wanted to know more. Years later, Mr Fountain recalled her searching for guidance and understanding of the region and country she lived in. 'She was someone who was looking for and developing a set of values to guide her. I remember having a conversation with her about the Tainui settlement ... and thinking she was someone a bit different. She really wanted to get her head around the whole thing.'

In Jacinda's search for values she found that she shared many with Mr Fountain. He set up a number of social activism groups at Morrinsville College and Jacinda was an enthusiastic member of all of them. One of these was the Human Rights Action Group, established in 1997, with Fountain as the supervising teacher. Like most school activism groups, it didn't change the world but members were at least vocal in their attempts. They wrote letters denouncing human rights violations in other countries, and supported prisoners of conscience. The group even held a Fax-a-Fascist day, inviting students to write letters to fascist leaders around the world denouncing their actions.

In the 1997 yearbook, the Human Rights Action Group photo shows twenty-six members, with Mr Fountain front and centre, Head Girl Virginia Dawson (a close friend of Jacinda's) to his immediate right and Jacinda to his left. A number of people pictured in that photo have no recollection of a) being in the group, or b) the group's existence. One student remembers Mr Fountain rounding up random students to be in the photo and inflate the group's numbers. In reality, most of the 'action' in the Human Rights Action Group was undertaken by the three members in the middle of the front row.

But Mr Fountain was popular. Enrolments in history classes at Morrinsville College increased during his time there, and not because of a sudden love for the subject. However, he was never going to stay in Morrinsville long. He was a big fish in a small pond and, like Jacinda, was destined for greater things. He taught Jacinda in each of his three years at the college and left after the 1997 school year to teach at a private school in Hamilton. He went on to work at a number of schools around the country and in 2018 became the principal at Wellington College, his own alma mater and one of the most prestigious state schools in New Zealand. One of his first moves as principal was to research and establish a set of school values.

When Gregor Fountain left Morrinsville College, Jacinda still had one more year of schooling left, but he maintains that he already knew Jacinda would go far. 'I absolutely thought she was someone who would change the world.'

But before she set about changing the world, Jacinda worked to change her small town – by leading SADD (Students Against Driving Drunk). In rural towns all over the world, drink driving is a problem. No public transport at night, minimal police presence, and not a lot to do: it all comes together to result in casual driving under the influence and, if luck is on their side and nothing worse happens, the occasional car through a farm fence. The SADD group at Morrinsville College advocated about the issue and even staged a dramatic re-enactment of a car crash on the school field in an attempt to discourage students (and the wider community) from driving drunk. But it wasn't all just messaging. Jacinda didn't drink, so she took it upon herself to ensure that her friends who did stayed safe. After the school ball in 1997, acting as both student rep and SADD member, Jacinda organised buses for students to get home. If they missed the bus, she drove them home herself.

A decade later, as a member of parliament, Jacinda would be criticised for being a 'career politician', meaning she had only ever worked in politics and never as a 'regular' New Zealander. It remains a fair comparison: many politicians had full careers in other professions before going into politics. It overlooks one thing though. While Jacinda never worked outside politics as an adult, as a teenager she had the most Kiwi of jobs imaginable: working the Friday night shift at the local fish'n'chip shop. After school on Friday, while her classmates were getting drunk in a field somewhere, Jacinda worked the busiest shift of the week at the Golden Kiwi.

The Golden Kiwi, technically a takeaway shop, specialised in the national food of fried fish and chips. The shop opened in 1963 and was owned by the Covich family. Thirty years later, son Grant, who still runs the business today, gave fourteen-year-old Jacinda a job, after she dropped off her CV with her mum. The Golden Kiwi harks back to days of old in its refusal to refurbish. Long after most fish'n'chip shops became exclusively takeaway, the Morrinsville shop kept its original wire seating, chequered cloths and table service. It was young Jacinda's job to take orders, serve food to diners, and wrap orders for the takeaway customers. Acutely aware of her daughter's inexperience, Laurell bought half a head of cabbage and instructed Jacinda to practise wrapping it at home.

Working at a fish'n'chip shop has come to serve Jacinda well, for in New Zealand nothing says 'of the people' more than having served the people deep-fried food wrapped in newspaper.

Jacinda's school years in Morrinsville stand out not for how extraordinary she was, but rather for the opposite. She did well academically but wasn't considered a genius, worked part-time for a local establishment, and, according to virtually everyone in Morrinsville when asked about her, 'never put a foot wrong'.

Flick through her school yearbooks and Jacinda's name features heavily. Debate team, speech competition winner, writing competition runner up, science competition winner. There's a Board of Trustees rep blurb featuring a headshot of Jacinda wearing sunglasses and blonde streaks in her hair. Not cool, but not *uncool*.

The one surprising entry is Jacinda's inclusion in a senior basketball team photo. Were it revealed that prime minister Jacinda Ardern was also a star athlete in her youth, not many people would question it, such is her reputation for overachievement. But sports seemed to be her equaliser. Perhaps her ability to deftly coordinate the many viewpoints of the student body as a Board of Trustees representative came at the expense of her ability to deftly coordinate her own limbs. The basketball team was a social one, and some doubles work with Louise on the badminton court wasn't exactly reminiscent of Venus and Serena. But she played with full enthusiasm and earnestness, and would go on to be a vocal supporter of increasing girls' participation in sports. Enthusiasm and earnestness, two qualities so often frowned upon by the desperately nonchalant New Zealand psyche, and two that Jacinda displayed in spades even as a teenager.

At a Board of Trustees meeting in 1998, seventeen-year-old Jacinda argued on behalf of Morrinsville College students that girls should be allowed to wear shorts if they wanted to. She herself was happy to wear a skirt, but that was beside the point. Jacinda was the voice of the students and she took her role seriously. If that was the change the people wanted, she would work hard for it. After a number of long Board meetings, she convinced the parent and staff representatives of a traditional rural college to change the school uniform for the second time in two years. Jacinda never did wear shorts to school, but visit Morrinsville College today and you'll see a number of girls do.

At the end of 1998, as Jacinda and her classmates packed up their lockers and prepared for the real world, everyone voted on a list of character titles and predictions. Funniest, best dressed, friendliest, best couple. Not every student received an accolade and only three predictions were made. Jeremy Habgood was predicted to be the first to become a millionaire. The most likely to succeed was Head Girl Virginia Dawson.

And most likely to become prime minister? Jacinda Ardern, of course.

2

Leaving the Church

There was one other thing that set Jacinda Ardern apart from many of her schoolmates: her religion. Raised in the Church of Latter-Day Saints, Jacinda and Louise went to church on Sundays. Mormon kids weren't allowed to drink alcohol, smoke or play sport on Sundays – in sport-loving New Zealand, it was the latter that was often the giveaway of Mormonism. That, and what they wore on mufti days. Mufti days have always been a chance for kids to show off their best gear. In 1980s Morrinsville, that meant Starter jackets and Origin jeans. But for those who came from more religious families, it was long skirts. Long skirts and no Coke, because the Mormon church considered caffeine a drug: it was out of the question for the Ardern kids.

Apart from these almost 'quirky' habits, being Mormon was never near the top of the list of descriptors for Jacinda. Had her classmates paid more attention, they may have found a connection between her lack of enthusiasm for partying and dating and the conservative beliefs of the church. But Jacinda's social inclinations seemed inherent rather than learned, as if her natural sensibilities just happened to work within the church's teachings rather than being dictated by them. Louise was perhaps the more stereotypical Mormon teenager: she broke the rules regularly, arguing with her parents and threatening to run away from home. It seems as if Jacinda felt more naturally comfortable with the demands of the church, though she has never talked about it. She did, however, dye her hair and pierce her nose, two unusual style choices for an earnest Mormon teenager with a love for student politics. Rebellion manifests in many forms.

Known for its door-knocking missionary activities, the Church of Jesus Christ of Latter-Day Saints, started by Joseph Smith in the United States in the 1820s, is a comparatively new religion. Often associated with the fundamentalist practice of polygamy, Mormonism in New Zealand is seen as a thinly connected branch of Christianity, most notable for its condemnation of sexual relations outside of marriage and same-sex relations full stop. According to her own recollections and those of friends, Jacinda's decision to leave the Mormon church was gradual. Always socially liberal, Jacinda's beliefs around LGBTQIA+ rights never aligned with those of the church. Historically, the Mormon church believed homosexuality to be a curable disease and sought to 'convert' its gay members to heterosexuality. Only as recently as 2018 did the church announce it would no longer actively attempt to change members' sexual orientation. However, its stance is still firmly anti-LGBTQIA+. Of course, it's not unusual for members of a particular religion to subscribe to some but not all beliefs and practices. But Mormonism is not a religion for casual believers. You are either all in or all out. And when it comes to sexuality, those who 'choose' to be gay are all the way out, whether they want to be or not. Eventually, it was this that would prove to be a catalyst for Jacinda leaving the church.

★★★

After school, Ardern moved away from Morrinsville to the University of Waikato in Hamilton, where she spent three years studying a bachelor of communications, with a semester abroad at Arizona State University. Nowhere is New Zealand's drinking culture stronger than at university. But as an undergraduate Ardern was still very much a practising Mormon; she didn't drink and was otherwise studious. Consequently, her time at Waikato seems to have been unremarkable – no photos, videos or stories of student debauchery have come to light. She was still close to home (the campus was in Hamilton and she commuted the thirty minutes from Morrinsville) so university was essentially an extension of college rather than a whole new world.

It wasn't until she moved to Wellington, a bleeding-heart liberal metropolis compared to Morrinsville, that Ardern really encountered a world more diverse than the one she was born and raised in. And some things in this new world caused her to question her faith, particularly as she interacted more and more with out and proud members of the gay community – especially in her work within Young Labour, a youth wing that had spent decades supporting the rights of the LGBTQIA+ community.

Ardern had volunteered for Labour MP Harry Duynhoven's 1996 campaign for the New Plymouth electoral seat while she was still at Morrinsville College. Her aunt, Marie Ardern, a longtime Labour supporter, had put her in touch with his office. After graduating from the University of Waikato in 2001, Ardern found work

with the one Labour contact she had. Duynhoven was a
rank-and-file MP, so this wasn't the most glamorous move
for an aspiring Labour candidate, but it was a foot in the
door. Ardern was still there in 2003, as Duynhoven's private secretary advising on energy issues, when she caught
the attention of the Young Labour committee. They were
looking for fresh faces to join the leadership group and
Ardern's name was floated by committee member Tony
Milne, who'd befriended her and was telling anyone who'd
listen that one day she'd be prime minister. He wasn't very
convincing, but it was easier to sell the idea of Ardern as a
Young Labour leader. 'She's very good at her job,' he said.
'She worked for Harry Duynhoven, which is a bit weird,
but she's great. She's Mormon, which is also a bit weird for
a Young Labour member, but again: she's great. And she's
a woman.'

There weren't a lot of women running for anything in
Young Labour at that time, so everyone agreed that to find
not just a woman for the leadership team but an extremely
competent one, was a huge get. She was also 'cool' (the bar
for being considered cool being lower in politics than it is
in high school).

It didn't take much convincing from Milne for the
committee to elect Ardern. By all accounts, Ardern didn't
campaign for her own election, but Milne wouldn't have
nominated her without notice. Once within the leadership ranks of Young Labour, she set about organising events
and boosting community engagement. Her big project, for
which she did the vast majority of organising and preparation, was the Young Labour Clarion Tour. Beginning after
Christmas in 2004, ten Young Labour members drove a
minibus from the top of the North Island to the bottom of
the South Island, stopping in small towns along the way to

do community work: things like cleaning up beaches to help protect native birds, or distributing condoms to the public on New Year's Eve. They travelled to Whanganui, Levin, Nelson, Kaikōura, Ashburton, Balclutha and Invercargill. Nine days over the summer holiday period, and ten Young Labour members in their mid-twenties spent it sorting rubbish from recycling at the tip and promoting democracy in small town centres. Definitely not cool but not *uncool*.

At that time, Ardern had 'half-and-half' hair. The top layer was dyed the blondest of blondes, and underneath was dark. Was it her natural brown, or had it been dyed to almost black? No one is sure. But when tied in a ponytail, as it often was, there was a perfect line: light on top and dark underneath. Sure, it's not good form to discuss the physical attributes of female public figures, and really it's not important. Except it's hugely important because it means a current world leader rocked a half-and-half hairstyle frankly not that long ago.

A now-deleted video documenting the Clarion Tour of '04/'05 opens with Ardern and Milne jokingly explaining what Young Labour is all about, with Ardern delivering the punchline 'Meetings … oh, and teleconferences … did we mention social justice?' It's not embarrassing in a genuinely horrific way like the allegations that former British Prime Minister David Cameron put his penis inside the mouth of a dead pig while at Oxford University, or that Australian Prime Minister Scott Morrison drunkenly shat his pants at a McDonald's after his favourite rugby league team lost a grand final. It's embarrassing in a more acute sense: who among us has not tried very hard to look like they're not trying hard? Ardern trying something and not quite succeeding, even if it was something as insignificant as delivering a line in a video hardly anyone has seen, is

reassuringly comforting. Her backstory was otherwise
edging dangerously close to Theresa May territory. The
former British PM claimed the naughtiest thing she had
ever done was 'running through fields of wheat' as a child.
But while May's anecdote felt calculated, if Ardern said
her most rebellious act as a child was jumping a fence and
running through someone's field it would ring true.

Young Labour had strong LGBTQIA+ representation in both its membership and its committee, so equal
rights issues were often prominent in their campaigns.
When Ardern was twenty-four, the *Civil Union Act 2004*
was passed, affording same-sex couples the same rights and
obligations of marriage in every way apart from the name.
The bill was promoted by two Labour MPs and was treated
as a conscience vote: MPs did not have to vote along party
lines. Forty-five of the sixty-five votes in support of the bill
came from Labour MPs. Ardern's two worlds – her church
back home and the Labour Party, now a big part of her
life – collided. The church she had grown up in was vocally
against the bill. But at work, she and her colleagues (many
of them gay themselves) were in full support of equal rights
for everyone. Until this time, Ardern had refrained from
drinking, even while working in the notoriously boozy
halls of parliament. She never passed judgement on those
who did drink – nor on those who smoked or took part
in any number of other behaviours prohibited within the
church. She simply didn't join them.

In 2005, while working in Prime Minister Helen Clark's
office in the lead-up to the general election, Ardern shared
a flat on the central Wellington street The Terrace with three
colleagues, all of whom were gay. The Out Takes Gay &
Lesbian Film Festival that year featured *Latter Days*, a 2003
film about a gay Mormon who has to choose between his

sexuality and his faith. Ardern's flatmate and friend Milne recalls the film as rather forgettable, with a few moments of emotion but nothing too dramatic. However, when the lights came up at the end of the screening, he looked over and saw that Ardern was in tears. It was a turning point in her relationship with her faith.

Leaving a church as insular as the Latter-Day Saints isn't simply a matter of deciding to drink alcohol. Ardern's family, including more distant relatives, were and still are active members of the church. To leave is to separate, in one way or another, from the family and community in which you were raised. While she has rarely opened up about it, in 2016 she revealed she had yet to speak to her father about her decision to leave and offered only that her mum was 'very disappointed'. For something that played such a big part in her childhood and created an absence in adulthood, Ardern is notably reluctant to speak about her relationship, or lack thereof, with the Mormon church. She maintains that her emancipation from the church has not negatively affected her familial ties, and perhaps that is where the reluctance to speak publicly about it stems from. Nothing like disparate religious beliefs to shut down family dinner conversation. Better to simply ignore the differences of opinion and focus on what everyone can agree on. Speaking to *Stuff* shortly after becoming prime minister, Ardern was careful to point out that she parted ways with some of the church's beliefs, but not the people. 'I can't separate out who I am from the things that I was raised with,' she told a reporter in 2018. 'I took a departure from the theology, but otherwise I have only positive things to say about it.'

Ardern now identifies as agnostic: she often clarifies that she's open to others' beliefs but without her own. In May 2019, her aunt and uncle, both elders within the church, presented Ardern with her family genealogy in two volumes, and were hosted by the prime minister at the Beehive (where government sits) accompanied by Russell M. Nelson, the current president of the church. The meeting would have been significant for Ardern's family, but it wasn't unprecedented: other New Zealand prime ministers have hosted church leaders, including Nelson, at the Beehive.

There's no way of knowing if Ardern's move away from her family's church was at all politically motivated. Religion and social conservatism are not uncommon in parliament, but they are less common in those that sit left of centre. And even in a country with a broad religious landscape, to be a Mormon in parliament would typically be seen as limiting one's appeal to voters and outright alienating some.

Working within the Labour Party and being Mormon was always going to come to a head for Ardern. Making that decision years before entering the public eye as a Labour list MP, whether deliberate or not, worked out in her favour. Ardern being a member of a conservative church for well over half her life is now simply a fascinating aside and not considered a reflection of her as a person, her beliefs or her values. Whether or not she continues to be influenced by her religious upbringing outside of service and community, only she could say.

3

The Apprenticeship

Jacinda Ardern may have been kind and earnest, but she wasn't naive. She knew that in order to get opportunities in her political career, she had to impress the right people. And to do that, she had to meet them and develop working relationships with them. Ardern didn't form friendships around parliament for cynical reasons, but it would be foolish to believe they weren't without an element of strategy. After spending a short time in Harry Duynhoven's office, Ardern applied for a position in the office of Phil Goff, Minister of Justice and Foreign Affairs. With great references from within Labour, she got the job.

She didn't spend long there though, because she caught the attention of the prime minister. Helen Clark was coming to the end of her second term in government and facing a difficult election in 2005 against National Party leader Don Brash. Conscious of the need to appeal more to young voters, she brought Ardern into her office as a policy adviser and Young Labour connection. Being noticed and promoted by the prime minister was a big deal for Ardern;

she was only twenty-four and still a novice at party politics, but she was moving up fast. She was now Vice President of Young Labour and heavily involved in their work increasing Labour votes among 18- to 24-year-olds.

During the 2005 election campaign, Young Labour took it upon themselves to make Clark cool – or at least not *uncool*. After Brash delivered a race-baiting speech in Orewa in January 2004, there had been a massive surge of support for National in the polls. Brash had called for an end to what he considered the special privileges afforded Māori. In reality, Māori continue to be over-represented in crime, poor health outcomes and prison statistics, as well as having poorer educational outcomes and a higher poverty rate, but he hit a nerve: support for National increased from 28 to 45 per cent in the two weeks following this speech.

Both the candidates were older (Clark in her fifties and Brash in his sixties) but of the two, Brash deliberately courted the older vote. Brash had never been, and would never be, popular with young voters, and in an attempt to attack him in an accessible way, the Young Labour minds sharing a flat on The Terrace came up with a genius plan. They set up a number, 0800 BRASH, and posted it around Wellington, inviting the public to call in. Anyone calling the number would reach an automated voice instructing them to dial different numbers for various unpopular policies Brash was campaigning on. 'Press one to sell off state assets, press two to ...' It was effectively a voluntary prank call. And it worked. Hundreds of Wellingtonians called the number, which was in fact connected to the landline at Ardern's flat. It was shouted out on popular national radio programmes and soon the hundreds became thousands. The stunt was more successful than they could have imagined, except even Ardern, the master organiser, didn't think to plan for one thing: the phone bill. After the flurry of phone activity to their flat, the four friends, all junior Labour staffers, so not flush with cash, received a bill from their telephone company. The amount owing was in the thousands of dollars. They didn't have the budget to cover such an astronomical bill without forfeiting meals, so Ardern, ever the negotiator, managed to talk the phone company into massively reducing the rates and lowering the amount owed.

While she was worrying about the cost of the Young Labour campaign stunt, Ardern was also making the most of her time in Clark's office, soaking up the habits and techniques of the first woman to be elected prime minister in New Zealand. She wasn't in the office simply to learn, either. Clark had tasked her with putting together policy portfolios in a number of sectors for the election campaign. And it was here that Ardern's reputation as a policy wonk was born. She read everything and asked endless questions. And when the campaign began, she observed every speech, interaction and tactic to see what worked and what didn't.

No one could say which way the 2005 election would go. But as a young person in politics, just beginning her career, Ardern had some decisions to make. One thing she knew for certain was that once the excitement of the campaign and election night was over, she wanted to leave. Go overseas. Expand her horizons. At least for a little while. So when Labour secured a narrow victory on election night and Clark returned to her office on the ninth floor of the Beehive, Ardern headed for the airport.

Pākehā have few cultural traditions as strong as the university graduate pilgrimage to the UK. If they've been raised with any semblance of privilege, they live in London for at least a few years, often longer. In the early 2000s, between 15,000 and 20,000 New Zealanders per year moved to the UK on a mid- to long-term basis. Of them, the vast majority lived and worked in London. Living in London as a New Zealander is about the safest form of adventure one can have. UK work visas allow for two years of residence, rather than the usual one, and the lifestyle shift is minimal. The 'Kiwis in London' Facebook community page has over 80,000 members. Most find they've simply transplanted their home environment into a different, but really quite similar, city. Chances are you'll wind up living with someone who you met once at a street party in Dunedin. Ardern's move was no different.

But before she made it to the UK, in early 2006 Ardern started her time abroad in New York. She was only there for six months, and was unable to work under her travel visa, so spent time helping with a workers' rights campaign. She also volunteered at CHiPS, a soup kitchen in Park Slope, Brooklyn, making meatballs. This soup kitchen would eventually be mentioned in nearly every overseas profile of Ardern, because she referred to it in her maiden speech to parliament. Ardern volunteering in a New York soup kitchen was narrative gold. A young socialist who spent time in New York feeding the homeless: beautiful. It made for an easy throwaway line in international profiles of the 'new hope' in world politics. But cynicism aside, there is no doubt that Ardern did volunteer there, because she has never been known to lie.

As the months in New York ticked by with no money coming in, Ardern needed work. So she turned to the UK and applied for a job in Tony Blair's Cabinet Office as an adviser. She was almost disappointed when she got the gig. Blair was clearly on his way out by this stage, and was best-known for sending British troops to Iraq in 2003, for which he was accused of being a war criminal. So Ardern would have had ambiguous feelings about the role, but she needed the work. 'It was totally pragmatic. I wanted to live overseas,' she told a reporter in 2017. 'I wanted to have that time and experience abroad. I was doing amazing voluntary work that I loved, but I needed to live, so I took the job.'

Blair later visited New Zealand, in 2011, when Ardern was a Labour MP. She bought a ticket to his event, and copped some criticism for doing so. By then, there was consensus among the left-leaning that Blair had done more harm than good. Ardern attended and was unimpressed with the soft questions from Blair's interviewer. She'd wanted to hear his reasoning for some of his more unpopular political decisions. So when the audience Q&A began, Ardern asked Blair if he regretted his decision to go to war in 2003. 'Knowing what you know now, what would you have done differently?' she asked. 'I would have prepared to be there longer,' he replied. So perhaps it's not surprising that Ardern is quick to distance herself from her work in Blair's Cabinet Office.

However, Blair and Ardern have some things in common. Blair started in politics as a young MP too, entering parliament as a 30-year-old for the Labour Party. He was also suddenly promoted to party leader after an abrupt departure (in Blair's case, the shocking sudden death of John Smith, in 1994), and went on to win the 1997 election in a landslide victory for a party that had struggled in opposition for eighteen years. Blair repositioned the left-wing Labour Party as a more centrist party and promoted policies that would normally be seen on the right, like being tough on crime. He brought about the Third Way, a combining of right-wing economic policies with left-wing socialist ideals, essentially creating a centrist way of governing. The philosophy was popular, with Bill Clinton adopting it in America, but has since fallen out of favour, as the right moved further right with the likes of Bush, then Trump, May and Johnson. Ardern would repeatedly label herself a 'pragmatic idealist', perhaps the most centrist way of defining oneself without using the actual word.

But while she was in London, Ardern never worked directly with Blair. Instead, she worked alongside Sir William Sargent in the Cabinet Office and Department for Business and Enterprise, where she was an assistant director working on regulatory issues, and with Sir Ronnie Flanagan on a policing review. Not cool but not *uncool*.

On weekends, she travelled with her sister, who was also living in London; to the Netherlands and Scotland and, at the end of 2007, Argentina. The pair spent a month in Buenos Aires, learning Spanish and sharing a windowless room, with Ardern's bed being couch cushions on the floor. Almost everywhere they went, Ardern had friends – thanks to her involvement in the International Union of Socialist Youth (IUSY).

Ardern's first role within Young Labour was international secretary. The international part centred on Young Labour's inclusion in IUSY. Every Young Labour party in the world is a member, as well as other socially democratic parties. IUSY began in 1907 and was established as a way for socialist parties in developed countries to share their knowledge and methods with those in developing countries. Thousands of young people around the world were part of IUSY. For many, it meant being involved in youth politics in their own country, then having a fun trip to a conference in another country once a year. For most, IUSY involvement was minimal. But Ardern was a consummate politician and knew how to build relationships. By the time she moved to London, she had made connections with delegates from all over the world. In every country she and her sister travelled to, Ardern caught up with IUSY friends. It worked socially and it was effective politically. Ardern's friends would remember her when it came to making decisions concerning leadership.

As international secretary and therefore a New Zealand representative, Ardern was eligible for leadership roles within IUSY at both a regional (Asia–Pacific region) and global level.

Being a global union means delegates from particular countries and regions are regarded in much the same light as their national governments, rather than as individuals. In 2004, the Asia Pacific region was almost forgotten, with the European regions being most dominant. Delegates from New Zealand were greeted kindly by all, simply for the fact that New Zealand had remained largely inoffensive in its foreign relationships and delegates from there would often act as mediators in discussions between countries with a less-than-friendly history. Classic New Zealand, just wanting everyone to get along.

What New Zealand delegates, or any delegates from the Asia Pacific region, weren't known for was climbing the leadership ladder. More often than not, the IUSY president was from Europe, and these leaders often went on to become key cabinet ministers in their respective countries. Ardern served as the president of the Asia Pacific region and attended conferences around the world to discuss strategies and share knowledge.

In 2004, Ardern and Milne attended an IUSY Congress event in Hungary, where global political issues were discussed and delegates voted on motions according to their country's interests. The voting determined the outward stance of IUSY. The Congress events were all business, with only a few hundred delegates attending from around the world.

The IUSY World Festival, held every four years in a different location (think the Olympics for politics nerds) was another story altogether – more like a week-long party. In 2006, it was held in Alicante, Spain, and Ardern attended. Thousands of delegates flocked to the city, taking the opportunity to travel overseas under the guise of work. Workshops and lectures may have been held during the day, but the most important and most attended events on the timetable were at night.

The New Zealand delegates, however, didn't view it that way. A team of ten Young Labour members had spent a full year fundraising in order to get to Spain, and they intended to take the trip seriously. Unlike some of the European delegates whose travel costs were low, they actually attended the daytime lessons and made connections with delegates from more influential countries.

Many people don't develop networking skills until they're well into their careers, and some never quite get the hang of it. Even in politics, the profession where forming connections is most critical, some seasoned players struggle to network in a way that feels genuine. But even in her early twenties, Ardern was a natural. She was such a master networker that her friends and IUSY colleagues, and maybe even herself, never saw the ladder she was building with her friendliness and charm.

But in 2006, her work paid off. Having moved to London earlier that year, Ardern was deemed ineligible to be the New Zealand representative on the IUSY board as she was no longer working within New Zealand Young Labour. She was made aware of this by her IUSY colleagues and reluctantly set about finding someone within

Young Labour to nominate as her replacement. She found Kate Sutton, her regional vice president and successor as the Young Labour international secretary, having taken over once Ardern moved overseas.

The plan was for the IUSY board to meet in Alicante, where Ardern would step down from her position and nominate Sutton as her replacement. Instead, Ardern entered the meeting and emerged as the nominee for IUSY president in 2008, when the current president would step down (elections were every two years).

Conversations would have been had in the lead-up to that meeting, both with and without Ardern, and a consensus was evidently reached that her leadership was more important than the fine print of IUSY's governing rules. For someone to be unanimously championed like that was rare. But for a New Zealand delegate to win over the rest of the world, despite conflicting interests and ambitious delegates surrounding her, was unheard of. It was cause for celebration both for Ardern and for her friends in the New Zealand delegation. And somehow, among all the celebration, it was forgotten, or perhaps ignored, that Ardern had supposedly gone into the meeting to resign.

Promising a promotion to a friend and ending up appointed yourself is the move of a ruthless operator. But though Sutton was disappointed personally, she said she felt happy for Ardern and excited that New Zealand would have its first ever IUSY president. When sharing the news, Ardern appeared to be genuinely upset – not that she had successfully secured a hugely prestigious position, but that she had let her friend down.

Of course, there's no such thing as an accidental or unintentional presidential election. Ardern's rise to the top of IUSY was groundbreaking (she was the first New

Zealand president and only the second female president in IUSY's 100-year history), and must have taken years of work behind the scenes. That a fellow New Zealand delegate suffered a minor loss as a byproduct of her success was acceptable collateral damage. Few people would turn down the offer of such a significant leadership role in order to keep their word, but perhaps only Ardern could do so without ruining or seemingly even affecting her relationship with Sutton. In 2006, the smiling assassin was born.

Ardern returned to London with her position secure and went back to work. When she got a call from Phil Goff, asking her to run for Labour in the 2008 election, Ardern said no. This was the beginning of what would become a pattern in her political career: initially declining when asked to put herself forward for a position. When Goff asked a second time, she said yes.

Ardern was sworn in as president of the International Union of Socialist Youth at the beginning of 2008, as planned. She travelled to an IUSY conference for the official ceremony and in doing so, missed Tony Milne's wedding, where she was supposed to be his best woman. Milne didn't mind – he said he was very happy for her.

★★★

Six months prior to the 2008 general election, Labour's Wellington regional list of election contenders was leaked to *The Dominion Post*. The top five listed were the five sitting MPs Labour had in Wellington already, but the reporter expressed mild surprise at the sixth name on the list: Jacinda Ardern. Ardern had been in London for two years and was described only as 'a former staff member in

Helen Clark's Beehive office'. There had been no hint that Ardern planned to return for the election, let alone run as a candidate, yet she was placed higher on the list than other confirmed candidates.

When Labour's selection committee met in Auckland to work on the overall party list, Ardern was high on the agenda. She had a history of leadership within Young Labour and was about to become President of IUSY. It was widely agreed that she would make a welcome addition.

Paul Tolich, representing the unions, put Ardern's name forward. The unions play a heavy hand in the nominations both for the list and for leader. That Ardern had the faith of Tolich from her time in an energy minister's office (Duynhoven) and from coordinating the relationship between Labour and the unions during the 2005 Clark campaign was massive. Did Ardern know that Tolich would be a valuable voice on her side even as a young staffer? Almost certainly. Was it still surprising that she'd left such an impression that he'd remembered two years later and offered up a strong endorsement? Almost certainly.

To have the heavily male-dominated unions put forward a young woman felt like progress. Clark, then prime minister and present at the meeting, also thought highly of Ardern and agreed that she should be given a generous debut list placing.

The Labour list is sorted by regions. And while the diplomatic approach would be to insist that there are strong candidates put forward every election from each region, Auckland and Wellington most often present the greatest number of qualified or experienced candidates. A hopeful candidate may receive a regional list ranking of fourth in Auckland when, if they'd been based in the South Island, they would have ranked first.

Ardern, who grew up in the Waikato but had lived most recently in Wellington, had to decide where she would run. Or rather, Ardern's friends and advisers still in New Zealand, like Tolich, had to determine where she'd be most useful. Though she'd appeared on the leaked Wellington list, there was no shortage of valuable candidates in the capital. It was decided that Ardern would be better placed in Waikato.

At the Labour meeting, Tolich assured Clark and the other attendees that Ardern was waiting in the wings and that they'd set the stage for her arrival. He made a strong case, but it was helped by the fact that Labour still needed more women.

Clark knew that all too well. In 1981, when Clark first entered parliament, politics after hours was all whisky and cards, and only boys allowed. Clark succeeded within the party despite her gender disadvantage, and wanted to make sure that the women following in her footsteps would have a fairer go. During her time as prime minister, the number of female Labour MPs increased greatly but Labour women still weren't winning electorate seats – they were getting into parliament on the list. When Labour was in government they were able to bring MPs in from deep on their list and thus present a party with a respectable gender balance. But Labour did not expect to win the 2008 election. After three increasingly unpopular terms in government, polling suggested New Zealand wanted change. And if Labour MP numbers dropped, women – from the list – would be the first to go.

Even within Clark's cabinet, only five of twenty ministers were women in 2005. At most, in 1999, she'd had seven women in her cabinet. The number of women in parliament overall had slowly increased since then, but their positions were not ones of power or longevity.

When Sutton was elected to the Labour board in 2006, she ran on a campaign of 50/50 gender balance for Labour MPs. Senior Labour Party members had been told to keep an eye out for promising women who could join the ranks. But as with any attempt to bring diversity (as incredible as it is to consider a woman a diversity hire) into an institution, there was pushback and suspicion that unqualified candidates would be promoted simply because they were women.

Ardern was the perfect antidote to this concern. She was young and would work well as a new face for Labour, but also had the respect of the unions. In a rare showing of unity in the factioned selection meetings, everyone agreed on Ardern.

When the list was released on 1 September, two months before the election, it represented a generational change in the Labour Party. It featured Phil Twyford (45 at the time), the former global head of Oxfam whom Labour had been seeking for years; Kelvin Davis (41), Māori education advocate and school principal; Carmel Sepuloni (31), who would go on to become the first New Zealand MP of Tongan descent; and Stuart Nash (41), whose grandfather was former prime minister Walter Nash. But the real winner was Ardern who, at twenty-eight and still in London, debuted higher on the party list than all of them. She was guaranteed a seat in parliament barring a catastrophic showing from Labour on Election Day.

It felt inevitable given her experience both within the party and with IUSY. She had the background and the pull, as well as the youthfulness that Labour were after. What she didn't have was a New Zealand presence. No one outside of Labour and the youth socialist movement knew who she was. And evidently she didn't particularly want to come back home. As a list-only candidate, Ardern asked to remain overseas and campaign from London. Her plan, as proposed to the board, was to form a New Zealand London Voters group. Droves of recent graduates flock to London every year for their overseas experience. The goal was to tap into a voter market largely left ignored by major parties during election campaigns. Ardern's job was to inform New Zealanders in London that there was in fact an election happening at home and that they should cast their vote in it.

Her proposal was accepted and she remained in London. That is, until Clark put her foot down. She stressed that Ardern needed to be in New Zealand, showing her face and proving her commitment to the campaign. The implication was that Ardern needed to earn her list placing, and being in London didn't cut it. It wasn't the only issue. Ardern wasn't running for an electorate seat. To be voted into parliament purely on party votes, and not even attempt to win a seat as an electorate MP, was brazen. Too brazen for a young woman running in her first ever election.

She has to contest a seat, said Clark. She doesn't have to win it, but she has to contest it. Contesting a seat would allow Ardern to get her name and face out there on the hoardings and through door-knocking. It would test Ardern's ability to connect with voters on a personal level and she could earn their trust by showing she was willing to put in the work on the ground.

Two weeks after the list was announced it was revealed that Ardern would be Labour's candidate in her home region of Waikato. The newly formed seat brought together various parts of surrounding electorates, most of which had been National strongholds for over forty years. The rural communities wanted nothing of Labour's social democracy, and not even a hometown girl would change that. Clark knew that. She had run in the same area, then Piako, in 1975 as a 25-year-old and been beaten comprehensively. Unlike Ardern, Clark had not been placed high on the party list and her loss was just that: a loss. However, it served as good practice for campaigning. Perhaps that is why she insisted Ardern contest an unwinnable seat thirty-three years later.

Ardern couldn't make a dent on Waikato and everyone knew it. She returned to New Zealand three weeks before Election Day, and valiantly campaigned around her hometown and region. Among the sea of red hoardings, Ardern's face beamed out, all teeth and brown hair. For the first time since she was a teenager, the blonde was nowhere to be seen. It didn't help: she lost by an astronomical margin. If National had stood a broomstick and bucket in the Waikato electorate, it would've won.

Ardern lost the Waikato seat, and Labour lost the 2008 election. John Key, who had only been in politics for six years, was elected prime minister. A fresh face, he was immensely likeable, in contrast to the impersonable Clark. It was the end of an era for Labour, but a flock of young MPs joined the opposition backbenches. Elected from the list, Ardern was one of them. Fellow newcomerss Grant Robertson, Chris Hipkins, Stuart Nash, Carmel Sepuloni and Phil Twyford were also elected. Perhaps because of her time overseas, perhaps because of her age, perhaps because she was a woman, the media didn't consider Ardern as exciting as the others. Nash and Twyford in particular were touted as future stars of the party.

Given her transparent interest in youth wellbeing, a consistent theme in her few interviews as a candidate, Ardern was made Labour's spokesperson for youth affairs and associate spokesperson for justice – youth justice.

When asked what she hoped to achieve as an MP, Ardern's answer was that of a diplomat rather than a politician. 'I am the youngest new MP. I hope to be part of a generation in Parliament that increases the participation of young people and engages them more in political debate.'

She had good reason to say this. National had also seen something of a generational change. On the other side of the aisle, Nikki Kaye (twenty-eight), Simon Bridges (thirty-one) and Amy Adams (thirty-seven) – someone who will never be able to effectively set a Google alert for her own name – also entered parliament. And Prime Minister Key and his deputy, Bill English, were just forty-seven and forty-six respectively: relatively young as leaders.

Clark was almost sixty and her deputy, Michael Cullen, was even older. Her 'team' were two generations removed from the likes of Kaye and Ardern, and everyone wondered how many party veterans would vacate their seats before the 2011 election and how many would hold on.

Clark and Cullen announced almost immediately that they would be gone by 2011, opening up opportunities for the newest recruits to make an impact. Their maiden speeches were their first chance to do so.

Maiden speeches are a chance for new, perhaps relatively unknown, MPs to tell their colleagues and opponents about themselves: where they've come from and what issues they're most passionate about. It's one of few opportunities – for some the only time – for first-term MPs to address the House at length with a broad scope.

Ardern gave her maiden speech, as the youngest member of parliament, on 16 December 2008. She thanked Clark for being a role model within the party and joked that 'Maiden statements are a bit like words spoken in a heated argument; like it or not, they will come back to haunt one.'

Ardern briefly outlined her life to date and spoke passionately on the issues she would fight for.

Being the youngest member of parliament meant Ardern was speaking from a generational viewpoint not shared by the vast majority of her colleagues. Where politicians in New Zealand have a tendency to appear a lot older than they really are, both incidentally through their sensibilities and political speak, and deliberately through their stances on particular issues, Ardern set herself apart from the beginning. She didn't try to fit in with the old boys' club. She was young and she was going to act in politics as a representative for young people. She had no intention of acting like an old politician in a young person's body.

And she made that distinction clear when she delivered a searing indictment on the government's inaction over climate change. 'I fear that our pride in New Zealand's clean, green reputation is already misplaced. It is shameful enough that we are about to lose New Zealand's most proactive legislation in response to the impacts of climate change that we have seen to date. It is unspeakable that, in addition, we now have a parliamentary select committee to question the science of climate change itself. We had the potential to be a world leader. National told us we should be fast followers, but now all I see are the many, many losers – the future generations whom some people in this House do not yet believe they have a responsibility to. Well, I do.'

Ardern and the other first-term MPs on both sides of the political aisle represented a new generation of politicians. Climate change was in the front of their minds; not exactly common in parliament a decade ago. Ardern presented two pillars of motivation: the environment and children. If her maiden speech was anything to go by, she planned to make some changes. She concluded by inviting scrutiny, perhaps not anticipating the degree to which she would eventually receive it.

'It is the things I have seen, the lessons I have learned, and the people of New Zealand whom I wish to serve that have brought me to this place. These are the very things that I wish to haunt me for as long as I have the privilege of serving here.'

4

A Rival

On paper, Jacinda Ardern was the perfect Labour candidate for Auckland Central, an electorate seat that encompasses the suburbs of Ponsonby, Grey Lynn, Westmere and Herne Bay, stomping ground of wealthy boomers and renting young professionals. In the 1970s and '80s these suburbs were home to migrant Pacific communities before they were priced out of the housing market. The old cultural churches are still there but the average value of a home in Central Auckland is now almost two million dollars.

For nearly a century Auckland Central had been a safe Labour seat. But in 2008 a young up-and-comer became the first National MP to hold the seat. Nikki Kaye was a 28-year-old overachiever, known for being incredibly competent, socially liberal, outspoken on conscience issues, and a rising star in a major political party. Sound familiar?

Kaye and Ardern were the same age and each was on a rising trajectory within their respective party. They were always going to be compared, whether or not they competed directly against one another. But it didn't take long for their paths to cross.

When Kaye won in 2008, rumours circulated that Phil Twyford, a Labour rising star, would be deployed to the Central seat to win it back. He lived in Kingsland (a bordering suburb) and had set up an office in the city already. It looked clear that he was set to become Labour's Auckland Central candidate. Ardern moved from the Waikato to Central Auckland in September 2009, igniting speculation that there'd be a contest within Labour for their candidate. It would soon go to Ardern, while Twyford would later insist that he was more than happy to move to West Auckland and contest the Waitakere seat instead.

Before Ardern was formally elected to stand for Labour in Auckland Central, *NZ Herald* journalist Patrick Gower described the potential contest in four words that would go on to haunt both Ardern and Kaye for nearly a decade.

'A political "battle of the babes" is set to play out in Auckland Central,' Gower wrote. 'With Parliament's two youngest members, Jacinda Ardern and Nikki Kaye, contesting the seat.'

'Battle of the babes'. The words were put in quotation marks, even though nobody had said them except Gower. It didn't matter: the phrase stuck.

It was inherently sexist, of course (can you imagine a battle between two male 28-year-old politicians being given the same tagline?). But people could see where Gower was coming from. In the 2010 annual survey by Durex (the condom manufacturer) on New Zealand's hottest celebrities and politicians, Kaye won in the female politician category. In 2011, the all-important election year, Ardern won and Kaye placed second. At the time, Ardern compared a survey on politicians' looks to 'asking someone to pick their favourite chocolate and then only giving them the choice of fruit and nut'. Both a self-deprecating joke and a roast on her fruit-and-nut colleagues, most of whom didn't make the list at all. (In the same survey, Winston Peters was crowned 'Slipperiest Politician' in a landslide victory, gathering more than 55 per cent of the votes.)

With politics usually an old man's game, the conversation around attractiveness was perhaps less about their actual looks and more about the fact that two young women were vying for the same position. Political lightning had struck twice and the media were appropriately dazed.

Even the most seasoned of political journalists struggled to avoid mentioning either woman's looks while writing about their respective campaigns. A well-respected political reporter called Ardern 'easy on the eye' in a profile. Another press gallery reporter warned of a close fight in 2011 because Kaye's new opponent was 'at least as bright, and at least as attractive'. A veteran magazine editor profiled both women and mused that Ardern's features were 'more pronounced, even the ears, which tonight she has proudly on show'. Ardern was never asked to confirm whether she had indeed proudly shown off her ears that night, or whether they were simply there, on either side of her head.

Politically, Kaye had every advantage. She was an electorate MP, having spent half a term acting on behalf of Auckland Central which, thanks to gentrification, was sliding steadily towards the political centre. She had experience in winning a tough contest as an underdog. And she was in government, while Ardern was in Opposition as a list MP. By all accounts, Kaye had the edge. Yet they were often discussed in the media as equals. Perhaps because Ardern had an edge over Kaye in her effortlessness.

In New Zealand, desperate modesty is a virtue. Even to suggest that you would like to be better than others at something is frowned upon. If you succeed, kia ora, but don't make a big thing out of it. New Zealanders are experts in tall poppy syndrome – no New Zealander experiencing fame and fortune overseas has escaped the machetes of the Kiwi psyche. If you do not humble yourself, everyone else will do it for you. It's endearing to a point, this insistence that everyone in New Zealand is simply stumbling upon their success, but eventually it gets tiresome. Election campaigns are uncomfortable affairs: politicians wear their efforts on their sleeves, and often those efforts reek of desperation. Elections are a desperate thing. Candidates do whatever they can to convince the public to vote for and therefore hire them. New Zealand prides itself on not stooping to the fluff and spectacle seen in politics overseas, and the last thing anyone wants to see is a tryhard.

Nikki Kaye tried hard. She was an athlete, an Auckland middle-distance running champion and an ultramarathon competitor. She took part in the 2008 Coast to Coast marathon, a 3-kilometre beach run, 70-kilometre cycle, 33-kilometre mountain climb and 67-kilometre kayak. It should have been the perfect side story, since so few politicians are athletic. But nobody likes hearing about how much work and training you had to do to complete an event 99 per cent of people would never think about attempting. Nobody likes a tryhard.

Kaye did have the advantage of being a local, though. Her background was that of an Auckland Central resident. Leafy suburbs and private schooling, followed by science and law degrees, her upbringing was in contrast to Ardern's in Morrinsville. But despite different beginnings, the two women's CVs had striking parallels. They both worked in party leaders' offices in the early 2000s – Ardern with Prime Minister Helen Clark and Kaye with Leader of the Opposition Bill English. Kaye worked in Europe in 2003 on government policy projects. Ardern arrived two years later, working under Sir Ronnie Flanagan in policing. While Ardern was working her way to becoming president of the International Union of Socialist Youth, Kaye served as the vice chairperson of the International Youth Democratic Union, who describe themselves as a 'global alliance of centre right political youth organisations united by a common desire for greater freedom and less government.'

Both women returned to New Zealand in order to run in the 2008 general election, though Kaye moved home in 2007 to put up a serious, and eventually successful, bid for the Auckland Central seat, while Ardern arrived a month before the election simply to make a showing in Waikato.

Both women were frequently described in the media as 'earnest'.

Cursed by their own similarities, the two women never got close; admittedly, the nature of campaigning made actual interactions rare. It was as if they both knew that they'd be compared to each other for the rest of their careers and were destined for a lifelong rivalry.

Kaye tried hard, and so did Ardern. But Ardern alone succeeded in making her campaigning feel natural. Kaye was vocal, presenting her ideas around public transport and small businesses whenever possible. Ardern simply went to events and had a chat to people. And oh by the way, vote Labour.

Of course only female politicians are 'tryhards'. Male politicians try hard all the time; their failed attempts to be relatable or funny are met with a grimace and then shrugged off. Women in politics are rarely afforded such a luxury. Kaye was competent, knowledgeable, pleasant and earnest. But by virtue of being less personable than Ardern, she was marked as the underdog in an electorate she had already won once before.

Ardern was a familiar face. From a crop of promising new MPs in 2008, she emerged victorious in claiming the Young Guns spot on *Breakfast*, the nationally broadcast morning show. Young Guns was a regular political segment featuring a young MP from Labour and National debating the issues of the week.

Ardern represented Labour and Simon Bridges National. Kaye made a few appearances, particularly early in 2009, but the chemistry was noticeably different. While Bridges and Ardern, and later Jami-Lee Ross and Ardern, appeared happy to sit beside each other and share a joke, when Kaye appeared on the segment there was a 30-centimetre gap between the two MPs and a distinct lack of humour. It felt bitter rather than collegially competitive. To put it plainly, the chemistry between Ardern and Bridges made for better television.

Getting face time on national television once a week all year round was a coup for Ardern and Bridges as back-benchers, where half the job is trying to get voters to remember your name. While Bridges fared better than Kaye on Young Guns, Ardern was the clear star. Being in opposition worked in her favour. She was able to criticise the government's latest decisions without having to defend her own party's actions. And no matter how serious the topic, Ardern made sure to get in the last laugh. Literally. Almost every interview ended with Ardern laughing and, more often than not, Bridges looking slightly hard done by.

Whether intentionally or not, Ardern was building her profile in a way rarely seen in politics. She was becoming a celebrity first. People in their twenties today remember hearing Ardern in the background as they got ready for school in the morning. They wouldn't have been able to tell you her role in parliament or her policy interests, but they knew Jacinda Ardern was a politician. That's a significant achievement for a first-term list MP in opposition. Being known personally more than politically would become a sticking point for Ardern years later when she campaigned to be prime minister, but in 2010 it served her well.

By standing Ardern in Auckland Central, Labour were fighting fire with fire in more ways than one. Kaye and Ardern agreed on a lot of things. When the National government proposed mining on Great Barrier Island – which fell in the Auckland Central electorate – Kaye took a stand against her own party. It didn't win her any favours: National supporters called her a traitor, while opponents accused her of grandstanding in order to curry favour with her socially liberal constituents.

In 2012, the Barbara Lee Family Foundation published a report titled *Pitch Perfect: Winning Strategies for Women Candidates*. In it, they refer to their own 2010 research which found that 'voters were perfectly willing to vote for a male executive they thought was qualified but did not particularly like. However, we found that they would not vote for a woman they found unlikeable even if she were qualified.' Women candidates must be both qualified and likeable, and each affects the other. Men candidates are not affected by that correlation. The report found that 'because qualifications and likeability are so closely linked, there are dual negative consequences for women when they make mistakes on the campaign trail'.

It's a double bind for women: being competent won't make you likeable, but being incompetent will certainly make you unlikeable. Ardern and Kaye were both competent but Ardern was the more likeable. Why? It's hard to say. Perhaps she simply had more of a sense of humour. Kaye was liked, and her stance on the Great Barrier Island mining proposal would later be regarded as honourable, but at the time it was framed by media commentators as a woman attempting to undercut her own party.

The Auckland Central contest was distinctively urban and liberal. Ardern and Kaye were running in the electorate most populated with young professionals and small business. They were also by far the two youngest serious candidates in the election. Auckland Central in 2011 was the perfect contest to showcase social media as a campaign tool, and the two young women were the perfect politicians to test drive it.

Ardern was first, creating her Twitter profile in March 2010, with Kaye following suit soon after, in June. The two quickly found their respective strengths: Kaye posted policy-heavy updates with the occasional personal aside, usually a self-deprecating joke. Meanwhile, policy came in second for Ardern, who regularly posted jokes about her parents and herself. Where Kaye sought to campaign as a National party member, promoting both herself and the party's policies as a whole, Ardern seemed to be campaigning alone. She rarely used party lines and, to an uninformed viewer, might have been mistaken for running as an independent. According to their Twitter updates, a vote for Nikki Kaye was a vote for National while a vote for Jacinda Ardern was a vote for Jacinda Ardern.

On election night in November 2011, the live updates showed a tightly fought contest. Kaye took an early lead as the votes came in, but with 22 per cent of votes counted she held a lead of only seventy-seven.

At 10.40 pm, after a campaign vocalising tangible policy far more than her opponent, Nikki Kaye delivered a victory speech to her supporters. She retained her Auckland Central seat with a majority of 717 votes. National stayed in power and Ardern returned to parliament as an opposition list MP.

Three years later Ardern would again challenge Kaye in the Auckland Central seat, and once again the Battle of the Babes moniker was wheeled out. With nobody replacing them as the young stars of New Zealand politics, the two women remained the exciting, liberal contest to watch.

In the three years since her first defeat, Ardern had worked hard to boost her profile in the business and arts scenes. She was prolific, not only appearing regularly around the Auckland music and comedy scenes, but seemingly becoming friends with everyone in those communities. She attended cultural festivals, held frequent coffee shop meetings, and represented the Labour Party at the annual Auckland Pride Parade. She'd succeeded in gathering support, or at least everyone seemed to like her. But everyone liked her in 2011 and Kaye still won that contest. Ardern needed to show she had the policy conviction to back up her interpersonal skills. Evidently, her party thought she did. By January 2014, Ardern had been promoted to Labour's front bench.

Unfortunately, while Ardern's profile was rising, the Labour party as a whole was crashing. Going into the 2014 election, Labour experienced some of their worst polling in party history, thanks to incessant infighting. The election was considered a hopeless fight, and MPs were desperate to win their electorates just to secure a seat in the House. Ardern had an uphill battle ahead of her, with the left-leaning suburb of Grey Lynn being moved out of the Auckland Central electorate that year.

Ardern's campaign reflected the fracturing within the party. Billboards were put up with #AskJacinda in large font. They invited voters to write questions on the hoardings which would then be answered by Ardern. It wasn't #AskLabour, it was #AskJacinda. A study of the two women's campaigns in 2014 found that in the four weeks leading up to election night, as Labour struggled to communicate a concrete policy plan, Ardern tweeted only three times about Labour policy. Labour weren't expected to put up any fight on election night, but maybe Ardern could pull off a minor victory.

The contest was even closer than in 2011. With two-thirds of the vote counted, Kaye was ahead: by just over 200 votes. By the end of the night, her lead had widened, though not by much. The party vote in Auckland Central was overwhelmingly National; unsurprising, given the state of the Labour party throughout the campaign. In the end, Kaye won her seat yet again, with a winning margin of 600 votes.

Ardern was 0–3.

Kaye defeated Ardern in two consecutive elections. She went on to become education minister in the National government. In 2016, Kaye stepped away from politics after a breast cancer diagnosis. But she recovered and retained Auckland Central in 2017. When the moment comes, it'll be a brave soul who'd underestimate a general election with Ardern and Kaye as party leaders. It will almost certainly have a better tagline.

5

The Rise Begins

Everyone in New Zealand knows someone who claims to have dated Jacinda Ardern. Notoriously private when it comes to her closest relationships, Ardern didn't publicly appear with a partner until 2014, when she was thirty-four. Until then, the most Ardern would disclose was that she wasn't in a serious relationship. That didn't stop everyone around her from trying to set her up on dates though.

In September 2014, speculation emerged that she was in a relationship with Clarke Gayford, after they were seen together at the World Press Photo Exhibition launch, and then again at various bars and restaurants. But the couple didn't make an official public appearance together until November, when they attended Lorde's music awards afterparty.

Gayford was as well known as Ardern, if not more so. He was a media celebrity and, on paper, the very opposite of Ardern. She was an earnest politician, 100 per cent committed to her work, who had, according to vague answers given to women's magazines, been single for a while. He was a radio and television host, who'd recently separated from a *Shortland Street* star. He was known around town as a party boy and had had a number of high-profile relationships. Not what would be considered a safe option for a rising political star: more like fodder for the gossip magazines, or a distraction.

Which makes the story of how the two met all the more surprising. According to Gayford, in 2013 he had concerns about a proposed surveillance bill that he believed would erode the privacy of New Zealanders. Gayford described himself as having been, prior to this, politically 'apathetic'. But now he took his concerns to Ardern, his local opposition MP, and she agreed to meet him for coffee to discuss them.

The two had met before, it turned out, though only briefly. At the 2012 *Metro* Restaurant of the Year Awards, Ardern was the plus one of model and friend Colin Mathura-Jeffree. Mathura-Jeffree had embarrassed Ardern all night by introducing her to everyone as 'the future prime minister'. He introduced her to Gayford and the two chatted for a while. A year later they sat at a local cafe, discussing an amendment bill and realised they both liked the same local drum and bass band, Concord Dawn.

Gayford and Ardern became friends and eventually he asked her out on a date: fishing. Having grown up on the East Coast, Gayford's one true passion was the ocean. And as he got older, he negotiated time slots on the radio that would allow him to go out on the water after work. Ardern had never fished before but proved good at it from the beginning. 'It was a champagne day,' Gayford later told a lifestyle magazine. 'The sea was glass flat and we had a huge pod of dolphins join us. It was literally Jacinda's first cast.' Over the next six years, writers around the country and the world would exhaust every possible fishing allegory when remarking on the couple. But on that champagne day, Ardern had her first cast and first catch. She pulled in a 5.4-kilogram snapper and with it, Gayford's heart.

The pair were constantly in the public eye. With Ardern the spokesperson for arts and culture and Gayford a television personality, they attended numerous awards ceremonies, gigs and book launches. Despite that, the couple kept things fairly low-key at first – they rarely featured in each other's social media feeds. And despite the unlikeliness on paper, the relationship worked.

Gayford maintained his own career, hosting and producing *Catch of the Day*, a fishing show filmed around the world. Their lifestyles matched. Ardern travelled regularly, flying to Wellington for parliament sitting days, and around the country when portfolio matters required it. Gayford filmed his material in all seasons, often making longer trips to the Pacific Islands and beyond. Among their busy schedules, they bought a house in Point Chevalier and renovated it together.

★★★

In a slightly damp flat in central Auckland, one month before the 2014 general election, a group of university students were disappointed by what Jacinda Ardern was saying to them. Ardern was standing in the kitchen, holding court and eating from a packet of salt and vinegar chips the flatmates had generously provided. Speaking candidly, or as candidly as a local MP on a house call can, Ardern was insisting, not for the first time, that she didn't want to be prime minister. In fact, she didn't want any sort of leadership position within the Labour Party. 'I've seen how hard it is to raise a family in that role,' she told them. 'And that's what I want to do.' At this point, Ardern and Gayford had not been publicly confirmed as a couple but had been dating for several months.

The students were disappointed – not because they were anti-family, but because, well, they liked Ardern. Three of the friends, all women, had attended a 'Locally Left' discussion at a local Returned Services Club, to see her speak. They were the youngest in the modest crowd by a solid three decades. After the event, they had a drink with Ardern and complained that their flatmates were apathetic about the upcoming election and didn't intend to vote. Without hesitation, Ardern offered to come round to their flat to see if she could stir up some interest in democracy. Two weeks later their dining room furniture was pushed to the side (they didn't have a lounge: the Auckland rental market had forced them to convert it into an extra bedroom) and a dozen of their friends were listening to Ardern in the kitchen.

She spoke about policy and Labour's plans for a new government, but even the most politically apathetic among the students knew Labour were doing terribly. So they asked her: do you want to be prime minister? And she said no.

It was disappointing to the students because although Labour had churned through several leaders in the last few years, it was Ardern a few rows back who appeared the most competent to them. And she was different. Well, at least somewhat: she wasn't a middle-aged white man.

When Helen Clark retired after the 2008 election, the party leadership reverted to type: a middle-aged man, in the shape of Phil Goff, with Annette King, a three-decade veteran Labour MP, as deputy. King was only the second woman to be deputy leader, but Goff and King were hardly representative of a new generation within Labour, and in 2011 they suffered a convincing election loss. Goff stepped down and was replaced by David Shearer. At this point, Ardern leapfrogged from a ranking of nineteen to become the highest-ranked woman in the party – at number four – and one of only two women on Labour's front bench. It was a big jump for Ardern, but not surprising given Labour's distinct lack of female representation high on the list. There were still more men named David on the front bench than there were women – a grim statistic critics liked to cite.

Under Clark, Labour had worked towards gender balance, but although the number of women MPs had increased, few of them rose to the higher echelons of the party.

In 2012, now on the front bench and therefore the front-line, Ardern's public profile lifted dramatically. Articles were written framing her as the next star of the Labour Party, but in interviews for these profiles Ardern emphasised her lack of ambition, at least as far as leadership went. 'There's something about politics where people always assume people's motivations are very particular,' she told one reporter. 'We all obsess about leadership far less than everyone else assumes we do.' Ardern must have only been speaking for herself, because the Labour Party was about to go through the worst period of leadership upheavals in its history, demonstrating just how much everyone in the Labour Party was obsessing about how they wanted to be leader.

But while those around her were spreading discontent in Shearer, a leader who was most famous in 2012 for delivering the inspiring line 'I don't believe I am not, not connecting', Ardern was dealing with her own issue: condescension. Having been given the substantial role of spokesperson for social development, Ardern found herself

up against veteran National minister Paula Bennett. The
two couldn't be further apart in how they conducted themselves in parliament. Ardern had preached a number of times
on the need for more kindness in politics, and when asked
how she would like to be remembered, she cited policies
she'd helped to craft around child wellbeing and families
'but ultimately I think I would just like to be remembered
as someone who has integrity'. Bennett, meanwhile, was
known by some as 'Bruiser Bennett' and had made headlines in 2009 for releasing the benefit details of two women
to the media after they criticised the government for stopping a particular allowance for beneficiaries. Attempting to
hold Bennett to account would prove a test of Ardern's goal
to bring kindness into the House.

In November, after asking a question of the minister, Ardern and her fellow opposition MPs interrupted
Bennett's answer. Heckling from the other side of the
debating chamber is common, and often descends into
incoherent yelling from both sides. Bennett responded with
'Zip it, sweetie.' Labour MPs were outraged and Trevor
Mallard objected on Ardern's behalf, but his objection was
dismissed. New Zealanders would go on to vote 'Zip it,
sweetie' as the quote of the year.

In his second term, Key's popularity as prime minister
had dipped, but he was still polling miles ahead of any given
Labour leader at the time. Shearer wasn't bad, thought the
public, he was just not quite right. He had been made leader
after only two and a half years in parliament, and many
believed that to be too soon. In August 2013, while arguing
against a proposal from National for a quota on snapper,
Shearer produced, seemingly out of nowhere, two dead
snapper and held them aloft in the House. It was a stunt,
sure, but to what end? Shearer never explained where he

had got the fish from, how long he had been carrying them around in his briefcase, or even what he did with them once he'd presented them in parliament. But he resigned two days later, saying he sensed he no longer had the full confidence of many of his colleagues.

One David stepped down and another took his place. From the beginning David Cunliffe had, at best, the support of half his caucus. Ardern had been public in her support for Grant Robertson, who'd unsuccessfully put himself forward for the position. Cunliffe wasn't good. He was only leader for twelve months, and during that time he managed to get himself immortalised as being bad with words. He criticised Key – a successful investment banker before he went into politics – for living a lavish lifestyle, and then had to defend his own multi-million-dollar Auckland home. And while speaking to a Women's Refuge symposium, Cunliffe uttered his most famous words: 'I'm sorry for being a man.' In fairness, had Cunliffe said that in 2019, the worst he would have suffered was some memes at his expense. But in 2014, Cunliffe's broad stroke apology did nothing but alienate half the country. He held on until the 2014 election, delivered Labour its worst election result in nearly a century, and somehow had plans to remain leader until the 2017 election. He was convinced he wasn't the reason for the catastrophic result, and though he was made to resign, he initially planned to run for the leadership again. Two weeks later he pulled out of the race, though he remained within the party until 2017.

Finally, women began entering the leadership fray. Sort of. Ardern and King were both recruited as deputies to aspiring leaders Grant Robertson and Andrew Little respectively. Robertson announced that, for the second time, he would be seeking the leadership position, and this time he was running with a pre-selected deputy in Ardern. At the launch, Ardern was met with the biggest cheer of the day and emphasised her connection to the younger voters she wanted to represent. 'The new generation of leadership is going to have to take on the next generation of challenges,' she said. That became the unofficial tagline of the Robertson–Ardern, or 'Gracinda', ticket. A new generation of leaders. The pair also presented a progressive front, with Ardern a woman and Robertson gay, though neither liked to focus on those things. In fact, Robertson found himself having to repeatedly steer conversation away from his sexuality. To avoid it, he was often introduced or referred to, rather over-emphatically, as a 'rugby-loving bloke'.

Robertson was the early favourite for the job but along came Andrew Little, a former union guy, who the National party had dubbed 'Angry Andrew', thanks to his impassioned speeches in parliament. Little won the leadership, but like Shearer before him, his effectiveness as an opposition MP did not translate into effectiveness as a leader. Once again Labour had a leader who couldn't connect with voters, and it's no surprise there wasn't much change in poll results. Position Goff, Shearer, Cunliffe and Little in a row and it would be a difficult game of Guess Who?

As all this turmoil within the party unfolded, Ardern stayed well out of it, which was particularly remarkable for such a high-ranking MP. Her addition to Robertson's ticket felt more like a favour as a friend than a real political power move. And after Robertson lost his bid for the leadership, she was back where she seemed most comfortable, among the team. 'Your time in this place is so fleeting and it'll only take a couple of decades before people look quizzically when your name is read out,' she told a reporter. 'So I think just always keeping a sense of the fact that you are just here for a particular time and place, you do the best you can, but no one is bigger than the party and parliament and the job you're doing.' This environment was where Ardern operated, and from where she confidently expressed her lack of leadership ambition.

The young women who invited Ardern to speak to them at their flat that day in 2014 hoped that one day they could say they'd had the prime minister over for dinner (read: three packets of chips with no dip). But it seemed like they'd be disappointed, as Ardern thought the leadership was too big a sacrifice for someone who wanted kids and a life outside of politics. No doubt Ardern didn't much fancy the scrutiny she'd come under as PM either. As an opposition MP, Ardern had faced little critique from the media, and she preferred to connect directly with the public, telling one interviewer, 'When I first came into parliament I had that breakfast media slot on TV where I could be myself and sometimes we could chuck in a bit of humour. I was a brand-new backbench MP. That is a very different form of engaging with the public than when you're leader having to do a stand-up with the media every day.'

Even in 2017, mere months before she would become leader and then prime minister, Ardern was adamant she didn't want anything to do with the job. 'It's me knowing myself and knowing that actually, when you're a bit of an anxious person and you constantly worry about things, there comes a point where certain jobs are just really bad for you,' she told *NEXT* magazine in June. 'I hate letting people down. I hate feeling like I'm not doing the job as well as I should. I've got a pretty big weight of responsibility right now; I can't imagine doing much more than that.'

But perhaps what Ardern didn't count on in 2014, when she was a safe distance from any leadership position, was that Labour would inevitably turn to her, even if she didn't want them to. She was the highest-ranked woman in the party and was a leap ahead of her female contemporaries when it came to public and party perception. People within Labour have reflected that if Ardern had been a man with the same skillset, she probably wouldn't have been promoted so quickly. She would almost certainly have gotten there eventually, but when a party is struggling to show it values women in its ranks, and you come along as a qualified woman, the path is faster. There were other women in the party – Nanaia Mahuta was also on the front bench – but none close to Ardern in popularity and stature.

Apparently everyone in politics knew that Ardern would be prime minister long before she did.

★★★

Shortly before Christmas 2016, two years into his third term as prime minister, John Key resigned. There was no warning, no scandal pushing him out, no internal coup bubbling up. He simply decided he didn't want to do the job anymore and resigned.

No fanfare surrounded his resignation. The only hint that something was amiss was that Key moved his regular Monday press conference to earlier in the day, at lunchtime. But nobody, on either side of parliament, predicted he would step down from the top job. To the press, Key explained that he simply wanted to spend more time with his family. 'Just a few days ago I marked the anniversary of my eighth year as prime minister and my tenth as leader of the National Party,' he began. 'Such an occasion seems a fitting time to not only take stock of the past ten years, but to look forward. Throughout these years I have given everything I could to this job that I cherish, and this country that I love. All of this has come at quite some sacrifice for the people who are dearest to me – my family.' Despite plenty of speculation around his announcement, no scandal or other reason for his resignation was uncovered.

Key had been successful before politics and he'd continue to succeed after it. Some of his appeal lay in the fact that he wasn't a career politician. And never was that more evident than in his decision to resign while still a popular prime minister. Leaving well before the next election was deliberate, as Key suggested a clean handover of leaders would work well for the party as they entered campaign season. He said he'd support whoever the party elected as his successor, but would be voting for his deputy, Bill English, if English put his name forward.

Across the halls in the offices of the opposition, Ardern and other Labour MPs were as shocked as the press gallery. 'I don't think anyone, hand on heart, could claim they saw that coming,' she remarked later. But Key's resignation was a potential lifeline to Labour. Key, nicknamed 'Teflon John', had been a charismatic, seemingly untouchable leader. Scandals, policy balls-ups, social faux pas: they all rolled off Key like butter off a pan. And now he was gone. Even the smoothest leadership changeovers had shown a dent in party popularity as voters stepped back from the uncertainty of a new leader. And English was no Key. He didn't have the same pull. Maybe Key's resignation was exactly what Labour needed to kickstart their ascent.

'There was a flash of hope,' Ardern remembered in 2019. 'Uncertainty as well, but I do genuinely remember there being a flash of hope. But it just didn't translate.'

She was right: when English was confirmed as the new leader of the National party six days later, he took over a steady ship. Labour hadn't been able to capitalise on the change in leadership and were still floundering in the polls. If change in National wasn't going to do it, maybe change in Labour would.

David Shearer, who had been Labour leader from 2011 to 2013, resigned from parliament three days after Key. His abrupt departure forced a by-election in his Mt Albert seat.

A week later, Ardern announced she would stand for Labour in the by-election. It was, she explained, a case of moving with the electorate, since a large chunk of Auckland Central had been rezoned into Mt Albert. Political commentators couldn't help but speculate that perhaps she simply wanted to finally win a seat. 'Everyone knows I lost twice [to Kaye] – the results are pretty clear. But no,' she answered at the time. 'I still genuinely believe Auckland Central can be won and I intend to work closely with whoever is the new candidate.'

Although Ardern had maintained her disinterest in the top job, standing in Mt Albert was a helpful step towards it. Everything she said was supporting the narrative of a complacent MP, while everything she did was a positive step towards leadership. Conventionally, those running for prime minister are electorate MPs. The only list MP to run was English in 2017, but that was after he voluntarily stepped back from his electorate seat. If Ardern ever ran for prime minister (even though she said she wouldn't), it would be helpful to be holding a seat already.

The moment Ardern looked likely to stand in Mt Albert, questions began about the deputy leadership. Annette King had announced that she wouldn't be running in her Rongotai electorate in Wellington at the next election but insisted she had no intention of stepping down as deputy. Meanwhile National announced that they wouldn't be contesting Mt Albert, all but handing the seat to Ardern. As the February by-election drew near, calls intensified for Little to promote Ardern as Labour supporters yearned for fresh, younger faces. King had acted as a mentor to Ardern (she was the only woman more senior than Ardern within the party, and had been in parliament since 1984), but from 2014 on the two women were inadvertently pitted against each other. Ardern shied away from the suggestion that she should take over as deputy leader, not least because she didn't want to overstep her mentor in the process. But every time there was trouble within the party (which was often between 2014 and 2016) calls came for change. Those suggesting that King step down never considered her performance a detriment to the party. Political pundits across the spectrum agreed that she was one of the more respected MPs in parliament. They just thought Ardern would be better. 'No indictment of King – but there is a bit of magic about Ardern,' one columnist wrote.

Unsurprisingly, Ardern won Mt Albert in a landslide. It was dubbed 'the most boring by-election in living memory'.

As calls for Ardern's promotion increased, King, now sixty-nine, labelled such calls 'ageist' and reiterated on 26 February that she wasn't going anywhere. Except she was. Just three days later, King quit as deputy leader and announced she would be resigning from politics after the forthcoming September election. Ardern was swiftly nominated by Little and voted in by caucus, including King, as the new deputy leader.

It was a lot of change in a week. While many celebrated the potential of Ardern, some commentators – particularly female ones – mourned the loss of King. Veteran columnist Jane Clifton believed King should have been leader. 'That she didn't put herself forward despite being so obviously qualified may be another sign of our chronic workforce imbalance and the distance women still have to travel before being promoted and paid equally to men,' she concluded.

Ardern never put herself forward for the deputy role, King didn't want to give up the role, yet somehow after a week of speculation, both women were in positions they never sought. Reflecting in 2019 on these events, Ardern told a book festival crowd in Auckland that she was 'still very sad' about the way it had played out.

King and Ardern had been close for years, and close outside of politics too. Ardern joked that King always tried to set her up on dates with people before she met Gayford, and that Ardern would buy random clothes for King if she thought they'd suit her. The two women shared an interest in each others' personal lives, so to be pitted against each other was upsetting.

'I know we both found it really awkward, we would talk to each other about it,' Ardern later said. 'Particularly because there was a lot of rumour. So I knew when she was going to stand aside as deputy, but I didn't know she was going to quit politics. And it wasn't until we were on a phone call together as a caucus, when she told everyone on the call. I was gutted, I felt like it was my fault somehow.'

Whether or not Ardern had reason to feel guilty, her fellow party members were excited to see her in her new role. Little wrote an inexplicably long Facebook post endorsing Ardern, including in it a comparison with recent world leaders.

'At a time when many talk of political apathy rising, and we look around the world to the US and Europe, where reactionary politics dominates, Jacinda – perhaps more than any other MP across the House – sparks a light in people and encourages unity.'

But not everyone was so enthralled. 'So, Andrew Little has landed himself a show pony in Jacinda Ardern, to jazz up the image of his dour leadership,' wrote one veteran right-wing columnist.

'Show pony'. Of all the names Ardern had been called – and there'd been a few – this was the one she'd mention in future interviews as having pissed her off.

Almost immediately after being promoted to deputy, Ardern overtook Little in the preferred prime minister polling.

People wanted her to be in charge. The left-leaning media were cautiously hopeful about her potential but didn't feel that she'd given any solid indication she could lead the party. As a backbencher, she'd largely stayed out of trouble, for better and for worse, and wasn't one of the heavy hitters in the debating chambers, despite a back-ground in the sport. So Steve Braunias, an acclaimed writer and friend of Ardern's, invited her to be the guest speaker at the Wintec Press Club.

In theory, Press Club was a triannual gathering of jour-nalists, politicians, and the best students from Wintec Journalism School to eat lunch, listen to a guest speaker and share knowledge. In practice, it was an excuse for journalists to get day-drunk and argue with whichever divisive politi-cian was invited for laughs. Braunias ran Press Club, and he wanted to give Ardern a chance to show some of the media what she had to offer. For balance, he would invite National deputy leader Paula Bennett to be the guest speaker at the next event. The Ardern Press Club was a popular one. Journalists and miscellaneous media personalities drove the two hours from Auckland to Hamilton, ready to see some life and hope injected into a deflating Labour party. Nearly everyone, including Ardern, left disappointed.

Braunias, who relished in creating awkward environments, didn't hold back in his introduction of Ardern. He presented a timeline of her appearances in women's magazines, appearances she later defended as being pragmatic, knowing she'd reach a wider audience of voters that way. At Press Club, though, it didn't sound good. 'In short, I know pretty much absolutely fucking nothing about Jacinda Ardern,' Braunias told the packed room, including a number of Green Party MPs. 'Neither would anyone reading this sort of pleasant garbage, and I think it's one of the reasons why she's widely regarded on the right as an MP of little or no substance, and as a politician as likeable but ultimately vacuous as John Key. What has she achieved?' It was hardly a glowing endorsement, though Braunias did finish by saying he hoped Ardern would be the next deputy prime minister.

Ardern gave a speech, reading off cards, that is mostly remembered for being entirely unmemorable. But her strength had always been answering questions intuitively, and her audience posed good ones. 'Does Andrew Little dull your shine? Do you ever want to push him off a cliff?' She answered diplomatically that it was her job to help voters get to know Little. When asked if Labour would negotiate with Winston Peters were he to have a deciding vote again in forming parliament, Ardern said yes. Someone called out, 'Can you not?'

'Do you sometimes feel like a winner in a loser party?' 'You have a man above you that you've refused to roll. What does that say about you?' The questions were tough, and all the tougher for coming from people who supported Ardern. The people in that room had watched for years as Labour leader after Labour leader rose to the top only to

prove themselves incapable of staying there. Everyone in
that room knew Little wasn't the best person to lead Labour
into the next election, and they wanted Ardern to agree.
They wanted her to get worked up and show that she had
the fight to take on National. They wanted her to show a
conviction they hadn't seen on the cover of *Woman's Day*.

But Ardern didn't give them what they wanted. She
dutifully defended Little and Trevor Mallard, but began to
get flustered by the onslaught. After a while, she started to
bite back, her answers becoming snippy. When asked why
voters should opt for a career politician like her rather than
an outsider, which Trump's recent election had shown was
a positive for voters, Ardern snapped. 'What, so you elect
a professional arsehole, instead?' And when asked if Peters
was racist, Ardern paused perhaps a fraction too long before
answering. 'I think Winston knows what he's doing.' She
went back to the question later to clarify: 'I'll tell you why
I paused – I truly do have to ask: is he genuinely racist? I
don't know him well enough.'

By the time Braunias stepped in to wrap up the Q&A
session, Ardern looked like she'd had enough. And when he
said there was time for a few more questions, she quipped,
'Do we have to?' It could have been a joke but it didn't
sound like one.

Mingling afterwards, journalists wondered if Ardern had
underestimated the event and come ill-prepared. No one
left the lunch particularly pleased with the outcome.

Ardern would go on to hold countless press conferences
and take thousands of questions from gathered journalists, but none would get under her skin quite like that first
experience at the boozy Hamilton lunch known as Press
Club. Perhaps it served as a lesson that once you're a leader –
even a deputy one – there's no such thing as an easy crowd.

Ardern was no longer simply an MP, which meant there was nowhere to hide.

Speaking in 2019, Ardern had enough distance to reflect on the trajectory she'd started on by moving electorates. 'I sometimes think had I not decided to run in Mt Albert, would I have then ended up as deputy leader, and then would I have ended up as leader?' The short answer is no.

By moving to the Mt Albert electorate, Ardern could showcase her strengths in a weakened by-election. It got her name out as coverage increased, and in doing so, presented her as an alternative option to both King and Little. It took all of three days for media speculation to result in King stepping down as leader and Ardern stepping up. Ardern may not have been able to see the woods for the trees at the time, but others did, including Little.

Because at the start of August, five months into Ardern's role as deputy leader and three months after her disastrous Press Club appearance, Andrew Little resigned.

6

The Press Conference

It's easy to look back and say that things couldn't have happened any other way. Of course Andrew Little would step down as leader of the Labour Party and nominate Jacinda Ardern as his successor. The signs were all there: the plummeting poll numbers, the murmurings within caucus, the prominence of Ardern in preferred prime minister polling. But on the morning of Wednesday, 26 July 2017, in the middle of an election campaign, Little had no intention of stepping down.

He and Ardern were in a meeting with the bosses of Weta Digital, the Wellington-based visual effects company famous for its work on *The Lord of the Rings* and other Peter Jackson projects, to discuss the controversial 2010 'Hobbit Law' that removed film workers' right to collective bargaining. Little was there as leader of the opposition in an election year, and Ardern as both deputy and spokesperson for arts and culture. It was her thirty-seventh birthday. She had come straight from a campaign appearance at the Tawa Rotary Club, where she'd been presented with a birthday cake. Cutting into it revealed a classic gag from club members: beneath the icing, the cake was entirely blue, National's colour. She laughed good-naturedly and made sure not to be photographed holding the blue cake as she was leaving. It would be eaten by Labour staffers, but the optics were the last thing a poorly polling opposition needed.

In the meeting with Weta, Little's phone vibrated. He ignored it. But when it vibrated again moments later, he furtively glanced at the screen. A message showed that internal polling by Labour had returned their worst result in party history: 23 per cent. In Little's own words, it was a 'double-take moment'. Ardern received the same message.

Later, back at parliament, Ardern sent Little a text message encouraging him to 'hang in there'. She'd later vaguely describe the message as being 'something Pollyannaish', a reference to the Eleanor H. Porter heroine who always tried to find the positive in everything.

That afternoon, they met in his office. For the first time, he floated the option of stepping down, saying, 'I don't know if I can do it.' 'You must stick at it and carry on,' he recalls Jacinda saying in response. So he did.

One poll can be an anomaly. And an internal poll need never be seen by voters. But of course Labour weren't the only ones polling. On Friday, TVNZ released the results of their Colmar-Brunton public poll. Labour sat at 24 per cent.

At 24 per cent, Labour would get fewer MPs from their list into parliament. Fewer MPs meant fewer resources. Fewer resources meant an even tougher battle in the 2020 election. If Little resigned as leader and Ardern took over they'd at least have a 'fresh approach', as their hoardings determinedly advertised. It might lift the party a few points and allow for a respectable showing in opposition. Then they could build for 2020. With Labour having hit rock-bottom in the polls, that was starting to look like the best possible outcome for them.

Questions around Little's leadership were raised on Saturday, this time at Ardern's home in Auckland, and this time by senior MPs. Speaking to *Stuff*, Little recalled one senior MP 'was very clear that they thought it was time for me to step aside'. But still he hesitated. It was barely eight weeks until the election. Little had seen Labour through some of their toughest years and had only recently succeeded in presenting a united party, without public disagreements or infighting. The party may have been going down in flames with voters, but at least they were going down together. Like all the toys holding hands in the incinerator in *Toy Story 3*.

The next day, Little shared his struggles – and in doing so, hammered another nail into the coffin of his leadership. In an interview with TVNZ's Corin Dann, he revealed that he'd discussed the option of resigning with senior colleagues. But in the same sentence he insisted that he was 'in this fight, and they support me in this fight'. Viewers were unconvinced.

Little's equivocation over the leadership became less and less attractive to voters with every passing day. On Monday a *Newshub* poll, conducted independently from the TVNZ one, also showed Labour at 24 per cent. Once is an isolated incident. Twice is an unfortunate coincidence. Three times is a trend.

On top of everything, Ardern had polled ahead of Little in the preferred prime minister polling, at 8.7 per cent to his 7.1 per cent.

That night, back in Auckland again, Little met with his team – including his chief of staff, Neale Jones, and his chief press secretary, Mike Jaspers – in the foyer of the Stamford Plaza Hotel, where they were staying. They again discussed Little's options. All three men phoned senior colleagues throughout the night, including Annette King, chief whip Kris Faafoi, and Ardern. While still supportive of him as leader if he chose to stay on, they expressed that it was becoming a more and more difficult decision to support.

Meanwhile, four suburbs over, Ardern was having a late birthday dinner with friends. They ate chicken and drank tea, and discussed the possible scenarios that could play out in the coming days. Over the course of the dinner, Ardern expressed to her friends both that she didn't want the job and that, if asked, she would accept it.

Little says he made the decision to step down as leader of the Labour Party at 'about half past ten that night'. But if so, he didn't share his decision with his team. Not that night, and not the next morning – although he did ask Jaspers to cancel his appearance on *The AM Show*. If he was about to step down as leader, it would be best not to appear on a live morning show. It was understood that in cancelling, Little had taken the first step in giving up his position, but no one knew for sure what was happening.

Ardern was on the same flight to Wellington as Little, and saw his group in the departure lounge. There was a brief, slightly awkward acknowledgement between Ardern, Jones and Jaspers.

At Wellington Airport, Mei Heron, a press gallery reporter from Radio New Zealand, was waiting when Little landed. She was as surprised to see him as he was to see her. Airport stops are always popular among political journalists, and any travelling politician with a story around them would expect at least a few journalists to be waiting for them in the arrivals lounge. The story all over the country that morning was whether Andrew Little would or wouldn't resign. Despite Little's schedule, which the media kept track of, clearly indicating which flight he'd likely be on, no one was waiting at the gate except Heron. She had almost accepted that she'd gotten the time wrong when Little emerged, entirely unprepared for any questions.

'Are you going to offer your resignation?' she asked, walking through the airport alongside him.

He responded, 'Um no, look, these issues are for a separate discussion.'

'So you're not going to offer a vote of confidence?'

'No,' he replied. 'There's none that I'm aware of and I'm certainly not putting one up.'

As they spoke, Ardern walked past, having disembarked from the plane shortly after Little. She smiled at Heron knowingly. It was a smile that said 'better him than me'. Heron smiled back and watched as Ardern continued walking and left the airport uninterrupted. Ardern wasn't the story. It would be the last time for a long time that Ardern would walk through Wellington airport and not be considered the story.

In the crown car on the way to parliament via Little's home in Island Bay, Jones asked him what he was planning to do. They'd cancelled his morning media and then moments later he'd told a reporter he wasn't going anywhere. They needed to get the story straight. So what was it going to be? Little had made up his mind. 'It's over,' he confirmed.

Jones made some phone calls. The first was to Ardern to inform her that she was about to be the leader of the Labour party. Her immediate response was a resigned sigh. She would later reveal while speaking to a group of teenage single mums that she'd been discussing the prospect of taking over with Little for days. 'From the 26th of July to the 1st of August, every single day I was asked and I said "no, no, no".'

Then Jones called the deputy chief of staff to organise a staff meeting that morning and arrange for new contracts to be written up. He called the press team to organise a press conference at 10 am, when Little would announce his resignation. And finally, he rang chief whip Faafoi and asked for caucus to meet after the press conference.

Jones and Jaspers had an hour to plan Little's resignation speech and they were still sitting in a crown car. When they arrived at parliament, Labour staff were told that Little would be resigning. It was emotional. They had, after all, been working tirelessly on what felt like an unwinnable election campaign, and now their leader was quitting. As exciting a prospect as Ardern was as leader, a change so late in the game was challenging. But staffers serve the leader, not the person, and they quickly moved on to figuring out how to make the transition as smooth as possible.

Little held his press conference in the second-floor caucus room, with Carmel Sepuloni and Kris Faafoi, the two whips, there in support. 'As leader you have to take responsibility and I have, and I do,' he said. It was, strangely enough, one of his better press appearances. Liberty makes a man light. 'It is my judgement that the party and the people who we are campaigning for would be better served by a new leader who can bring a fresh face and a fresh voice to this vital campaign.'

History – at least so far, since 2017 – has been kind to Little. The decision he had made in the lobby of the Stamford Plaza Hotel would be considered one of the toughest and greatest strategic moves in New Zealand politics. But that morning, as he promised to 'stay in the fight', it looked cowardly. Little had seen Labour through some of its most tumultuous years and succeeded in uniting a broken party – so much so that even his resignation was handled without drama. But as he fronted the media to hand the steering wheel of a sinking ship to his deputy, opinions came thick and fast, and they weren't particularly kind.

Hot takes, by their nature, are formed by impressions rather than comprehensive understanding. And the impression Andrew Little gave on the morning of 1 August 2017, was one of a man passing the buck at the eleventh hour.

In caucus moments later, Little nominated Ardern for leader and the movement was unanimously supported. Grant Robertson, who many would have picked to be deputy, instead nominated Kelvin Davis for the role, and that too was unanimously supported. It was the most seamless and, bar Little's personal struggles, painless leadership change the Labour Party had experienced in years.

A press conference had been scheduled for 2 pm. Little's advisers, now Ardern's, gathered with her to plan her introduction to New Zealand as leader of the opposition. They had one hour. When asked if there was anything in particular she wanted to say, Ardern said she'd written down a few ideas during the flight that morning. The men glanced at each other. Politicians always have ideas for their speeches and many fancy themselves bona fide wordsmiths. It often falls to their advisers to politely suggest alternative (read: better) talking points. But in this case they had no notes. After Ardern read out what she planned to say they left her to it and busied themselves with arranging the chairs.

A portable banner with the Labour logo was positioned behind a lectern. Ardern entered first in a red blazer, closely followed by Davis and Sepuloni. Moments later, Megan

Woods, Chris Hipkins, Kris Faafoi, David Clark, Phil Twyford, Grant Robertson, David Parker and Stuart Nash, all senior Labour members, joined them. The mood was sombre. Labour MPs had become accustomed to looking morose in press conferences.

Ardern began: 'Thank you everyone for joining us this afternoon. I want to start by giving a brief statement and then we'll allow time for questions at the conclusion.' It was as if a relief teacher had entered the classroom. Everyone present was analysing her delivery, trying to determine if she'd be able to handle the class or not. In this case, the class was an unprecedentedly flailing Labour Party and a packed press gallery, waiting to pounce on any sign of weakness. Her short speech, though predictable, was delivered confidently, the debating student in her coming to the fore. Her support team remained stoic.

Ardern thanked Little and then reassured the public that Labour was a strong party and this incredibly undesirable circumstance was in fact totally fine. She concluded: 'I'm privileged and honoured to be the leader of the Labour Party. I am looking forward to the challenge of the election campaign, where I will get the opportunity to talk to New Zealand about Labour's plan for a better and fairer New Zealand. This is what Labour has always stood for and under my leadership it is what we will continue to stand for. I am happy to take questions, I am sure there are many.'

At that last line, some of the ministers standing behind Ardern laughed, perhaps in relief. It was a good speech, well delivered. But they couldn't quite breathe easy yet: the press conference had only just begun. It could go downhill at any moment.

Those watching around the country – the students tuning in during university lectures, office workers with an extra tab open, and every working journalist – held their breath. Even those with the highest of hopes had seen enough of Labour's undoing in recent years to know they had to couple them with the lowest of expectations.

For many watching, both in the room and around the country, Little stepping down looked like a desperate attempt from Labour to save the furniture. No matter who was leader, it was too late to turn around their polling. But someone like Ardern; young, energetic, fresh, may be able to shake things up just enough to save face. It looked like a desperate move, and one that may sacrifice her in the process. Becoming leader simply to lose an election gracefully is hardly an ideal starting point for a politician.

But there she stood, as she opened the floor for questions.

Barry Soper, a veteran press gallery reporter of more than two decades, called out first. 'Do you think you're up to the job of being prime minister?'

Jacinda didn't hesitate. 'Yes, I am, Barry, and my team would not have selected me if they didn't believe that also.' Her delivery wasn't particularly noteworthy, and the line even less so, but the fact she addressed Barry by name was unexpected.

During the next twenty minutes of questions, she kept up the personal approach – much like a teacher moderating a class discussion. 'Sorry, what was that, Audrey?', 'Andrea', 'Alex', 'Chris', 'Look, Paddy', 'Katie', 'We're not going to come out of the election with 24 per cent, Corin.' This would be normal for a prime minister, who has weekly post-cabinet conferences with the press gallery, but it wasn't anticipated from a leader of the opposition who'd been in the job all of two hours. This was the first indication that, despite being thrown a hospital pass by her colleagues, Ardern was more than prepared for her moment.

Before long, a reporter directed a question at Davis, the newly elected deputy leader. As he stepped forward to answer, Ardern stepped back, but not completely behind him. Deliberate or not, it showed how comfortable she was with being front and centre.

A reporter asked a question in te reo and Davis answered in kind. It was a rare moment in New Zealand politics and helped Labour look friendly to Māori, something the socially liberal party had struggled with, largely due to distinctly anti-Māori moves made by the previous Labour government under Helen Clark.

Ardern shut down suggestions that there were factions once again within the Labour party and admitted that she had recently been quoted as saying she did not want the job. 'I have been asked to take on this challenge. I have accepted,' she stated simply.

She answered questions around the Memorandum of Understanding that Labour had with the Greens, who seemed to be catching up to Labour in the polls, firmly: might they be a key to Labour forming government? 'Transparency with the New Zealand public around who we would intend to work with if the public give us the opportunity and the privilege to be in government, I think that transparency is important and it remains. But I want to be very clear. This is a Labour campaign. We will be focused on Labour's policies and ideas. I do not want to be drawn into conversations about other parties, plans or policies.'

The statement was delivered with force. This was no longer a flailing Labour Party, searching desperately for allies with which to join forces. This was the second most powerful political party in the country, and they were going to act like it. If any doubt remained at this point, this declaration made it clear that Ardern was very much in control.

Being able to handle a large press conference is a unique skill that few MPs possess, and even fewer possess intuitively. Often they, and the public, don't find out whether they are good at it until they have to front the full press gallery and answer questions during a live broadcast. MPs will speak to reporters individually or in small groups, but the full gallery is a different beast. Many a politician has been undone by such occasions, most notably former National MP Jami-Lee Ross. Ross called a press conference in October 2018 to resign from the party and to allege that Simon Bridges, his party leader, had broken electoral law. Upon finishing his outrageously long prepared statement, Ross stood on the chequered tiles of Bowen House and answered questions for a further thirty-eight minutes. He didn't know how to walk away, and wound up revealing a whole lot more than he originally intended. Ross, now an independent, spent much of 2019 sitting in the farthest corner of the debating chamber, alone. His chances of ever becoming prime minister are slim.

Ardern's first major press conference was a completely different story. Her support crew behind her were visibly relaxing as she answered each question with aplomb. This was, they started to realise, unlike any Labour presser in the past five years. Ardern was genuinely positive and full of confidence. And it was starting to rub off on everyone else.

When asked about Labour possibly working with the Māori Party, Davis responded with the confidence of a deputy leader expecting to win an election. 'If the Māori Party is still standing after the election, they'll have to up their game if they want to work with us.' Just a reminder: at this point, the Labour Party was polling at 23 per cent.

The decision to promote Davis, the most senior Māori MP in the party, to deputy was clearly tactical but nonetheless welcomed by Labour supporters. Labour had positioned themselves as a socially liberal party committed to raising New Zealand's standard of living, an issue faced disproportionately by Māori. But Labour had a fraught reputation with Māori. The last Labour prime minister, Helen Clark, had overseen the *Foreshore and Seabed Act 2004*, a law widely considered to be an act of oppression against the already historically oppressed Māori.

Since 2004, Labour had attempted, rather unsuccessfully, to regain Māori support. Having Davis as deputy, the first Māori deputy leader of Labour in its history, had symbolic power. Davis was also running in a Māori electorate, and the Māori seats were vital for Labour if they were to hold or gain ground.

Perhaps the most defining moment of the conference came in the final minute. A reporter addressed a question to Stuart Nash, who was standing conspicuously at the very end of the support line-up. 'You said yesterday Labour shouldn't change leaders this close to the election ...' As the reporter spoke, Sepuloni looked across at Nash and smirked. Davis looked to be laughing. Nash had been the lone MP to speak out strongly against a leadership change. As he stepped forward to respond, he was beaten to it by Ardern, who answered before the question was even finished. 'Stuart has acknowledged to me that he was wrong.' The whole room laughed, and Nash stepped back into place at the end of the line.

Ardern's transition from deputy leader to leader both in title and in commanding presence overnight was extraordinary to behold. Six months earlier, Ardern and Nash had been more or less equals in the party. But in that instant, their new relationship was instantly and convincingly established. It sent a clear message: Labour would no longer allow infighting or members speaking out of turn. After five years of a very public struggle for loyalty and cooperation, Labour's new leader making a point of putting a colleague in his place was refreshing.

While all this was unfolding, Little was packing up the office that was no longer his. He'd promised to support his successor in her campaign, but he needed to take a few days to mourn his lost ambitions. By the time Ardern returned to the offices of the opposition, she would find an empty workspace ready for her across the hall from her old one. Little would be gone, driven home with a box of his possessions.

When the last question was answered, Ardern thanked the room, smiled and led her team out. As they made their way past the mics, which were still picking up sound, health spokesperson David Clark could be heard muttering 'nailed it' under his breath. He wasn't wrong.

7

The First 72 Hours

The 'Jacinda effect' was immediate.

It's hard to overstate the excitement with which even the most cynical journalists reported Ardern's appointment as leader. New Zealand politics hadn't had such a charismatic leader in decades. John Key had been affable in a Kiwi Bloke sort of way, but Ardern was something else. It had been so long since Labour had dominated the news cycle for a positive reason that even right-wing commentators couldn't help but get caught up in the buzz.

Breathless live crosses from outside the Beehive dominated the six o'clock news, and the front pages of the major newspapers around the country the next morning declared: 'Labour's golden girl steps up' and 'Labour's A-bomb has the X-factor'. They would continue to lead with Ardern for the next two days.

For nine years, National had sat in government and watched as their opposition scored own goal after own goal. But with a new captain, the Labour team was looking not just less downtrodden but actually hopeful. It was a shock for everyone, and National MPs didn't take to it kindly. Minister of Defence Gerry Brownlee went so far as to send Patrick Gower (he of 'Battle of the Babes' fame) a set of cheerleading pompoms with a note: 'Watching your unbridled enthusiasm yesterday in your live crosses I thought the props may help in the future.'

The excitement manifested in more concrete ways too. In the twenty-four hours following Ardern's first press conference, Labour received more than $250,000 in online donations, with a median donation of $33. At one point they were receiving $700 in donations every minute, unheard of in New Zealand politics. As well as the increase in donations, Labour received over 1000 new volunteer sign-ups in a day.

The extra help was much needed. The thousands of hoardings around the country showing Little and Ardern with their slogan 'Fresh Approach' didn't look so fresh anymore. On social media, people had no shortage of solutions to offer. Some pointed out that Little and Davis shared a similar enough build to make a clean swap of the faces. One user printed out a picture of Davis's face and stuck it over Little's to demonstrate. Others photoshopped a black X over Little and added an 'er' to make the sign read 'A Fresher Approach'. Some suggested that Labour simply cut out Little's face, leaving a hole that voters could put their own heads in, like the photo walls at county fairs. Jacinda and Me, walking together towards a better New Zealand. It wasn't the worst idea in the world. Labour themselves wanted to overhaul the entire campaign. They needed a fresh approach – without the slogan 'a fresh approach'.

Ardern had promised a new strategy within seventy-two hours and she delivered. Within three days, new hoardings had been erected. And on Thursday morning, forty-eight

hours after Little resigned, Labour scheduled a press conference to announce their new campaign. But while
volunteers were putting up the brand-new signs around the
country, Ardern was encountering her first real challenge as
leader. One that would show whether she was a leader with
steel, who could make cut-throat decisions, or that her critics were right and she didn't have the ruthlessness required
to be a successful politician. The question was whether or
not to axe a potential ally, Metiria Turei.

Turei was the co-leader of the Green Party, a left-wing
party formed in 1990 with a focus on environmental issues
and socialist economic policies. The Greens were the third-
largest party in New Zealand, though significantly smaller
than National and Labour. Since the turn of the century
they had typically received between 6 and 12 per cent of
party votes in general elections. Because New Zealand has
a mixed member proportional (MMP) electoral system,
the Greens play a crucial role in giving support to either
side within parliament. On most issues, Labour and the
Greens agree.

In May 2016, Labour had been looking for allies. They
signed a Memorandum of Understanding (MOU) with the
Greens, 'to work co-operatively to change the government
in the 2017 election'. It was a historic move, interpreted as
Labour coming to terms with the fact that it looked near
impossible for them to beat National on their own.

But in July 2017, Labour were floundering in the polls
and the Greens wanted to seize the chance to sway unde-
cided left-wing voters. So Metitiria Turei took a risk. A
calculated risk, though commentators from both the left
and right would later agree it wasn't calculated enough.
At the party AGM, where Turei and her co-leader James
Shaw outlined their campaign policies, she admitted that

as a young single mum she had committed benefit fraud. It wasn't a slip of the tongue and it wasn't a play for headlines. It was intended to start a conversation around welfare and whether it is possible to survive on the benefit in New Zealand. It succeeded. But it also started another conversation: should Turei, someone who'd admitted to breaking the law, be in government?

Turei's team had discussed her speech with Little's team before the conference (as part of their regular meetings under the MOU), and Labour had advised against it. If there's one thing that unites all voters, they felt, it's a disdain for those who breach the social contract. Not paying taxes or taking more than you're entitled to are considered equal sins. *We all agreed to follow these rules, how dare you get greedy.* Never mind that one is called benefit *fraud* and taps out at tens of millions of dollars a year, while the other is tax *evasion* and totals in the billions of dollars of unpaid tax annually.

As a 23-year-old single mother studying law in the '90s, Turei did not disclose that she had flatmates paying rent to her – so that her benefit wouldn't be cut for being over the income threshold.

Her admission dominated the news cycle for a few days, and brought the Greens back into the election conversation. The ministry of social development launched an investigation into Turei's benefit history on the same day that the poll results came out, Ardern's birthday. The same poll that showed Labour polling at their worst since 1995 showed the Greens at an incredible 15 per cent.

Voters to the centre of Labour saw a left block imploding and fled to New Zealand First, while Labour voters who were tired of the lack of conviction their party was showing felt they'd found a worthy alternative in the Greens. Turei's honesty and frankness touched many New Zealanders, who empathised rather than saw her as a criminal. Labour were dropping in the polls, yes. And they were heading for an election loss to National anyway, yes. But Turei's move meant the Greens were also taking Labour votes.

Looking back, Metiria Turei's speech could be seen as the catalyst for Jacinda Ardern becoming prime minister. Had Turei not taken the risk, Labour would have probably continued polling in the high 20s and Little would have had no reason to consider stepping down at the eleventh hour. But Turei did take that risk, Labour's support plummeted, and Little had no choice but to go, leaving Ardern to step up.

On the morning that Little resigned, the Greens were looking at a potentially record-breaking election result. There was still much criticism of Turei's admission in the media, but polls showed a lot of voters supported her. When Little resigned seven weeks before the election, many expected an even bigger surge to the Greens, as more disgruntled Labour voters turned their backs on red. Instead, by the time Ardern had wrapped up her first press conference, droves of left-wing voters were flocking back to Labour.

It should have been a win–win situation. The Green Party was finding its feet, getting media attention and starting conversations around the policies they wanted to implement. And Labour had a rising star as their new leader, who'd just exceeded everyone's expectations in her first media challenge. But the media wasn't done with Turei yet.

On 3 August, while hundreds of thousands of dollars were being donated to Labour, *Newshub* reported that Turei had enrolled to vote in an electorate where she was no longer living. Voting in a different electorate to the one you actually reside in isn't uncommon. People move and don't bother changing their address on the electoral roll all the time. But when asked about it, Turei replied that she'd stayed enrolled at her old residence in order to vote for her friend, who was running a joke campaign for that seat. This was the beginning of the end for Turei. On its own, it was nothing. But paired with her earlier confession, it was damning. Although most people believed Turei had been wrong to claim an increased benefit, there was a lot of sympathy for her and understanding that she did it out of necessity, not greed. But when it was reported that she also committed electoral fraud simply to vote for her friend, she started to seem like someone who broke the law recklessly, for the fun of it. It sowed doubt in a lot of voters' minds. If Turei had admitted to benefit fraud, and then confessed to have also committed electoral fraud, what else was there to find in her past? As it turned out, nothing. But it was too late.

Predictably, after Turei's AGM speech, National MPs had spoken out strongly against her actions. Right-wing commentators had called for her to be prosecuted. But Little had said he thought Turei was brave for admitting it, and that he would support her and continue to support the MOU.

But when the *Newshub* report came out, Little wasn't the leader anymore. With Ardern in charge, would Labour stick by Turei and the Greens or would they cut them off like an infected limb?

Appearing on *The AM Show* the morning after the *Newshub* report was published, deputy leader Davis didn't hold back in distancing himself and Labour from Turei and the Greens. 'The Greens, they've made their bed and they're going to have to lie in it,' he said. 'We're just going to have to have a good discussion about how this is going to affect us, because we don't want to be seen to be condoning this sort of stuff.'

Labour scheduled a press conference for 12.15 pm on Thursday, 4 August, two days after Ardern became leader. The purpose was to unveil Labour's new slogan and campaign look. There would also be questions about Turei. It was far too early for Ardern to have blood on her hands, but she needed to show she was able to make the tough decisions.

That morning, Ardern assigned two members of her team to pass on a message to James Shaw and his team. One of the messengers was heavily rumoured to be Grant Robertson and the other chief of staff, Neale Jones. They told the Greens that if asked about Turei's potential role in a Labour government, Ardern would say she would not assign Turei a cabinet or ministerial position. This was huge. The two parties had a memorandum of understanding. For Ardern to rule out the co-leader of their potential coalition partner from any ministerial role was essentially a disowning. On top of that, Ardern, known for being the most empathetic MP in parliament and criticised for being 'too nice', hadn't even passed the news on herself.

In order to save face, Turei scheduled her own press conference for noon, leaving Labour to push Ardern's back to 1 pm. In Turei's presser, she announced that she would not be putting herself forward for a ministerial position if Labour got into government but would remain as co-leader of the Greens at least until the election. Turei insisted that Labour hadn't pressured her to step back. It was hard to believe (what MP, having spent a decade in opposition, would willingly rule themselves out of contention for a ministerial position?) and became even harder to believe once Ardern held her own press conference an hour later.

Ardern stated that her team had 'conveyed' her view to Turei that morning that Turei had no place in a Labour–Greens government. With Labour experiencing a rare surge of power and support, the future of the Labour–Greens alliance was looking shaky.

By the end of the election campaign, the consensus was that Turei had been brave in admitting both her struggles and the unlawful behaviour it took for her to survive those struggles. But in politics, honesty is no substitute for strategy, and had the Greens plotted out her admission more stringently (for example, if she had made a point of paying back what she had been overpaid in the '90s, now that she was a high-earning MP, *before* the speech), things may have turned out very differently. Instead, Turei's admission set in motion a series of events that would ultimately end with her own political downfall and Ardern's accelerated ascension. Ardern's dismissal of Turei in that moment was widely praised. The politician judged for a decade as 'too nice' had dispatched an ally with ruthless efficiency. It reassured Ardern's supporters that she could play the game.

Supporters of Turei and the Greens saw things differently. To them, Ardern had failed at her first opportunity to put her 'kinder politics' into practice. In standing by Turei and supporting the kaupapa (principles) they shared, Ardern could have demonstrated a new way to govern. The compassionate leader would have done that. But in August 2017, it looked like the compassionate leader wouldn't win an election. In that moment, the kinder, empathetic approach was set aside in service of the bigger picture. As Ardern would later say whenever speaking about the less savoury parts of her job: 'It's all politics.'

Five days after telling media she wasn't going anywhere, Turei resigned from her position as co-leader of the Greens and left politics altogether. She has said on more than one occasion that she has no regrets and if she had the choice, she'd do it all over again. If it weren't for Turei's speech and its flow-on effects, Little would have remained leader and the Labour–Greens unit would have stayed in opposition. In the same way that Little deserves credit for knowing when to quit, Turei deserves credit for taking that risk and accepting her own demise. She disappeared from public life and refused to speak about the events of that week in August. Today, she is an artist, specialising in embroidery and digital mediums.

So consider this: Ardern managed to replace a leader in her own party and axe one from another party within the space of a week – yet her popularity only grew in response. The smiling assassin now had cheerleaders.

Having shown her political steel, Ardern moved swiftly on to the real reason for her press conference: the new look campaign. What Little had been trying to do wasn't working. And though the easy option would be to simply swap drivers, Ardern and her team decided to swap out the whole car. Virtually overnight, any hint of Little was scrubbed. Labour had initially promoted Little and Ardern as a team, while National's hoardings showed only Bill English. When Labour's new hoardings went up, Davis was nowhere to be seen. It was Ardern alone versus English. One on one.

The switch in imagery was drastic. The loyal reds of Labour had been swapped for a clean, almost angelic white. Ardern smiled out, alone, also in white. It was crisp, and felt modern even on the most traditional advertising platforms. Volunteer t-shirts were printed with the new slogan in white-on-red, in a style not unlike artist Barbara Kruger, and later the Supreme clothing brand: 'Let's do this.'

Ardern's first post on Facebook as leader, aside from live-streaming her press conference, was on 2 August. It was a photo of Ardern leaving the conference, captioned 'Yesterday was not quite what I was expecting! Overwhelmed by the wonderful messages, and the possibility. Let's do this. #changethegovt'

A journalist asked Ardern the next day if 'Let's do this' was her campaign slogan and she denied it, but also said she wasn't ruling it out. Labour MPs had already begun using the term in their own posts about her leadership coup, and a video created and shared by the Labour Party ended with 'Let's Do This' on a still red frame. By the time the seventy-two hours was up, 'Let's do this' was already synonymous with Ardern's Labour Party.

Everything was accelerated, from the changeover, to the donations, to the campaign overhaul. Events that typically took weeks to plan were being executed within days. The wheels were turning and everyone in Labour was simply trying to keep up.

The election was only fifty days away.

8

The Campaign

An election campaign informally begins on the first day of any election year. And seven weeks out from the big day, the schedule's locked in. Every appearance, speech, announcement or ribbon-cutting is confirmed. Little and Ardern had formed a campaign schedule tailored to their strengths and campaign priorities. Now, with Ardern as leader, it was obsolete.

First, Ardern gathered with staffers and some of her old friends in Fraser House, below the Labour headquarters, to figure out her policy framework. She kept most of it as Little had devised, but she wanted to shift the emphasis. Most importantly, she wanted to focus more on the environment and climate change.

And she had in mind a different way of communicating, too. Unlike perhaps any other politician in New Zealand, Ardern could conduct herself authentically and appealingly on social media – apparently effortlessly. As one of the youngest members of parliament, she was an experienced user of social media. Ardern promised early on in her campaign that as well as caring about getting Labour votes, she would also work to get more people voting full stop. To do that, she felt politics needed to be more accessible to regular people. So she promised to go live on Facebook at least once a week throughout the campaign and give regular voters the chance to ask her questions and have them answered immediately. 'I want to reach everyone,' she said.

For every policy announcement, she scheduled a Facebook Live event later that day, in which she would explain the policy further in a more casual setting (often at her home), before answering questions that comment- ers submitted during the broadcast. Ardern was cutting out the media middle man and allowing members of the public to act as their own press gallery. A lot of New Zealanders weren't particularly interested in Labour's freshwater policy or their plans for a fuel tax, but they were interested in Jacinda Ardern. What Ardern achieved with those live videos was a promotion of democracy and policy to audiences that typically did not engage with politics. Everything's just that little bit easier to understand when someone you genuinely like is explaining it.

Ardern's Live videos were popular, and her written posts even more so. Thousands of people liked, commented on and shared them. Once again, even as leader this time, the focus of Ardern's social media campaign was more on her own actions and views than Labour policy. It was a deliber- ate move, and one that made New Zealand politics more like American politics, where campaigning is heavily slanted towards the individual candidates rather than their parties.

When it had been a matter of Little versus English, Labour's campaign had been a traditional one. Both men were notoriously dull. Likely neither of them would have a significant presence online if their jobs didn't call for it. But Ardern was a digital native and she took her campaign online. She was a natural, and her posts were not the predictable, carefully crafted political messages voters had come to expect from their politicians.

During a media statement early on in the campaign, Ardern recalled one of her political influences, former prime minister Norman Kirk, and his philosophy for a better New Zealand: 'All Kiwis want is someone to love, somewhere to live, somewhere to work, and something to hope for.'

She was that hope, as the flood of donations and volunteers in the days since her promotion indicated. But could this translate into votes?

Ardern herself tempered her expectations of what she could achieve in seven weeks. A protective mechanism. Reflecting later, she said, 'There was a little piece in the back of my mind where I would tell myself, "you're here to save the furniture".'

Ardern's first policy announcement as leader was on a Sunday in downtown Auckland. It wasn't a particularly inspiring subject: public transport. Yet hundreds of supporters turned up, not to hear about the light rail network proposal, but to support their new favourite politician. It was a big venue – the Cloud, a massive, ugly building on Auckland's waterfront built to host events for the 2011 Rugby World Cup – but the space was packed. In that moment, seeing 'a lot of people who've come to hear about trains', Ardern first thought that maybe, just maybe, Labour had a shot after all.

The crowds didn't go away. For the next six weeks, everywhere Ardern went she was surrounded by people. Sometimes there were volunteers wearing Labour t-shirts, almost always there were children.

Working day to day and planning events at such short notice meant Ardern spent a lot of time in one particular place: schools. The optics were good: children are the future and if the children seem to like the leader that's always good for media. They also operate in large groups. No politician should ever be pictured alone on a campaign trail. Yet more than one image of English standing in an abandoned warehouse had been released *by his own team*. It made him look unsupported. In contrast, Ardern shared photos from a school visit every other day, surrounded by dozens of smiling children and looking extremely popular.

Ten days after Ardern became leader, *Newshub* and Reid Research released another poll. As expected, the change in leadership and almost universally positive reception to Ardern had led to a jump for Labour. They had risen 9 percentage points to a respectable 33.1 per cent. But the Greens had dropped nearly 5 full percentage points to 8.3 per cent.

After the failure of polls in the United States to predict Donald Trump's victory over Hillary Clinton, or UK polls to predict Brexit, Labour supporters were hesitant to get too invested in their first positive poll results, but it was hard not to. The preferred prime minister polling showed English had a slight increase to 27.7 per cent and Ardern had an extraordinary jump from 8.6 to 26.3 per cent. No Labour leader had gotten that close to leading in the preferred PM polls since Helen Clark early in the 2008 campaign, when she was the incumbent prime minister.

Labour had seven weeks to turn their campaign around, and they'd made enormous strides in just a fortnight.

But even as her popularity soared and she eased into her new role, Ardern was still at pains to make it known that she had never wanted this. When asked about her ambitions to be prime minister on a Facebook Live chat, Ardern replied: 'I've always had the view that I could achieve what I want to achieve by being a member of a team that's in government and by being a minister. But we have to be in government. So the team asked me to help with that job, and that's why I'm here. I'm not here because of my own personal ambition. I'm not here because I want to be the big cheese or the top dog, I'm here because I want to bring in a team of New Zealanders who care deeply about making this country better. They just so happen to have chosen me to be at the lead.'

The day after the *Newshub* poll came out, Ardern's mentor and predecessor as deputy leader Annette King left parliament after thirty-three years. King had served in the Labour Party from when one of Ardern's favourite politicians, Norman Kirk, was in power in the early 1970s, and through two more Labour governments. Her farewell speech included a special note of encouragement to her mentee: 'I have a feeling you will lead the party for years to come and you are going to be one of our most loved and effective leaders and prime ministers.' It was a powerful statement from a woman who had spent half her life within the halls of parliament and earned the respect of politicians throughout the House. And King backed up her words by staying on enthusiastically as an unofficial adviser to Ardern for the rest of the campaign.

The apex of Ardern's pre-election popularity was her official campaign launch. On 20 August, three weeks after taking over and just shy of five weeks before the election, Ardern launched the Labour Party campaign at Auckland Town Hall. It was a modest venue (for comparison, National held their launch at an indoor arena), but of course the venue had been booked when Little was still the leader.

Now supporters lined up early on Queen Street in downtown Auckland, hoping to get a seat inside. Not everyone did. The hall reached capacity early and the remaining hopefuls were forced to flock to the theatre next door to watch the event on a screen. Even then, people were turned away due to overcrowding.

The launch had an energy unlike any New Zealand political event in recent history. A sea of red flooded the city, with flags, signs and streamers everywhere. Supporters chanted, 'Let's do this!' There was optimism and genuine excitement. Veteran political commentator and author Colin James, who had covered fifteen elections, wrote that the feeling at the launch was 'as if a thick, dark curtain had been pulled back to let midday summer light in on Labour'.

During her speech, Ardern addressed one of her touchstone policy areas, a point of difference from Little: climate change. She spoke about the urgency with which New Zealand needed to act. Climate change, she said, 'is my generation's nuclear-free moment, and I am determined that we will tackle it head on.'

Of course, this was a hit to the Greens. The environment and sustainability had always been at the forefront of their policies. With Labour catering to centre-left voters, the Greens typically secured the left left with their focus on climate change action. Ardern made a statement to that effect and predictably it was repeated by media and supporters throughout Labour's campaign, playing to those exact Green voters.

The campaign launch was a resounding success. Ardern had cemented her position as a serious threat to the National government, and had shown how 'youth-adjacent' she really was by focusing her party's attention on climate change. This was the biggest issue for young people and Ardern showed she knew how heavily it weighed on their shoulders.

When speaking to a high school in Christchurch, Ardern again stressed the importance of taking action on climate change. 'One of the reasons that we've started talking about this issue as much as we have is because … if we don't start tackling it now, you'll find when you're in positions of leadership that you'll be picking up the tab.'

Openly acknowledging the seriousness of climate change on the campaign trail was a step in the right direction, though not a huge surprise for those who had followed Ardern's career and her stance on the issue. It was, however, a welcome point of difference between New Zealand and its western neighbours. While politicians in Australia, the UK and the US continued to debate whether global warming was even real, New Zealand politicians were debating how best to tackle it.

In unfortunate timing, in August, not two months before the election, Deputy Prime Minister of Australia Barnaby Joyce was found to have broken Australian electoral law by holding dual citizenship between Australia and New Zealand. Joyce was born in Australia, but his father was born in New Zealand. The Australian Constitution dictates that those with dual citizenship cannot be legislators. In the previous year, many members of parliament had been outed (or outed themselves) as dual citizens, causing electoral havoc. The crime was a victimless one, but Australian voters were tired of the mess. More pressingly, if Joyce were made to step down by the Australian High Court, Malcolm Turnbull's government would lose its one-vote majority.

The scenario was exactly the sort of thing comedian John Oliver would love to pick apart. But for Turnbull's government, it was no laughing matter. Foreign Minister Julie Bishop took aim at the New Zealand Labour Party and accused them of colluding with the Australian Labor Party (also in opposition) in revealing Joyce's dual citizenship. She went so far as to say: 'If there was a change of government, I would find it very difficult to build trust with members of a political party that had been used by the Australian Labor Party to seek to undermine the Australian government.'

Bishop's comments weren't to be taken lightly. Australia is New Zealand's closest ally and a major trading partner. For a senior representative of Australia's government to say that they wouldn't be able to form a relationship with one of New Zealand's major parties was, well, major. Would Ardern stand up for her party and country, like Hugh Grant in *Love Actually*, or would she defer to the more powerful player and apologise, like most diplomatic encounters outside of the movies? Well, call her Hughcinda because she wasn't taking any of Bishop's shit. She called in the Australian High Commissioner and informed him that any claims of Labour's involvement were untrue and unfortunate. She then tweeted: 'I value our relationship with the Australian Govt highly. I won't let disappointing & false claims stand in the way of that relationship.' She had also noted earlier that she 'would happily take a call from Julie Bishop to clarify matters'. It was a firm but fair stance, basically asking that Australia keep their shambles of a political landscape to themselves, please.

Bishop refused to apologise and never backed down from her claims, but was widely regarded by New Zealanders and Australians alike to have lost that scuffle.

Joyce would eventually be declared ineligible and made to stand down until the next election, where he would win back his ministerial position before losing it again after revealing he had separated from his wife of twenty-four years and was expecting a child with a former staffer. Joyce was jokingly nominated as New Zealander of the Year in 2017 but did not make the shortlist.

Meanwhile, Ardern went from strength to strength. When *One News* and Colmar Brunton released their latest poll on the last day of August, just three weeks before the election, the country gasped. For the first time in twelve years, the Labour Party was polling ahead of National. At 43 per cent to National's 41 per cent, the result was better than anyone on the left could have dreamed.

The Labour campaign, which had until very recently looked dead in the water, was alive and functioning. Ardern and her team started to realise that seven weeks could be plenty of time to win an election. But they were about to learn that it was also plenty of time to lose one.

***

'It has been said that introducing a capital gains tax is political suicide. I take a different view.' So wrote Jacinda Ardern, in the *New Zealand Herald*, in 2011.

In the 2011 election, capital gains tax was the centre-piece of Labour's tax package. They proposed a 15 per cent tax on gains made through the sale of shares, companies and property, excluding the family home. It was expected to be a game-changer in a faltering campaign but proved to have little effect on voters. While approximately half of those polled thought a capital gains tax was a good idea, it wasn't considered important enough for them to switch to a Labour vote in the election.

When David Cunliffe again campaigned on a capital gains tax in 2014, it hung around like a bad fart. Nobody wants to hear policies explained at length by politicians, they just want to know what it means for them and their hard-earned money. So when John Key called capital gains tax a 'death tax', probably after watching an old *West Wing* episode, it derailed Cunliffe, who struggled to say why it wasn't. Instead of promoting all Labour's other policies, Cunliffe got stuck trying, and largely failing, to explain how a capital gains tax would or wouldn't affect the average New Zealander. In 2014, Labour suffered their biggest election loss in ninety-two years.

Now, six years after it had first been floated, Ardern wanted to bring the CGT back. In her 2011 column supporting the tax, she'd written 'Standing by and doing nothing while the country's economy becomes a housing market with a few extras added on and we sink into more and more debt and rising unemployment – that is the real threat.' There was a national housing crisis; the median house price in Auckland was nine times that of the median income. In these circumstances, a capital gains tax appeared reasonable – at least on face value.

But when Little had outlined his tax policy framework, he had ruled out a capital gains tax. With Ardern in charge, CGT was very much back on the table. New Zealand was one of few developed countries around the world to not tax profits made from the sale of property. Australia had a capital gains tax. Canada had a capital gains tax. The UK, Denmark, Sweden, France, virtually every country that New Zealand considered itself to be like had a capital gains tax. Implementing one wouldn't be a drastic move, argued its supporters, because it was already long overdue.

Time had passed since Cunliffe had failed to convince voters and if anyone was going to sell CGT to the country, it would be Labour's beloved new leader. Ardern announced that, as prime minister, she would form a tax working group and, if it came back with a recommendation for CGT, she would implement one before the 2020 election.

She'd made a 'Captain's call', she said, in deciding not to rule out a CGT in her first term. She wasn't going to campaign on it, but she wasn't going to rule it out as a possibility before 2020. Voters didn't like that. All they heard was that if Labour got into government, they'd implement extra taxes without warning or consultation. It scared people, and National pounced: 'Taxinda' or 'Let's Tax This' were their go-to lines in attack ads. It was a repeat of the last two elections and once again, it worked. Ardern had made her first bold call as leader and it backfired. Taxes rule the world and the fear of them rules voters.

Even though Labour had deliberately chosen not to campaign on the capital gains tax (the Greens were the only party to do so), by not ruling it out they once again found themselves spending precious airtime trying to defend it. As far as a tax policy went, Labour didn't have much. And their lack of clarity made them an easy target for National, who implied Labour were going to surprise New Zealanders with endless new taxes if elected.

Targeted attack ads aren't nearly as popular in New Zealand as in other democracies. Some might argue it's because there's a greater sense of decorum, others would argue it's because New Zealanders are so thin-skinned. Whatever the reason, there's an underlying sense of 'hey, don't be too mean' in New Zealand campaigning. And both Ardern and English, in their respective parliamentary careers, had established themselves as MPs who operated with a higher-than-average level of sportsmanship.

So when National released attack ads targeting Labour's tax policy, people were shocked. It showed that National were genuinely worried, probably for the first time in nine years, about losing their place in government. But it also showed that attack ads work. By claiming that Labour were planning to introduce a whole basket of new taxes (they weren't, but they also weren't getting that message across), the shine of Jacindamania began to dim.

In the first week of September, Grant Robertson released Labour's proposed budget. There was nothing ground-breaking in it. Until Steven Joyce, the finance minister, sent out a press release claiming there was an $11.7 billion hole in it. Labour staffers panicked. Was there a hole? How could they possibly have messed up calculations that badly? They called Robertson's economic adviser to triple-check, and were assured that this claim was bullshit. There was no hole. Not even a little hole that got blown out of proportion? No, not even a little hole.

They were right. There was no hole.

Ardern was at a Pink Batts insulation factory when the news broke. She stepped away from the media scrum that had followed her the entire campaign, and had a timeout with her staff as a giant guillotine loudly cut insulation nearby. When she returned to the media pack, she said some things about insulation and they asked her only about the hole. There's no hole, she said.

But Joyce didn't back down, and neither did the rest of the National party. Somehow this imaginary hole kept pop-ping up in debates and media stand-ups, and all Robertson could do was keep saying that there was no hole. It became a he-said, he-said situation, and National said it louder. By the end of the week's polling, Labour's popularity had dropped back into the 30s.

But Ardern was holding steady in other ways. In the televised debates between Ardern and English, she put in strong performances. The four debates, held between 31 August (the first debate was held one hour after the dramatic poll showed Labour in the lead for the first time in over a decade) and 20 September, were closely fought. There were no major breakthroughs or hits for either side – in fact, they were about as civil as close election debates get – but there were a few memorable moments.

At the end of the second debate, the two leaders were asked about abortion. 'At the moment it is actually illegal, under the Crimes Act, to have an abortion,' began moderator Patrick Gower. 'The main way that women get it is by saying that having a child is a serious danger to their mental health, and that forces a lot of women to lie. Should we change that law?'

He had barely finished asking the question before Ardern answered. 'Yes.'

'Will you do it if you become prime minister?'

Again, her answer overlapped with Gower's question. 'Yes. It shouldn't be in the Crimes Act.'

The passion and conviction in Ardern's response got a rousing ovation from the live studio audience. When pressed about whether she would make that change in government, Ardern was firm.

'People need to make their own decision. I accept that there will be people out there who disagree with abortion. I want them to have that as their right. But I also want women who want access to have it as their right too. This is about everyone being able to make their own decision.'

It was a moment of sure-footedness in a debate series between two politicians adept at speaking around a firm statement. With elections since 2008 being fought between a rotating cast of middle-aged men, abortion had unsurprisingly not been a hot topic for debate. But Gower wasn't wrong. Though abortion was technically available to women around the country – and it would be a shock to hear of someone being charged with a crime for terminating a pregnancy – abortion was still in the New Zealand Crimes Act.

The minutiae of tax policy and the guidelines for a tax working group were capital-P political issues, the types of things journalists and politics nerds on Twitter love to discuss at length in lieu of having a social life. Abortion was a conscience issue, and arguably a personal issue, and that's where Ardern's strength lay.

After the debate, Ardern sent a text message to Gower. 'You did a good job,' she wrote.

On the ground, Ardern was campaigning in a way that few politicians manage: by appearing to have genuine empathy and a sense of humour. Children, the great equalisers with no real interest in politicians, flocked to her wherever she went. In town halls all over the country, women spoke of how Ardern's success was inspiring them and their daughters.

But while Ardern kept a smile on in every selfie (and there were many), the campaign was taking its toll. At an event in Nelson, Ardern had called for more investment in health services and used the example of her grandfather having recently been discharged from Waikato Hospital at midnight as emblematic of issues within the system. Days later, as their campaign made its way along the West Coast, Ardern watched another National attack ad raising doubt about Labour's tax policy, and learned that the media were attempting to locate her grandfather to follow up on her claims. She started to doubt her own instincts. 'It absolutely gutted me. I thought, "Did I make a mistake in mentioning that? How can I protect my family?"' she recalled later. 'And in the course of all that, my grandmother had a stroke too and was admitted into hospital as well and started a steady decline through the election campaign.'

Understandably, Ardern remembers this as 'the real low point' of the election.

Among that, while having a sausage roll in a small-town cafe, Ardern reconsidered her captain's call on tax. Labour were bleeding and they knew exactly where the wound was. So Ardern called Robertson and they decided to walk back her captain's call. On 15 September, Robertson called a press conference and announced that Labour would not impose any new taxes, even if recommended by a tax working group, until after the 2020 election. There was one week to go until the election. They hadn't expected to peak so high, but they also hadn't expected to peak so early. If they could just hold on for another eight days, they might be able to pull it off.

On the morning of 19 September, Margaret Bottomley, Ardern's maternal grandmother who had lent her granddaughter a people-mover so she could campaign better for the 2008 election, passed away at Te Aroha Community Hospital. She was eighty-one.

The final leaders debate was the next day. Ardern briefly mentioned her grandmother's death in the course of campaigning, but the campaign continued as scheduled, as did the debate. Commentators unanimously considered this to be the least impressive of the four debates and called it a draw. There was nothing said that would change voters' minds at the eleventh hour. New Zealand election campaigns are relatively short, officially seven weeks, but by the week of the election, everyone was ready for it to be over. None more so, it seemed, than the candidates themselves.

Ardern's grandmother's funeral was held in Te Aroha, in the Waikato, on 22 September. It was a small service, and media largely kept their distance. One reporter remembers being sent to scope it. The reporter didn't want to go, and preemptively apologised to Gayford, having bumped into him that morning in Auckland. He gave a look but didn't say anything. Moments later, the reporter was pleasantly surprised to receive a call from Ardern, who was in the car on her way to the service, saying there were no hard feelings and she understood it was part of the job.

After the funeral, Ardern returned immediately to Auckland to attend the last few Labour events before electoral law dictated that she cease campaigning.

The election was just one day away.

9

Election Night

Nobody won.

This is a common downside of New Zealand's mixed-member proportional (MMP) governing system: it's entirely possible to not have a winner on election night. And in 2017, nobody won.

New Zealand used to operate under a 'first past the post' system, in which everyone got one vote in their electorate and whichever party won the most seats on election night became the government. The MMP system, introduced by referendum in 1993, means that every voter casts two votes: one for their preferred electorate candidate, who will represent their electorate in parliament, and one for their preferred party. These are helpfully referred to as the electorate vote and the party vote.

The New Zealand parliament is typically made up of 120 representative seats. In the 2014 and 2017 elections there were seventy-one electorate seats, with the remaining seats being filled by members from party lists, as determined by the party votes.

To win a seat, a candidate must win the most electorate votes in their electorate. For example, in 2014, Nikki
Kaye earned her seat in parliament by beating Ardern in the
Auckland Central electorate. To win the rest of the seats, it
takes party votes.

If a party wins more than 5 per cent of the party votes,
they are entitled to the same percentage of seats in the
House. When Labour suffered their worst election loss in
recent history in 2014, they received just 25 per cent of the
party votes (thirty-two seats). Because their members had
already won twenty-seven electorate seats, they were able
to bring in just five additional members from their list, one
of whom was Ardern. At the same time, the Greens won no
electorate seats but gained close to 11 per cent of the party
vote. All fourteen of their seats in the House came from
their list.

Since New Zealand switched to an MMP system in
1996, no party has been able to govern alone. In 2014,
National got the closest, gaining sixty seats in the House,
just one shy of a majority. In order to govern, they formed
a coalition with ACT (one seat), United Future (one seat),
and the Māori Party (two seats).

In 2017, with polling in the final week of the campaign
showing both major parties either in the late thirties or
early forties, it was clear that neither had a shot at governing alone. Whichever party became the government would
only be able to do so with the help of at least one other
party, but most likely one man: Winston Raymond Peters.

Peters was a parliamentary veteran. He had been in and
out of parliament since before Ardern was born. And in
those four decades, he had got a lot done and pissed off a
lot of people (read: every single politician). While studying
in the '70s, Peters joined the Young Nats, National's youth

wing. He stood for the National Party in the 1975 election and lost, but became a member of parliament for National in 1978. He stayed with National and was Minister of Māori Affairs from 1990 to 1991, when he was sacked from cabinet and eventually pushed out of the party following multiple instances of publicly going against his own party.

In 1993 he then established the populist New Zealand First and, thanks largely to his personal brand popularity with voters, easily won back his Tauranga electorate seat, along with four other seats.

In 1996, when MMP was introduced, allowing smaller parties to win a larger share of the seats, Peters' New Zealand First won a whopping seventeen seats. With neither National nor Labour winning enough seats to govern alone, New Zealand First held the balance of power. For the first, but not the last, time, Peters was the kingmaker, able to choose which party he wanted to work with and therefore who would become prime minister.

After a month of negotiating with both parties, Peters shocked everyone by choosing to work with the National party again, despite their very recent break-up. As part of his negotiations Peters was made deputy prime minister, but it didn't last. After health minister Jenny Shipley staged a coup to become National leader and PM, Peters clashed with his remaining coalition colleagues and by August 1998, Shipley sacked him from all his positions.

He stuck around for the next two terms in opposition, either winning his electorate seat or getting in on party votes, and in 2005, Peters once again held the balance of power. This time he went with Clark's Labour. The relationship ran more smoothly than his National ones, largely because Peters was outside of cabinet and able to criticise the government in areas where he disagreed. But, again, good things never last: in 2008, Peters failed to win back his Tauranga seat, and New Zealand First fell below the 5 per cent party vote threshold. At sixty-three, Peters was out of parliament for the third time. But he promised to be back. And he was.

Returning to parliament in 2011 Peters spent two terms in opposition. And come the 2017 election, all signs pointed to Peters being kingmaker yet again.

On the day of the election, Ardern was at home with her family. Early results of vote counting wouldn't be in until early afternoon so, like most New Zealanders, Ardern was watching TV and waiting for news. Earlier that day, perhaps to distract herself, she had painted her fence. The paint job wasn't perfect, but whose is?

For food, Ardern decided on the classic Kiwi dish of a sausage sizzle. Thin white bread, sausage ('the more processed the better'), maybe some onions if you're feeling fancy, and tomato sauce. Gayford was cooking up a fish dish, of course.

The campaign had been tough. Three years in opposition managed to cram itself into seven weeks and Labour had risen, fallen and risen again. The final poll of the campaign showed National at just under 46 per cent and Labour at 37 per cent. It was still a marked improvement for Labour, but, incredibly, National hadn't fallen at all since the same time three years earlier.

As always, what the varied election polls proved was that you can't trust polls.

It was possible to vote as early as three weeks before Election Day, and the turnout for early voting was the highest in history, at 1.24 million, around 40 per cent of the total vote. Also up was the youth turnout. If nothing else, Ardern had achieved her career goal of increasing youth engagement in democracy and voting.

While increased voter turnout was undeniably positive, the downside was that it made election night a lot less exciting. Because ballots had been cast early, vote-counting proceeded faster and by 7.30 pm, 10 per cent of all party votes had already been counted. By this stage in counting, it takes something unusual to upset the trend. And on Saturday, 23 September 2017, the trend was confirming the results of the final poll. National were comfortably ahead on 46.4 per cent, Labour on 36.5 per cent, New Zealand First on 7.1 per cent and the Greens on 5.9 per cent.

At 8 pm, the trend remained, and National were holding their not insignificant lead. Ardern was still at home cooking sausages, while Gayford served them to media camped outside their fence. Inside, Ardern paced around wearing a red gown and slippers. Peters was already at his party in Northland. In a beautiful example of the smallness of New Zealand, former prime minister Jenny Shipley (who acrimoniously severed ties with Peters in 1998) happened to be eating dinner at the restaurant next door.

As the night wore on, speculation grew around possible partnerships to form a government. National held a clear majority as a lone party, but they didn't have enough to govern alone. And if the initial trend shifted even one or two percentage points, all bets were off. One thing that remained consistent was the power Peters would have, regardless of the outcome.

The closest thing to a winner's speech on election night happened in the far north at a small gathering, before either English or Ardern had shown up to their respective events.

Shortly before 10 pm, Peters addressed his supporters early so that some of them could catch the last ferry home. 'As things stand, I believe that we do have the balance of legal responsibility,' he said. 'And we're not going to be hasty with that. We're not going to rush out and make decisions and make all sorts of statements.

'We have been strong enough and honest enough with our supporters to make it home and to have not all the cards, but we do have the main cards.' He said his party would not make a decision until all the votes had been counted (a small portion of special votes are counted in the weeks following the election), and urged the media to be patient. In true Peters style he preemptively berated those reporters present for any future transgressions around their reporting of his decision-making.

Technically, Peters had lost that night. National's Matt King had unseated him in the Northland electorate, meaning if New Zealand First had gotten under 5 per cent of party votes, they would've been out of parliament. Instead, they got a little over 7 per cent and held the balance of power. Even when Peters loses, he wins.

In brief, the parties that weren't currently in government (Labour, Green and NZ First) were projected to receive more votes than those that were. Green Party leader James Shaw told his supporters that he was happy with the result, and believed the mood around the country was clear. 'New Zealanders have voted for change.'

As Ardern left her home to go to the Labour event, she was asked about the result and her answer was simple. 'Obviously we hoped for better.'

When Ardern arrived at Aotea Centre twenty minutes later, Labour supporters were chanting 'Jacinda, Jacinda'. The mood among the crowd was one of renewed excitement. But Ardern's speech wasn't one of victory. She thanked her staff and volunteers, but not much more. She had three speeches prepared, for different scenarios: a concession speech, a speech for an incomplete result and a victory speech (though she later admitted to having spent very little time on the last one). The speech she actually delivered landed somewhere between concession and question mark. She said she felt privileged to represent a diverse range of New Zealanders and lamented the mildly disappointing result. 'I haven't done as well for them as I would have liked.'

At that, a female audience member gave a reassuring heckle: 'Yes, you have!' The crowd roared, and the rest of her speech was peppered with interruptions, mostly from women professing their support for her.

Offstage, Ardern's staff were despondent. Earlier in the night, they had seen the numbers: it wasn't looking good. They knew they'd lost. But they tried to convince themselves it was anyone's game, if only to stop the mood from dampening too much before Ardern's arrival. Technically it was anyone's game, and they wouldn't have been foolish to act more jubilant, but it felt wrong.

Within half an hour of Ardern's speech, English took the stage at National's party and delivered an unequivocal victory speech. The mood at National's event had until that point been cautious optimism, but English's confidence in declaring the election result a success lifted spirits immeasurably. He announced that he'd look to negotiate a deal with Peters as soon as possible so that National could continue to govern. If there remained any doubt over who had won, English did his best to erase it.

As Ardern finished her speech, there was a quick debate among her campaign staff about whether or not to let off the streamers they'd prepared. There was certainly reason to celebrate. Labour had performed astronomically better than anyone could have predicted two months earlier, and even had a shot at forming a government. But the thought of Labour not forming a government and Ardern being captured for eternity among streamers in a premature celebration made them hesitate. It would be a sad image and sad images don't fade.

The streamers stayed in their cannons and the wait for Winston Peters began.

***

For three weeks, from 23 September to 12 October, New Zealanders were left home alone without their parents. For all intents and purposes, a government's term finishes the day before the next election. English was still technically the prime minister, but no governing was happening – just negotiations with Peters.

Three days after the election, Peters held a press conference in the Beehive to give an update on New Zealand First's position. The next twenty minutes proved to be one of the more entertaining political press conferences in recent history. Peters began by scolding the press gallery journalists present, going so far as to single out a column from Patrick Gower – who always seemed to be in the middle of petty political dramas – that suggested Peters had a grudge against Steven Joyce of National. Peters rejected the claim and questioned Gower's character. He angrily stated that he would not be divulging any information about his party's process until 7 October, once every last vote had been officially counted. He then opened up the floor for questions but instead of answering them, told each reporter why their question was dumb.

With some reporters he bickered: they desperately pushed for an answer and he refused to give it. Others, he simply dismissed.

Reporter: What are your policy priorities going to be when you kick off negotiations?

Peters: Where are you from?

Reporter: Australia.

Peters: Yeah, it shows. Next question.

[laughter from the room]

Peters: Don't come and ask a silly question like that.

It was classic Peters, and a reminder why he was the most iconic (for better and for worse) politician in the country. He gave nothing away: there was no hint whatsoever about which way he'd lean in the coming negotiations.

Winston Peters had a big decision to make, perhaps the biggest decision a New Zealander could be tasked with making: he had to decide who would be prime minister and which party would lead the next government. But Peters, and only Peters, had made such a decision before. Twice.

In both cases, with National and with Labour, there had been issues; Peters was always reluctant to compromise within a coalition. Issues seemed to follow him around, and yet he was the longest serving politician in the country, with forty-two years to his parliamentary résumé.

In 2017, Peters once again had to decide between National and Labour. But it wasn't that simple. The MMP system tends to lead to coalition governments, with parties (sometimes from opposite ends of the political spectrum) forming relationships in order to govern. And in this election, Peters had options. Relationship options.

The first of these was a possible 'marriage' (coalition): because National won fifty-six seats, they only needed to fill five more seats to form a majority. With New Zealand First collecting nine seats, if Peters chose to side with National, they could govern with just the two parties, making the most likely relationship a straight coalition government. The two parties would govern together, on equal terms, with ministers from both parties presenting a united front and voting along their party line.

Alternatively, he might enter into a 'friends with benefits' (confidence and supply) arrangement. A confidence and supply agreement means a party agrees to vote in support of any issues that relate to confidence (supporting the government in its ability to govern) and supply (supporting the government's budget) while not being tied together as a joint government. A confidence and supply partner is like that guy you sleep with occasionally but would never call your boyfriend. Again, National had won enough seats to govern virtually alone, with New Zealand First in a confidence and supply agreement. In exchange for this support, New Zealand First could request support on some of their own policies and perhaps a nice, comfy position for Peters.

Labour did not win enough seats to govern alone with New Zealand First. Any negotiations between them would have to include the Greens.

Which brings us to the third relationship option: polygamy (coalition with three parties). Labour, New Zealand First and the Greens could enter into a three-way coalition and govern together. This option was deemed unlikely from the beginning as Peters had notorious disdain for the Greens, and with two fundamentally opposed parties in coalition, surely nothing would get done?

The final option was 'marriage with a side piece'. Labour and New Zealand First could get married (form a coalition) and then, in order to make up the seats, enlist the Greens as a side piece (in a confidence and supply agreement). Peters and his MPs would be very much in government with Labour, while the Greens would lend their support to the budget and push through their policies but otherwise act as an independent party. Like any spouse-and-side-piece arrangement, New Zealand First and the Greens would have little to do with each other.

Technically there were nine possible iterations of government for Peters to choose from, but those were the four most realistic options.

On 7 October, the special votes had all been counted and the official, truly final results were announced. Both Labour and the Greens picked up a seat in the historically left-leaning special votes, with National losing two. Peters was right: the specials really did change the game. Based on election night results, a Labour–New Zealand First–Greens agreement would have totalled sixty-one seats, meaning a one-seat majority. That would mean three years of stress that an MP might go rogue at any moment, defect from their party and ruin everything.

But the final result had the same agreement totalling sixty-three seats, a much safer scenario. National were still ahead (a National–New Zealand First agreement would be a 65-seat government), but it was a lot closer than initially predicted.

The negotiations, held in a meeting room positioned neatly exactly between the Beehive and the offices of the opposition, were almost comically mundane, in a bare setting with the occasional packet of biscuits for a snack. From the day the special votes came in to the day Peters made his decision, Labour's leadership team and Peters' team met nearly every day, sometimes twice a day. The meetings followed the same, simple agenda: each day the two leaders worked through a long list of policy areas to find out where they agreed and where they didn't. Ardern – for

most of the negotiations the only woman in the room –
had always been a policy wonk, always the one in meetings
who knew the finer details on any given topic. So, she was
in her element. And while Peters went off to have the exact
same meetings with National, Ardern and her team met
with the Greens.

She had a challenging task ahead of her. MMP had yet
to result in a government formed by the minority parties,
and if she wanted to be the first to make it happen, she
had to find a way to bring New Zealand First and the
Greens together.

Peters didn't like the Greens. He didn't want to meet
with them or have joint discussions, and he didn't like it
when they came up during his negotiations with Labour.
Peters was considering a deal with Labour. If Labour had to
sort something out with the Greens to make it happen, that
was Labour's problem.

As the meetings wore on, Peters was nothing but cordial.
He brought in various party members to discuss different
portfolios, and occasionally a random person that no one
across the table recognised but who would turn out to be a
friend of New Zealand First. It was understood that Peters
was being equally cordial with the National team, and he
gave no hints in his meetings with Labour that he was leaning one way or the other.

Winston Peters was the hot girl on campus and he knew
how to play the dating game.

Meanwhile, the New Zealand public carried on life
without a government and nothing much changed. Press
gallery journalists loitered around the parliamentary buildings, desperate for any sign of a decision. One day a Labour
staffer took ginger nut biscuits into their negotiation meeting (he was hungry, they were edible) and reporters rushed

to ask Peters if ginger nuts were his preferred biscuit. To no one's surprise, Peters answered by telling them off.

Near what turned out to be the end of negotiations, communication between Labour and New Zealand First dropped off alarmingly. Ardern's team waited anxiously for a call or message to continue talks but received nothing. By mid-morning, they were convinced that Peters had decided to go with National and began drafting up a press release announcing their withdrawal from negotiations. You can't be dumped if you dump them first.

Then Ardern rang Peters for confirmation and he said no, the negotiations were definitely still going, it was simply a miscommunication. The press release remained a draft.

It had been three weeks since the election and over a week since negotiations began. Press gallery journalists were going stir-crazy, and so were parliamentary staffers, who had very little to do besides wait to learn whether they'd be receiving a government pay cheque the next year or a much smaller opposition one. On the day of Peters' announcement, reporters heard a cheer erupt from one of the Labour offices and speculation began that they had just learned they would be forming a government. In reality, it was just some bored staffers cheering while watching *Family Feud*.

On 19 October, twenty-six days after the election, Peters called a press conference to announce his decision. He scheduled it for 6.20 pm, meaning it would interrupt the six o'clock national news bulletins. Classic Peters.

As he made his way to the Beehive theatrette, Ardern, her negotiating team, a few MPs and Gayford gathered in her office to watch the broadcast. No one in the room had any idea which way Peters would go. A poll by Gayford on the night revealed a split room.

Ardern's senior team were cautiously optimistic, as one of them had received a text message that morning from a known supporter of New Zealand First that said 'ka pai' (well done). It could've been a joke, but what a weird joke to make. They'd also heard that National hadn't received much communication from New Zealand First lately, but again, they weren't going to trust that intel.

'Let's begin by thanking both the National and Labour parties for the manner in which these negotiations have been conducted and the work that they've put into it,' Peters began. He wasn't going to give it up easily. He spoke about the election and about special votes. He described the swiftness of negotiations compared to those the German government, who were also trying to form a coalition, were going through concurrently. And he claimed, unconvincingly, given the staying power of Peters and the relative obscurity of his party members, that the decision was made by the whole of New Zealand First, not just him as leader. Nobody had referred to NZ First as kingmaker, the title was reserved for Peters alone. He spoke for a full six minutes about things that weren't The Decision, even managing to include a reference to the Rolling Stones' classic 'You Can't Always Get What You Want'. When he turned to the economy, Ardern's team groaned (Labour were not known for their economic policies).

But then he flipped the script: 'Far too many New Zealanders have come to view today's capitalism not as their friend but as their foe, and they are not all wrong.'

Ardern's office erupted, then quietened down. They knew they had won, but Peters, being Peters, still had to tease things out for the media some more.

'We had a choice to make, for a modified status quo or for change. That's why in the end we chose a coalition government of New Zealand First with the New Zealand Labour Party.'

Ardern jumped up with tears in her eyes and embraced Robertson.

Down in the theatrette, Peters opened the floor for questions and held a friendlier than usual session with the media.

But no one in Ardern's office was listening. She was going to be the prime minister. Labour were back in government. Three months ago they would never have predicted it.

Ardern ordered pizza and opened a good bottle of whisky. Tomorrow they had a lot of work to do: moving offices, beginning the transition to being in power. But that was tomorrow. Tonight, they would celebrate.

10

The Diplomat

There were a lot of happy people that night. New Zealand had voted for change (just) and they were about to get it. Pundits from both sides of the aisle were in agreement that Ardern becoming prime minister was exciting. Late that night, Green Party leader James Shaw told the press that party delegates had voted overwhelmingly in favour of entering into a confidence and supply agreement with Labour. Addressing caucus the next morning, Ardern was greeted with a standing ovation. 'This will be a government of change,' she told them. 'It will be a government we can be proud of. And this will be a moment in time that I hope all of us look back on with immense pride.'

As part of their coalition deal, Ardern offered Peters the position of deputy prime minister, which he accepted, as well as minister of foreign affairs and minister for racing (Peters was a big fan of the horses). His party also received four cabinet positions, a coup for a party of nine. The Greens received three ministerial positions outside of cabinet, which was as expected for a confidence and supply agreement.

Then it was time to go to work. Ardern released a 100-day plan, outlining the government's priorities. A year of free tertiary education beginning in 2018; cutting the tax credits the National government had promised, and redirecting that to a 'Winter Energy Payment' for pensioners and beneficiaries; an increase to paid parental leave; a family payment of $60 a week for parents of newborns; and banning overseas housing speculators to stem the ballooning market.

The number one priority, unspoken but at the forefront of everyone's minds, was staying afloat as a coalition. For the first time in MMP history, the party without the largest share of the vote was governing. And they were doing so with the support of two parties that couldn't be more opposed if they tried. Whatever ambitions Ardern and Labour had for their first 100 days, there were plenty of observers holding their breath, anticipating a coalition collapse almost immediately. As the leader of such a fraught arrangement, Ardern would have little to no room for error. She'd be rubbing her tummy and patting her head the whole time. One slip up and everything would tumble. And even if it didn't, many questioned just how effective a Labour–New Zealand First–Greens government could be in making real change. One commentator simply called it the 'coalition of losers'.

Ardern dismissed these concerns (publicly) and said her focus was on ticking off the items on her 100-day to-do list. And she did, sort of. Paid parental leave was extended, winter payments and family payments were introduced, the first year of tertiary education was made free from 1 January 2018, legislation was introduced to ban overseas speculators from buying (existing) homes in New Zealand, and the selling of state homes was halted. Labour had campaigned on a potential water tax, but that was scrapped

during the negotiation talks with NZ First. Student allow-
ances (for students from low-income families) and living
cost loans were increased by $50 a week. While this last
move was initially applauded for its acknowledgement of
the increasing financial pressures of renting while studying,
reports soon emerged that landlords were simply raising
their rents now they knew their tenants had an extra $50 a
week. Even when landlords lose in New Zealand, they win.

The two biggest, non-tangible moves the government
made in its first 100 days were to set up the tax working
group and to begin work on Kiwibuild. The tax working
group was tasked with assessing the viability of a number of
potential taxes in New Zealand. The most pressing one was
capital gains. The findings wouldn't be heard for months, but
it was a promising start, particularly for young voters who'd
already accepted that they'd never be able to afford a home
in the cities they grew up in. Then there was Kiwibuild.
Labour campaigned on a promise to build 100,000 affordable homes in ten years. That's a lot of homes. Even the
many people who supported the programme were sceptical
about the practical feasibility of building so many homes so
quickly. But Labour were confident and they began the first
steps in their flagship policy.

Ardern worked through her own firsts too. Not two
weeks after she was sworn in as prime minister, she found
herself having to walk a fine line of diplomacy when meeting with Australia's prime minister, Malcolm Turnbull.
Having watched from afar as 600 refugees were left
stranded on Nauru and Manus Island, refused asylum by
the Australian government and left living in conditions
worse than squalor, New Zealanders wanted to help. A
majority of New Zealanders were open to accepting more
refugees, according to 2017 polling. Back in 2013, John

Key extended an offer to Australia's Julia Gillard to take in 150 refugees. The offer was left hanging, and in 2017, Ardern reiterated it. This was a potentially risky move, as Ardern could have been seen to be undermining Australia's immigration policies on her first diplomatic visit as prime minister. But, she argued, 'We can also not ignore the human face of what Australia is dealing with.' Instead, the one-day trip went well. Turnbull did not accept Ardern's offer but Ardern returned to New Zealand having taken a stand on an important issue without entirely alienating a trade partner.

Ardern then attended her first international summit as prime minister, going to an APEC meeting in Vietnam. Having only earlier that year door-knocked alone in Mt Albert, Ardern was somewhat dismayed to find herself with a security team of six in Vietnam. Her food was tasted before she ate it, and a well-meaning agent attempted to shield her from an impromptu haka. Summits are the perfect time to have brief informal meetings with other leaders and potential partners, so Ardern tried to attend every one she was invited to. The problem was that after her surprise election win, and being the youngest female government leader in the world, a lot of people wanted meetings with Ardern. Building relationships had always been Ardern's biggest strength. But back-to-back bilateral breakfast meetings were made infinitely more difficult to stomach when coupled with morning sickness.

On the night Winston Peters made his big decision, no one had noticed that Ardern, a known fan of whisky, didn't drink any to celebrate the biggest moment of her life. Or if they did, it was dismissed because she was never a big drinker anyway. In fact Ardern wasn't drinking because, in the midst of negotiations with Peters, she had found out

she was pregnant. Ardern told no one, not even her closest colleagues. Instead, she carried on as normal, forming
a government and doing her best to not let world leaders
see that she was trying not to throw up while speaking
with them.

During the Vietnam trip, Ardern met President Trump
informally for the first time. When asked later for her
impression of the divisive leader, her answer managed to be
both diplomatic and brutal: 'He is consistent. He is the same
person that you see behind the scenes as he is in the public
or through the media.'

The diplomacy was somewhat undermined when Ardern
learned the hard way that as prime minister, you're never off
the record. Shortly after her return from APEC, Ardern presented an award at the New Zealand Music Awards. Waiting
backstage with comedian Tom Sainsbury, a friend of hers,
Ardern shared a humorous yarn from her trip. Four days
later she was being grilled on morning television about it.
In a radio interview Sainsbury had retold her story, saying
Ardern had said Trump had not only failed to recognise her
but had mistaken her for Justin Trudeau's wife. Sainsbury
reported that Ardern had said Trump was 'not as orange
in real life'. In damage control, Ardern later attempted to
clarify that she'd simply heard the story from someone else,
who'd allegedly witnessed Trump's confusion. It was a con-
voluted story and few believed her, but Ardern learned her
lesson. No more telling yarns. She made no further comment on how orange Trump was.

Despite the diplomatic speed bumps, by the end of the
first 100 days it felt as if Ardern had dragged her coalition
along without a lot of assistance. Robertson as finance minister had proven competent in his role, but many of Ardern's
ministers took a while to get used to being in government

for the first time. The coalition had survived, and that was no small feat.

Kaitiakitanga: Guardianship and protection

Cosplay: Portmanteau of costume and play. The practice of dressing up as a character from a film, book, or video game.

While commentators were reviewing the first 100 days of Ardern's government, Ardern went to Waitangi, where Te Tiriti o Waitangi (the Treaty of Waitangi) had been signed on 6 February 1840.

Every year on 6 February, New Zealand celebrates Waitangi Day. 'Celebrate' is perhaps the wrong word. Waitangi Day marks the signing of the treaty by British colonisers, on behalf of the Crown, and by Māori chiefs. In lieu of a constitution, the treaty is considered a founding document, even though a number of hapū and iwi didn't sign it.

The chiefs who signed the treaty thought little would change in regards to ownership and governance of the land. The translation of *kawanatanga* ('government') as 'sovereignty' from the Māori to English text has been one (but by no means the only) justification for the disenfranchisement of Māori. In the 178 years since the document was signed, many breaches by the Crown have left Māori overrepresented in incarceration, poverty and health statistics, and underrepresented in education and asset ownership. For many Māori, Waitangi Day is a day to reckon with historical injustices and some are compelled to protest.

For political leaders, this makes Waitangi Day a daunting day on the political calendar. In 1998, Helen Clark, then leader of the opposition, was prevented from speaking on

Te Tii marae, the site where the treaty was signed, because in te ao Māori, women are not permitted to speak on the pae (front bench) of the marae, regardless of status. Clark didn't take kindly to the restriction, but she wouldn't be the only leader barred from speaking on the lower marae. The right to speak is granted by marae trustees and in 2016, John Key was denied speaking rights on Te Tii marae, as was his successor, Bill English, in 2017. The trustees claimed it was simply a miscommunication while the PM's team claimed they weren't welcome. Whatever the case, both prime ministers chose to spend Waitangi Day somewhere else entirely.

In addition to the general New Zealand electorates (like Auckland Central and Waikato), there are seven Māori electorate seats, decided exclusively by the Māori electoral roll. Historically, Labour has dominated these seats. In 1999 and 2002, they held all seven. But in 2004, Labour's relationship with Māori was shaken by the Clark government's introduction of the *Foreshore and Seabed Act*. The Act concerned the customary ownership of New Zealand's foreshore (the area on the beach between the high tide and low tide marks) and seabed (the land under the sea surrounding the coast). According to Te Tiriti o Waitangi, which has since 1989 been used as the basis for settlement claims so that stolen land and assets can be returned to Māori, there is no reason for the foreshore and seabed not to be classified as Māori ancestral land. Yet the *Foreshore and Seabed Act* aimed to prevent iwi and hapū from establishing themselves as customary title holders to these areas. The Act handed ownership of the foreshore and seabed to the Crown, except for privately owned coastal land. This private, exempted land was largely owned by, you guessed it, rich non-Māori. The Act was racist and led one Māori Labour MP, Tariana Turia, to cross the political aisle and vote against her own party's legislation. She went on to start the Māori Party, and took many Māori Labour voters with her. Proceedings at Waitangi in 2004 were particularly fraught.

Labour lost five of its seven Māori seats in 2005 and Labour had to work hard to get them back – slowly they picked up one or two more each election, until by 2014 they were back to six.

During the 2017 election campaign, an Ardern–Davis ticket (Davis held a Māori seat) proved a winning formula for Labour, and they won back all seven seats. The Māori Party won no seats, and came in under the 5 per cent threshold, leaving them out of parliament for the first time since their formation in 2004. It was a Labour Act that proved the catalyst for the Māori Party's inception, and it was Labour that brought about its demise.

In late 2017 it was announced that after years of tempestuous encounters, the 2018 Waitangi Day proceedings would be moved to the Upper Treaty Grounds, the site of Te Whare Runanga, a carved meeting house opened in 1940 to celebrate the one hundredth anniversary of the signing. A more neutral territory, one might call it. This worked well for Ardern, who had by now announced her pregnancy publicly, and was no doubt hoping for a national day without incident.

In an unprecedented move, Ardern spent five days at Waitangi in the lead-up to 6 February. MPs rarely stayed more than one day in Waitangi, with many choosing to spend a cursory morning there before heading back to the city. Northland is one of the most economically deprived regions in the country. Many interpreted Ardern choosing to spend a meaningful amount of time there as a show of her commitment to engage with all Māori, not just those in leadership or business positions.

It wasn't the only break from tradition. With the change in venue came a change in custom, and Ardern was granted permission to speak from the porch of Te Whare Runanga, the meeting house on Treaty Grounds. It would be the first time a female prime minister was granted speaking rights on the grounds, and of course the first time a pregnant prime minister had visited Waitangi.

Titewhai Harawira, the same woman who challenged Clark in 1998, escorted Ardern during the traditional pōwhiri. The two held hands as they were welcomed onto the Treaty grounds.

Typically, after the dawn service on the morning of Waitangi Day, government ministers, including the prime minister, would share a breakfast with iwi leaders at the nearby Copthorne Hotel. Having spent nearly a full week meeting with various iwi, Ardern wanted to have breakfast with the community. She instructed the Waitangi organising committee to scrap the hotel breakfast and set up a public barbecue. She and her ministers would be in charge of cooking for everyone.

So on Waitangi Day 2018, with an expectation that 400 members of the public would show up, Ardern and her ministers wound up barbecuing for 800. Speaking briefly to the crowd, Ardern explained why she had decided to shift from tradition. 'Today felt like the day we could spend with the members of the community,' she said. 'And I prefer bacon butties over formal breakfast anyway.' Wearing matching aprons, Ardern, Davis, Little and a number of MPs in the new government cooked sausages, bacon and onions for the people of the north. For Ardern, it was a tangible way to show that the government saw their role as one of service. She'd expressed the same sentiments during her landmark speech at Te Whare Runanga the day before.

'We did not come simply for the beauty and the hospitality of the North,' she said. 'We came because there is work to do. Much mahi to do. And we will only achieve what needs to be done, together. So, in those five days, we have talked about education, health, employment, roads, housing. But now we must take the talk to action.'

It was Ardern's first Waitangi visit as prime minister, and her government had only been in power for three months. She knew this worked in their favour and asked to be held to account in coming years. 'When we return, in one year, in three years, I ask you to ask of us what we have done. Ask us how we have given dignity back to your whānau, ask us what we have done to improve poverty for tamariki, ask us what we have done to give rangatahi opportunities and jobs, ask us, hold us to account. Because one day I want to be able to tell my child that I earned the right to stand here and only you can tell me when I have done that.'

Ardern's Waitangi visit was deemed a universal success, perhaps the first time a prime minister left Waitangi more popular than when they arrived. One Māori commentator put it succinctly: 'Such a different vibe this Waitangi. It's almost like all you need to do is listen and be respectful of historical grievance for ppl to feel reassured and not throw stuff at you. WHO COULD HAVE PREDICTED SUCH A THING?!'

***

Ardern asked for her government to be held to account and she would get what she asked for.

Two months after Waitangi, she met the Queen. Travelling through Europe on a packed 'relationship-building' tour, Ardern met with a number of leaders. She spoke to an

audience of teenagers with Justin Trudeau, in a Q&A session
chaired by London mayor Sadiq Khan. During the discussion,
Ardern asked the students to put their hand up if they believed
in equality. Every hand in the room went up. 'You are all
feminists,' she said. More formal, private talks were held with
Emmanuel Macron and Angela Merkel concerning trade
deals, global warming and education. She was also invited to
the Queen's Dinner, a formal gathering of commonwealth
leaders and royals before the general meeting.

Before the event, Ardern was loaned a kahu huruhuru
(traditional Māori feather cloak) to wear to the dinner by
London-based cultural group the Ngāti Rānana London
Māori Club. Kahu huruhuru and korowai (another type
of traditional cloak) are typically made for either a specific
person (one was woven for Queen Elizabeth in 1954) or
a specific title (a kākahu, prestige cloak, was designed and
woven to be worn annually by the New Zealander of the
Year). A kahu huruhuru is made to represent the mana of
the wearer.

When Ardern and Gayford walked through the halls of
Buckingham Palace, Gayford in a tuxedo and Ardern visibly pregnant wearing a kahu huruhuru over her dress, the
effect was striking. Even the most cynical of cultural commentators couldn't help but be moved. It felt subversive in
many ways, but most presciently in that Ardern had chosen
to represent Māori while in the home of the monarchy, the
very family that had sent its people to colonise Aotearoa
two centuries ago. Ardern, a young, unmarried, pregnant
woman, attending a Queen's Dinner for world leaders at
Buckingham Palace with her partner, the host of a fishing
show, felt like a *Downton Abbey*-style rebellion.

Ardern was given the honour of proposing a toast at the
event. She stood in the kahu huruhuru, the wall behind

her covered in giant paintings of the monarchy, and recited a Māori proverb. 'He aha te mea nui o te ao?' *What is the most important thing in the world?* 'He tangata, he tangata, he tangata.' *It is the people, it is the people, it is the people.* The Queen's Dinner is not usually a widely broadcast event but thanks to Ardern, in 2018 it was. The photo of her and Gayford was shared thousands of times on social media. New Zealanders boasted about their new leader, who could go viral for presenting well, rather than the opposite. Americans, Brits and Australians shared the photo alongside comments decrying their own political leaders. Even those who staunchly disagreed with Ardern and Labour couldn't help but acknowledge that it was a great moment for a little country on the world stage. All politics aside, it was a cool photo.

But back in New Zealand, tension was building. Six cousins that had grown up at Ihumātao village, near Auckland airport, were gaining support for their fight against a proposed housing development on their ancestral land. The land was of historical significance. In 1863, an ultimatum had been given to the people of Ihumātao: pledge allegiance to Her Majesty Queen Victoria or be forcibly removed. Not wanting to be made to fight against their own kin, the people of Ihumātao left and headed to the Waikato. Their homes were destroyed and their land confiscated by the Crown. Three years later, recent immigrant Gavin Wallace bought two parcels of the land, 81 acres, for a total sum of £658. Two days after the confiscation of Ihumātao, British troops began the invasion of the Waikato, which would later be described as the turning point in the New Zealand Wars – a war in which the Crown continuously breached the Treaty of Waitangi and confiscated over a million acres of Māori land. In 1995, the Crown formally apologised to Waikato–Tainui for 'the loss of lives because of the hostilities arising from its invasion'. It was this apology, and the Waikato Invasion, that Ardern had learned about in Mr Fountain's classes at Morrinsville College.

The fight to protect the land at Ihumātao had been going on a long time, with mana whenua (indigenous people with rights over the land) of Ihumātao appealing to local government and the then National government to reverse a 2014 rezoning decision that would deem the land a Special Housing Area and allow the development to go ahead. Labour issued a press release from housing spokesperson Phil Twyford in August 2015 titled 'Taihoa at Ihumātao'. The release detailed their opposition to the rezoning and development and criticised National's housing minister Nick Smith for not doing 'his homework' and 'riding roughshod over the community'.

But by 2019 all attempts to stop the process, including three visits to the UN by the land protectors, had failed, and Fletcher Residential, who had bought the land from the Wallace family for a sum in the tens of millions, were getting ready to evict protesters and begin construction of 480 houses.

On 23 July 2019, Ihumātao protectors, who had been occupying the land, blocked Fletcher's diggers on the first day of construction. They called for the government to intervene, to buy back the land and make it a protected area. Ardern kept her distance, saying that because there were Māori on both sides of the argument (some were against the development, others had managed to negotiate the number of houses down with Fletcher and were therefore in support of it), it wasn't the government's place to intervene. The two highest-ranked Māori MPs, Deputy Prime

Minister Peters and Leader of the Opposition Bridges, were in rare agreement that the protectors should simply 'go home'. Ardern, however, brokered a deal to halt construction until a consensus could be reached.

Many opposed to the development were disappointed in Ardern's lack of engagement. Here was her chance to show she truly stood with Māori and had Māori interests at heart. Some accused her of simply 'cosplaying' Māori: wearing the costume in Buckingham Palace but not inhabiting the values. 'Entrusted to wear a kahu huruhuru and then watch on passively as our tapu [sacred] land gets monumentally desecrated, ya gotta do more than cosplay sis @jacindaardern smh,' one protector tweeted.

It was a lose-lose for Ardern. A history of fraught Treaty land settlements, many ongoing, suggested that if the government purchased this particular land they could open themselves up to over a trillion dollars of confiscated land buybacks. But the protectors weren't asking for the land to be returned, they simply didn't want it desecrated. And it was common for the government to purchase historically significant land. In fact, while the Ihumātao negotiations were happening, the government stepped in to purchase the family home of Kate Sheppard, the woman who led the movement that resulted in New Zealand being the first country to grant women the right to vote, in 1893, for $4.5 million. Repeated invitations for Ardern to visit Ihumātao were declined, and tensions grew between the peaceful occupiers and the heavy police presence at the site. In September 2019, mana whenua announced that they had reached a consensus: they wanted their land back. The ball lofted over Fletcher and into Ardern's court. How she chose to handle it would have a heavy impact on Labour's Māori seats in the next election.

When pressed by reporters on the issue, Ardern refused to rule out the government purchasing the land from Fletcher, suggesting that this might be where Ardern showcased her commitment to righting some of the historical wrongs done to Māori. As 2019 came to an end, protectors continued to occupy Ihumātao land, though the media attention and police presence had been greatly reduced, and negotiations between parties were ongoing.

In the same month, the government made a long overdue announcement. New Zealand history would be added to the national curriculum and made compulsory by 2022. All students would learn of Māori's first arrival to the country, the later arrival of the British, the New Zealand Wars, and how these shaped the country. The announcement was widely welcomed, although many older New Zealanders were reluctant to accept that the history they had learned may not have been entirely correct. Ardern had learned a more comprehensive New Zealand history as a student of Mr Fountain, but she was in the minority.

In January 2020, word came from Ihumātao that a resolution had been reached between the protectors, the government, and Fletchers. Hints were dropped that an announcement would be timed for Waitangi Day, 6 February. Shortly after, Peters told reporters that such claims were false, and no resolution was near. Despite the mixed messages being broadcast by the various parties, many believed a resolution would come before the next election, with the likeliest outcome involving the Crown purchasing the land from Fletchers.

Going into the election year of 2020, the Labour Party remained the only party in New Zealand politics without a Māori leader. Ardern still plans to visit Ihumātao.

Many may question what a

Ardern's first foray into politics was as Morrinsville College Student Council president.

Ardern joined the Young Labour Clarion Tour in 2004–05.

In her maiden speech, Ardern spoke of her commitment to social justice.

BREAKFAST   13
                                                                PMN
730 ▲67   FTSE 100 5524 ▲77   Dow Jones 12619 ▲8   7:56

Ardern shared a TV spot with Nationals' Simon Bridges as the 'young guns' of their
respective parties.

Ardern and Clarke Gayford initially seemed an unlikely couple, but their relationship has endured.

Ardern DJs at Laneway Festival in Auckland, 2014.

Ardern's first press conference as Labour leader.

Helen Clark, New Zealand's first elected female PM, was Ardern's mentor and supporter.

Clarke Gayford
@NZClarke

A year ago today @winstonpeters made a bold call that changed EVERYTHING. We watched on TV like everyone else, except I pointed a camera the other way. Here's a before and after thats never been seen.

What an incredible year it has been, what a year ahead. Welcome to the ride.

12:49 pm · 19 Oct 2018

The moment Ardern found out she was elected.

Ardern and her partner, Clarke Gayford, arrive at Buckingham Palace for a dinner with Queen Elizabeth II.

Ardern announces the birth of her child, Neve Te Aroha Ardern Gayford, on Instagram.

The Ardern–Gayford family snapped in a candid moment at the United Nations in New York.

Ardern hugs a mourner following the worst mass shooting in New Zealand's history.

Ardern was widely praised around the world for her compassionate response to the Christchurch mosque attacks.

11

Working Motherhood

Jacinda Ardern had been vocal about her desire to be a parent and there was no question in anyone's mind that she and Clarke Gayford were deeply committed. But did they have plans to marry? When interviewed during the 2017 election campaign, both Ardern and Gayford had made jokes about it but hadn't answered the question. After the interview, Gayford emailed the reporter: 'Honestly, I couldn't imagine life without her now, and I've got no doubt that we will get married at some stage, it was just a weird thing to have to verbalise, as if I was giving the game away by saying that, somehow.'

But they already shared a dependant. As they were both away from home a lot, a dog was too big a commitment, so instead they had chosen a cat: Paddles. Paddles was an SPCA rescue, white and ginger, and small. She had thumbs, too. A polydactyl. Paddles made regular cameo appearances in Ardern's social media feeds and was heard in the background of more than one policy announcement on Facebook Live.

When President Trump called Ardern to offer his congratulations after the election, Gayford had to take Paddles out of the room, as her meows were carrying down the phone line. Paddles was beloved, and had grown into her own celebrity. The Ardern-Gayford family was a trio.

On 7 November 2017, while Ardern opened parliament for the first time as prime minister, Paddles was dying. Ardern's neighbour was driving down their street when he hit something. A flash of ginger disappeared behind a fence. By the time he and another neighbour found her, Paddles was dead. The neighbour's daughter wrote a condolence card for Ardern and Gayford, and asked that Ardern not send her dad to prison. Instead, Ardern called him to thank him for the card and to apologise for what he went through. Months later, the driver bumped into Ardern on the beach and confessed to being the man who accidentally killed her cat. Ardern apologised to him again for the distress.

The nation mourned with Ardern and Gayford, now the most famous couple in New Zealand. The first family's house was a little bit emptier.

But a couple of months later, on 19 January, Ardern posted an image to Instagram of three fishing hooks; two big, one little. 'Clarke and I are really excited that in June our team will expand from two to three, and that we'll be joining the many parents out there who wear two hats,' she wrote. 'I'll be Prime Minister AND a mum, and Clarke will be "first man of fishing" and stay at home dad.'

The announcement was sudden and simple. A sparse press release was sent out soon after this. According to one of Ardern's staffers at the time, her pregnancy and the public aspect of it was the one thing that Ardern dictated entirely on her own. There was no team of advisers strategising about how her pregnancy and early motherhood would play out, and no one advising her on how best to navigate the inevitable media furore around it and possible backlash from the opposition. Ardern had maintained throughout her pregnancy that once her child was born, it would be strictly off limits to media, both within the walls of parliament and out in public.

Ardern had long since produced a plan, which she shared with only a few staffers and colleagues, for both her pregnancy and for her first few months of motherhood. There was never any danger of her losing her leadership because of a pregnancy, but even so, New Zealanders weren't unanimously overjoyed at the news. In fact, because Ardern had commented in interviews as early as 2014 that she wanted to have children and had referenced that desire as one of her reasons for not wanting to be prime minister, the questions around her family plans began within twenty-four hours of being made Labour leader back in August.

While most people were happy for Ardern personally, political opponents questioned how she would juggle pregnancy and labour with the demands of office. And many people were unenthused about Winston Peters acting as prime minister for a full six weeks while Ardern would be on maternity leave.

No one in the press team, or anywhere else, had experience in handling a prime minister's pregnancy because no prime minister had ever been pregnant while in office.

Ardern would be only the second world leader in history to give birth while in office. The first was Benazir Bhutto, who gave birth in 1990 while Prime Minister of Pakistan. Coincidentally, Ardern would end up giving birth on 21 June, Bhutto's own birthday. Half a world away and twenty-eight years later, Ardern would experience a drastically different pregnancy and childbirth from Bhutto, who had to hide her pregnancy throughout her term while fighting to keep hold of her leadership. Bhutto gave birth via caesarian section and did not take maternity leave, instead returning to work the very next day.

As the country awaited the birth of Ardern's first child with barely contained excitement, it felt like progress. Progress because Ardern was having a child and continuing in the top role in the country. Progress because such a situation hadn't presented itself in nearly thirty years and never so normalised.

***

But progress aside, nothing is more mind-numbingly boring than waiting for someone to give birth. The act of birth is itself fascinating – a wonder, a miracle. Waiting, not so much. But on a very cold day in June 2018, the whole of New Zealand became a hospital foyer as everyone waited for the prime ministerial baby to arrive.

The New Zealand media were faced with an unprecedented scenario; how were they meant to cover it? Perhaps the closest equivalent was royal births in the UK, which inexplicably capture the world's attention each time.

Public interest in Ardern's pregnancy had been huge. For many there was a sense of pride. New Zealanders had elected a leader who was about to have a baby. Ardern made everyone feel like they were her friend, so everyone wanted the best for her. Even political opponents put aside their differences and wished her well. Some went so far as to fight the media on her behalf, believing that while the government should be held to account, the prime minister's labour didn't fall under that umbrella. What many angry readers didn't realise was that the media *were* leaving Ardern alone. So alone that readers seeking labour details instead learned about the Cancer star sign and what it would mean for the baby to be born on Winter Solstice (it's a good thing, apparently).

Ardern's baby was due on 17 June so when the date came, the media were poised to make an announcement. Updates soon turned mundane as it became apparent that not only had Ardern not given birth, she wasn't even in labour. One local website, *The Spinoff*, began a live blog on the 17th, intending for it to be a funny gag until the baby actually arrived. Forty-eight hours later and the 19 June updates had taken an existential turn.

'2.13 pm: No baby.'

'3.19 pm: What is a baby? A baby is the perfect confluence of love and pain. It is the universe distilled.'

'3.44 pm: No baby.'

'4.01 pm: No baby.'

Three days later Ardern was still working at home (parliament wasn't sitting) and reading documents. She would officially be on maternity leave the day she was admitted to hospital to give birth: Winston Peters would be acting prime minister for the next six weeks.

Journalists took to interviewing a midwife, any midwife, about how long babies take to arrive after their due date. The answer: hard to say.

Gayford tweeted that they were #stillwaiting and this too was reported. History was about to be written and reporters needed to stay on the story. One outlet compiled a playlist of baby-related songs.

Finally Gayford drove Ardern to Auckland hospital on the morning of the 21st, a 12-minute journey from their home in Sandringham. The time taken could be reported with confidence as one unfortunate *NZ Herald* staffer was tasked with recreating the entire drive for a news video.

All media outlets immediately sent a field reporter to the hospital. The prime minister's office had issued strict guidelines to media about covering the birth. Accredited personnel were allowed into a designated room in the hospital, the main purpose of which was to store camera gear and make it easier for Ardern's press team to provide updates. Strictly no filming was allowed within the walls of the hospital. Instead, reporters set up live-cross stations across the road and desperately scrambled for things to talk about as the whole country was reminded that waiting for a baby to be born is extremely tedious.

Things New Zealand media reported in lieu of a baby announcement on 21 June 2018:

59,610 babies were born in New Zealand in 2017 (30,588 boys, 29,022 girls).

Charlotte was the most common girls' name that year. Oliver was the most common boys' name.

21 June is the birthday of actor Chris Pratt, Lana Del Rey, Prince William and (as noted by Megaupload founder and failed politician Kim Dotcom) Edward Snowden.

21 June falls in the Cancer zodiac sign.

The shortest day of the year is known as the Winter Solstice. In 2018, that day was 21 June (as reported from outside Auckland hospital, in the cold and rain).

Jacinda Ardern is not the first woman to have a baby (as reported by Mark Richardson on *The AM Show*).

Sometimes babies aren't born on their due date.

The most common time of day for babies to be born is 4 am.

Photos of every interaction Ardern had ever had with a child (usually her nieces).

Photos of other politicians holding their own babies.

'The average length of stay for a woman giving birth in our hospital is 2.3 days.Typically a woman will be discharged home or to Birthcare, depending on her requirements.' – statement from Auckland City Hospital

Some people standing outside Auckland Hospital on their way to work were excited about the prime minister's baby. Others didn't know what the reporter was talking about and just wanted to have their smoko in peace.

Once Ardern had arrived at the hospital, updates were given throughout the day to media gathered in a waiting room, but they were laughably mundane. Reports of flowers and well wishes being received from leaders around the world, but nothing on the actual labour.

But shortly after 6 pm, Ardern and Gayford shared the news of their new arrival the same way thousands of other New Zealand parents choose to: via Instagram. Ardern posted a photo, clearly taken on a phone, of herself holding a baby on a hospital bed, with Gayford kneeling at their side. 'Welcome to our village wee one,' she wrote. 'Feeling very lucky to have a healthy baby girl that arrived at 4.45 pm weighing 3.31 kg (7.3 lb) Thank you so much for your best wishes and your kindness. We're all doing really well thanks to the wonderful team at Auckland City Hospital.'

Media scrambled. For so long, the understood flow of information was from government to media to public. Embargoed press releases and 'not for publication' comments meant journalists always knew more than the public, and it was their job to pass information on in the most palatable and digestible way. But when it came to the history-making event of a sitting prime minister giving birth, Ardern showed them that they arguably had no role to play. Reporters sitting downstairs at the hospital found out Ardern had had her baby the same way every other New Zealand citizen found out: on social media.

Moments later, a press release was sent to media outlets repeating the information already provided in Ardern's caption. There was just one piece of information supplied by Ardern's press team that wasn't already public knowledge: her first meal after giving birth was the loudly patriotic Marmite on toast and a hot Milo. It was duly reported.

The interest spread overseas, with half of the coverage dedicated to baby updates and the other half to the ridiculousness of live-blogging a birth happening behind firmly closed doors. 'Jacinda Ardern #babywatch sends New Zealand media gaga,' read one *Guardian* headline, referencing the hashtag that had been adopted on that rainy Thursday.

As tripods were folded away and news crews left for the night, Ardern's baby remained nameless. A press conference was announced for the next morning, and would turn out to be the only occasion Ardern would answer multiple questions about her baby. Media once again gathered in a waiting room, along with nurses, doctors and patients who just happened to be walking by at the time.

Ardern and Gayford walked out with the baby in Ardern's arms. Gayford wore an extremely dad sweater and Ardern wore Chucks. The foyer was hushed except for the occasional click of a camera. Even hardened political reporters weren't so heartless as to make a baby cry, even if the baby was of political and public interest. Ardern addressed the crowd briefly, presenting her daughter to the world: Neve Te Aroha Ardern Gayford. Ardern, it was stressed, was a middle name, not a last name. The couple had chosen not to accept the gifted names from numerous iwi around the country.

To accept one and not another would have been awkward. And to accept them all would stretch the character limit of a birth certificate. Te Aroha, which means 'love' in te reo Māori, was chosen to encompass all the gifted names and represent the indigenous land of her home country, as well as being the name of the maunga (mountain) Ardern could see from her childhood home in Morrinsville. It was a surreal press conference for a prime minister to hold. No political questions were asked and details were largely inconsequential, but like the days prior, it felt important for the media to be there and report on what little information was provided.

Ardern's press team announced that the new family would be leaving the hospital through the back entrance. Media would be allowed to film from the side of the road as they drove by. So once again, political reporters who usually spent their days chasing down politicians and camping outside their offices for a scoop, stood outside in the wind and rain waiting for a baby. Across the road from the hospital, a local shop was selling copies of the national paper, featuring a very gender-binary pink-themed front page in honour of the birth of the prime minister's daughter.

After a long wait, Ardern's security detail car emerged, followed by the new parents. As they passed by the photographers, Ardern waved, in an action reminiscent again of the royal family. A moment later they were gone. Nobody cheered, nobody followed them, and nobody really cared. Because despite the ridiculous live-blogging, the themed front pages and the viral hashtag, the birth of Prime Minister Ardern's first child was really rather ordinary. Exactly as she had wanted.

***

Just as New Zealand had never had such a young prime minister before, they'd also never had such a young couple representing them on the world stage. Gayford embraced his new, rather unconventional, role wholeheartedly. He demurred to Ardern in interviews, always being sure to note that he had the easy job and simply did what he could to support her at home. As he'd said in his post-interview email earlier that year, 'It's a pretty strange time for us both. I just want to be the best partner I can be, in the background, gently nudging her to the greatness I know she's got inside her.'

At international events, Gayford would pose alongside the other spouses of world leaders, often the only man in the group. Just as Ardern stood out in the world leaders group photos, where the vast majority were older men, so too did Gayford stand out in the spouses photos. Because Neve was so young, and particularly when Ardern was still breastfeeding, Gayford attended a lot of events as a plus one. At the UN General Assembly, he and Neve turned heads walking through the halls of diplomacy. But perhaps Gayford's most notable outing with Ardern was before Neve was born, in the halls of Buckingham Palace. As Ardern walked through the halls of the palace, pregnant, and wearing a traditional Māori cloak, a photographer took a candid shot of the couple. Ardern walked in the middle, a look of purpose on her face. Gayford strode by her side, just a little bit behind.

★★★

Ardern spent her six weeks of maternity leave at her home in Sandringham with Gayford, but she wasn't entirely closed off. Excited locals posted stories of bumping into the new parents out for a walk with the pram. Temporarily free from prime ministerial duties, Ardern attended only a few events, one of which was the local launch of a parenting book.

The worldwide reaction to Neve's birth was overwhelming. Congratulations poured in from world leaders and celebrities alike. The Queen sent a message. The day after Neve's birth, a small graphic was added below the search bar on Google's homepage. It was an illustration by Wellington artist Stephen Templer of the three fish hooks Ardern had used to announce her pregnancy – a clear message of support from one of the biggest companies in the world. The graphic could easily have been overlooked: in fact, Ardern herself was unaware of it until someone from her office pointed it out to her.

The outpouring of support was a surprise to Ardern, who later revealed she had been nervous not just about the birth but about how the announcement of her pregnancy would be received. 'I didn't expect people to be so welcoming, so positive about me being pregnant while being prime minister,' she told *The Australian Women's Weekly*. 'I was really nervous about that announcement – really nervous. So that part surprised me – and then the follow on, which was, "And now that you've got her, we're here to help."'

When Ardern returned to parliamentary duties, her work life went back to normal, or as normal as it could be while accompanied by a baby at all times. On her first day back, Ardern had a round of media interviews. While some reporters focused on her return as a new mother, others simply picked up where they left off six weeks earlier: why was business confidence falling under a Labour government? It was politics as usual.

On days when the prime minister is required to conduct business within parliamentary buildings (cabinet meetings on Mondays, caucus and question time on Tuesdays, cabinet committee meetings on Wednesdays), Ardern would fly from her home in Sandringham, Auckland, to Wellington, where she, Gayford, Neve, and sometimes her mother or mother-in-law would stay in the Premier House residence.

A nursery was set up in Ardern's office on the ninth floor of the Beehive, for Neve to sleep and play while her mum worked. There had never been a part-time infant resident on the ninth floor before, but if there was ever an office that had the physical space to accommodate a nursery and an extra pair of hands, it was the prime minister's.

Media respected Ardern's desire for privacy for Neve. There was a precedent – other prime ministers had had children (though never any so fresh out the womb), and the media knew they were off-limits.

Ardern's transition was aided by the earlier arrival of two babies in the House, and by Speaker Trevor Mallard's ongoing mission to make parliament more friendly towards families, particularly mothers. Shortly before the 2017 election, Labour MP Willow-Jean Prime gave birth to a daughter, Heeni. Fellow first-term Labour MP Kiritapu Allan's wife also gave birth during the campaign. Mallard proved to be quite helpful with Prime's baby on the campaign trail, and once Labour were elected he encouraged her to bring her baby into the House if needed. She did, and breastfed within the debating chambers, a move now entirely accepted. Previously, MPs would leave the chambers to breastfeed. Now, Parliament's messengers, whose job primarily involved delivering papers between MPs in the House, would enter the chambers and deliver a baby to its mother to be fed.

In November 2017, Mallard himself cradled three-month-old Heeni while her mother debated a bill to extend paid parental leave. And within weeks, when that bill was passed and paid parental leave was extended from eighteen to twenty-two (and in 2020, twenty-six) weeks, Allan and Prime were both present in the House. As were their babies.

When announcing the bill, Ardern could barely contain her excitement. It was a change she'd supported her entire time in opposition, and one of the first actions her government had taken.

Because MPs are elected officials and therefore not employees, they're not entitled to paid parental leave. Ardern's six weeks of maternity leave were unpaid. Of course, MPs, particularly the prime minister, earn well above the average income in New Zealand and are therefore less affected than most New Zealanders by this rule.

Mothers in New Zealand parliament have a short history. In 1970, Whetu Tirikatene-Sullivan, a Labour member, became the first woman to give birth while serving as an MP. She returned to work two weeks later and cared for her baby in her office. The baby did not make any appearances in the House. Thirteen years later, Ruth Richardson breastfed at work, in a room specially designated for that purpose. In 2017, it took all of two weeks for the occasional presence of Prime and Allan's babies to become part of the furniture. By the time Neve was first brought to parliament in August of 2018, it was nothing new.

As one staffer recalls, it wasn't unusual for Ardern to walk into a meeting in her office while breastfeeding, or to disappear briefly to express. Neve was spotted by media or the public in various places around the parliament buildings, but she never made an appearance in the House.

Ardern said more than once on her first day back at work that she had no plans to bring Neve into the debating chambers. As the prime minister, Ardern was not required, nor expected, to be in the House for hours at a time. Typically, she would attend at the beginning of a session to answer questions from the opposition but once that was done, would leave for other engagements. Other MPs, particularly lower-ranked ones such as Allan and Prime, spent far more time in the chambers and Ardern acknowledged and supported their decisions to have their babies with them.

Ardern did her best to temper praise for her ability to run the country and have a baby. 'I'm very mindful that I don't want to be some kind of posterchild saying women can do everything, because it implies women should do everything, and I think women have enough expectations,' she told *The Sunday Times*, a UK publication. 'I can only do everything because I have help, by which I mean Clarke.'

Ardern breastfeeding Neve while fielding the always accusatory questions of the opposition would perhaps have been a step too far. During bill readings and prepared statements, sure. But Ardern wasn't often present for those. Were she to choose to bring Neve into the debating chambers, it would've simply provided fuel for those already accusing Ardern of favouring soft media and PR distractions over the realities of running a country. Instead, Neve remained a faceless presence in New Zealand, only occasionally contributing a gurgle during one of Ardern's Facebook Live announcements or featuring as a bundle of blankets in the few photos released by the prime minister's office.

That is, until she accompanied Ardern and Gayford to the United Nations General Assembly in September 2018. The UN General Assembly is held every year in New York. It's the most important gathering of delegates in the international calendar, with every country, regardless of size or influence, being granted the same one vote in deliberations.

The assembly spans a week at the end of September, and all 193 delegates, most of them presidents and prime ministers, are given a chance to address the assembly. The theme of the assembly in 2018 was 'Making the United Nations relevant for all people: Global leadership and shared responsibilities for peaceful, equitable and sustainable societies'.

Three-month-old Neve was issued an official UN ID lanyard, complete with headshot. It read 'Ms Neve Te Aroha Ardern Gayford – First Baby'. First baby in more ways than one. Ardern made history by being the first world leader to bring a baby to the General Assembly.

It's not typical for children or partners of world leaders to travel with them to events such as the UN General Assembly but Ardern was still breastfeeding Neve, so there was no other option.

When entering the building and flanked by world media, Ardern was careful to cover Neve's face in a blanket so no photos could be taken. At one point, as they walked by a wall of cameras, one of the photographers yelled out 'Congratulations!' Ardern smiled and thanked him before continuing into the building. She had promised herself and the media that she would keep Neve's life private until Neve was old enough to decide for herself. She wasn't about to break that promise so early, even in the process of making history.

On the day before the official debate began, Ardern spoke at the Nelson Mandela peace summit. Before she got up to address the assembly, Ardern was with other New Zealand delegates on the assembly floor. But Neve and Gayford were never too far away. Gayford took great delight in sharing the various spontaneous encounters they had with delegates from around the world. 'I wish I could have captured the startled look on a Japanese delegation who walked into a meeting room in the middle of a nappy change,' he tweeted. 'Great yarn for her 21st.'

While Ardern was delivering her speech, Gayford decided to take Neve down to visit her mum. As Ardern made her way back to her seat, she was shocked to find Gayford and Neve waiting there for her. She wasn't even sure they were technically allowed to be there.

The visit was largely uneventful, with those nearest to Ardern leaning over to say hello to the baby. What Ardern wasn't aware of was the photographer up in the gallery.

Ardern (and Mallard) may have been able to restrict the New Zealand press gallery in their reporting and photographing of Neve, but New York didn't play by the same rules. Reporters and photographers had flown in from all over the world to cover the event, and despite the importance and gravitas of the UN, the General Assembly is hardly a plate of riches for click-hungry media outlets.

Carlo Allegri, shooting for Reuters, snapped a series of photos of Ardern, Gayford and Neve. It's clear the photos were shot from a distance, and that neither Ardern nor Gayford were aware they were being photographed.

The resulting photos, showing Neve looking not so impressed with the whole thing, and her parents looking very much unprepared for an audience, were quickly released online. They were the first photos showing Neve's face and it was on one of the biggest political stages in the world. The images, so unprecedented an event they were showing, spread rapidly around the globe. They were viewed more than 195 million times worldwide.

The prime minister had been so stringent in keeping Neve out of the media. It was rather ironic that the first images showing Neve's face were zoomed in, slightly grainy, not exactly flattering snaps. And because of all those things, it's those photos that have been seen by millions of eyes around the world. Hardly ideal for any politician in a profession in which success so often relies on heavy-handedly controlling the narrative.

But what Ardern certainly knew, whether she liked it or not, was that kids are great for optics and babies are even better. And although Ardern could honestly express slight annoyance at being papped at the UN General Assembly (not often that sentence can be written unironically), it was all positive. People all around the world shared the photos and applauded Ardern for so comfortably being a mother at work. A spokesperson for the UN praised Ardern and hoped she wouldn't be an anomaly. 'Prime Minister Ardern is showing that no one is better qualified to represent her country than a working mother. Just 5 per cent of the world's leaders are women, so we need to make them as welcome here as possible.'

Ardern hadn't allowed media to photograph her baby until that point, and hadn't even posted any clear photos of Neve herself since the birth. But the new tenant in the prime minister's residence was never far from the public's eye, or at least ear.

Live videos on Facebook from Ardern's lounge, often discussing a policy or government announcement, regularly included supporting audio from Neve, just out of frame.

The presence of Neve in the periphery of Ardern's role divided voters. Many loved the normalising of a woman working while raising a child, and not shying away from either role. The consistent off-camera cameo appearances from Neve never failed to be reported on, and were always popular with readers. But just as many saw Neve's presence, and the subsequent reporting of every mild incident, as a carefully deployed distraction from the prime minister's office. It was never obvious. Both Ardern and her team were far too smart to have any 'Neve news' pop up conspicuously at the same time as negative press, but the spontaneous moments were often politically well timed for a leader already struggling with underperforming ministers.

Any adviser worth their salt would know that a prime minister having a newborn baby could be useful politically, particularly a prime minister as popular as Ardern. But New Zealand politics has never been as cynical as politics in the United States or the UK. So was Neve used, at least somewhat, as a political prop, or was it simply an authentic representation of a woman trying to run a country while raising a baby? The likely answer, like most of Ardern's political moves and motivations, lies somewhere in the middle.

Still, by performing prime ministerial duties and parenting a newborn simultaneously, Ardern made an impact. No, Jacinda Ardern wasn't the world's first working mother. But symbolism isn't always hollow. While some working mothers bristled at the overwhelming attention and praise Ardern was receiving for doing what thousands had done before her, young women all around the world saw a new normal. If a woman can run a country while parenting an infant, there was no reason for anyone to frown at any other woman in any other job doing the same thing.

12

Helen and Jacinda

There was another reason a pregnant prime minister – and then a prime minister with a breastfeeding newborn – felt like progress. It cast into sharp relief the experience of the previous female Prime Minister of New Zealand, Helen Clark.

Helen Clark, who was prime minister from 1999 to 2008, had much in common with Ardern. Both were born in the Waikato and raised in rural farming towns. Both were staunchly liberal despite growing up in conservative communities. Both were career politicians, joining the Labour Party as teenagers and entering parliament at a young age (Clark at thirty, Ardern at twenty-eight). They are the only women who have been elected as prime minister in New Zealand (Jenny Shipley served as prime minister from 1997 to 1999 after Jim Bolger was voted out of power by his own National Party, but was not voted in by the public) and share a unique bond as Labour prime ministers simultaneously dealing with sexism in both parliament and the media.

But despite their similarities, very few casual followers of New Zealand politics see a kinship between Clark and Ardern: they don't look or sound anything alike and they don't appear to share many personality traits. While they both experienced sexism, the nature it took was very different for each.

Clark approached politics with a view to beating men (and they were overwhelmingly men) at their own game. Parliament has been described as a 'bear pit': you either kill or be killed. The clearest sign of success is through collecting scalps, whether in the debating chambers or by undermining your opposition, usually through leaks to the media. Clark was ruthless, cut-throat, and not afraid to sacrifice her colleagues for the greater good. This was standard political behaviour, but jarring coming from a *lady*.

Being seen in the same light as her male counterparts worked in Clark's favour – to an extent. It's the same approach that a generation of female political leaders took all over the world. Angela Merkel, Hillary Clinton, Theresa May and the Iron Lady herself, Margaret Thatcher. They were stern, humourless (or at least perceived to be), tough, and scared of nothing except growing their hair beyond their shoulders. That's what was needed to succeed in the male–dominated, male-serving world of politics.

In Clark's biography, *Portrait of a Prime Minister*, released in her first term, her electorate secretary, Joan Caulfield, referred to her as being not a feminist leader but simply 'a woman who could be as effective and as good as any man could be'. But for all her efforts not to be seen as a 'female politician' Clark struggled to gain membership of the boys club of parliament.

Her deep voice helped. In the debating chamber, where soft speakers were shouted down and talked over,

Clark's baritone cut through interjections and demanded an audience. Her refusal to pander or engage in 'personality politics' set her apart, sometimes to her detriment but more often to her benefit. People affectionately joked that if someone had walked up to *Clark* on the beach and admitted to killing her cat that person would soon have joined the cat in the afterlife.

But while her deep voice and staunch posture were beneficial within the walls of parliament, they were turned against her outside it.

In 1981, when she successfully campaigned for the Mt Albert seat and entered parliament, Clark was unmarried. Her single status, 'unfeminine' fashion sense, and apparent lack of interest in starting a family led talkback radio hosts and political bloggers across the country to speculate about her sexuality. In 2008, when Ardern entered parliament, she was also unmarried. Neither woman had explicitly stated their sexuality, but no one suggested Ardern was a lesbian. Interest in Ardern's romantic life was sexist, to be sure (no one asked her male counterparts who they were dating), but it appeared to stem from simple curiosity. Who was she dating? Did she have any ex-boyfriends? Talk of Clark's love life wasn't curiosity, it was suspicion.

Clark was socially progressive, had gay friends and was a vocal advocate for more liberal abortion laws. She was everything the old conservative guard feared, and for her time was more radical than Ardern. It was all too much for the 1980s parliament. According to her biography, even fellow party members suspected Clark was a lesbian. When she began dating academic Peter Davis (a man), the rumours continued, with suggestions that their connection was simply a relationship of political convenience.

For the most part, Clark ignored the personal attacks, but she was politically pragmatic. In 1981, after a life spent dismissing the establishment of marriage and staunchly defending her decision to never marry, Clark got married. She didn't want to – in fact she hated the thought of it – but she knew that it would quieten at least a fraction of the unnecessary chatter surrounding her. She cried at the wedding registry. Questioned about the event years later, her sister Sandra said, 'Was it a happy occasion? It was an occasion.' Twenty years on, Clark still considered her wedding day 'a necessary evil'.

Thirty years after Clark married for political reasons, the landscape Ardern stepped into with Gayford was palpably different. While there was excitement in the general gossipy sense about the couple, their announcement that they were expecting a child was greeted remarkably positively. There was little to no commentary about the fact that the cohabiting couple were not actually married. Even Ardern's parents, practising Mormons, expressed only excitement at the news.

Clark never had kids. Going by her comments on the topic throughout the years, it was apparent she had never planned to either. And that worked against her as a politician. An opposition MP attempted to discredit Clark's family policies because she didn't have children herself. Detractors claimed her lack of interest in starting a family revealed a coldness to her, as if choosing not to have children meant she was incapable of experiencing maternal emotions, ones that were apparently vital in the dog-eat-dog world of politics.

The same type of detractors argued that Ardern's decision to have a child while in office revealed a lack of commitment to the role. To them, having a baby would be nothing more than a distraction for a new mother who would have to make drastic decisions on a daily basis. Unsurprisingly, the decision made by women in parliament to have children or not was a lose-lose.

Ardern did face sexist rhetoric, but not on the same level as that faced by Clark in the '80s and '90s. Clark was criticised as soft and emotionally vulnerable, simply because she was a woman, while also being criticised for being too masculine and not championing other women enough. She was ridiculed for her appearance and regularly described as unattractive. So much so that her biographer, Brian Edwards, made the bizarre move of including a number of quotes from senior male party members insisting that they in fact found Clark very attractive. Ardern, on the other hand, had her conventionally attractive looks used to discredit her as a member of parliament. 'Show pony', 'All style no substance', and 'Pretty little thing' were all used to describe Ardern as an MP. Even after becoming prime minister, comments under every online article accused her of only being successful because of her looks.

Ardern was certainly playing a much smaller violin than Clark, but she had learned from her Labour predecessor. Where Clark most often tried to ignore nasty asides, she was never able to address them without sounding defensive or weak. Ardern managed to defuse a number of incidents involving sexist remarks by insisting that while she could appreciate the issues around such comments, she herself wasn't bothered by them. It allowed her to present herself as not being 'too sensitive' (a perceived weakness for women in any industry) while also not endorsing such rhetoric.

When Patrick Gower labelled the Auckland Central contest a 'battle of the babes', it irked both Ardern and Kaye. But neither engaged with it, choosing instead to kill it with silence. It never went away, though, and Ardern would later lament that perhaps they had missed an opportunity to confront such labels.

The rhetoric stuck. In 2015, rugby league veteran Graham Lowe, a panellist on a morning television show, was asked about Ardern's potential in politics. His response: 'I'll tell you what, she's a pretty little thing at the moment ... She just comes across as the right image.' His comment sparked immediate outrage. One of the show's hosts, the beloved Hilary Barry, expressed her disappointment immediately via Twitter. 'Panellist describes @jacindaardern's skill in politics – "she's a pretty little thing." Rest assured he won't leave without bruised shins,' she wrote. Ardern replied, 'and for this, I thank you Hilary. I hope your shoes were pointy.'

The responses to Lowe were swift, but unlike in Clark's time, they were universally condemning. Lowe responded, explaining that he had been 'trying to compliment her. I come from an era where calling someone pretty was one of the highest compliment and so I did. I would worry about offending Jacinda herself, and if I did I apologise.'

Aside from her initial tweet, Ardern stayed silent. There were more than enough people leaping to her defence. Robertson posted a lengthy rant to his Facebook page, beginning, 'I am sick to death of the ignorant, sexist bullshit that my friend and colleague Jacinda Ardern has had to put up with in the past few weeks.'

The debate continued, and branched out from whether or not what Lowe had said was offensive, to whether or not it was true. What had Ardern done in opposition? Did she care more about aesthetics than policy? Ardern herself finally spoke publicly about it and insisted she wasn't offended. But when a right-wing commentator ended his critical column with the line 'Whether the 35-year-old is a

pretty little thing is in the eye of the beholder. She's definitely turned out to be pretty bloody stupid', Ardern had
had enough. She wrote her own column about the lose-
lose dilemma of dealing with sexism in the media.'Damned
if you do, damned if you don't,' the column began. Ardern
had debated countless times how best to respond to sexist
remarks or categorisations in her job. 'Maybe laugh it off
as flattering, but would that make light of something that,
really, we should be trying to stamp out? Or should I speak
up, and with that, risk being painted as humourless and
overly sensitive?'

Sure enough, the whole saga didn't do Ardern any
favours. The most common critique was that coverage of
her had been more personal than political. By creating a
front-page story about whether or not she was offended
by an old man's remark, she only added fuel to the fire.
Ardern must have learned from the experience because
two years later, she'd handle similar situations almost
to perfection.

In Ardern's favour in 2017 – in comparison to Clark in
the 1980s – was the noise of social media. When Clark's
detractors started rumours and speculation about her, she
was left to handle them on her own. In 2017, when Ardern
found herself on the receiving end of bad lines from *her*
detractors, she didn't have to look far to find a well of
support. In fact, she didn't have to look at all. Ardern had
been the most online politician since being online as a
politician was a thing. She had thousands of supporters,
even if that support didn't always translate into votes. So
when the brand new Opportunities Party leader Gareth
Morgan tweeted 'Jacinda should be required to show she's
more than lipstick on a pig', the response was immediate. He got thoroughly ratioed, and then Prime Minister

Bill English announced that he wouldn't work with the Opportunities Party if Morgan had that attitude. Instead of admitting to a bad choice of words, Morgan doubled down on his statement.

By the time a reporter asked Ardern for her comment the next day, she didn't need to directly address Morgan. He'd already been defeated. Instead, she could (perhaps honestly) say that it didn't bother her. 'It was aimed at me and the question was whether I take offence and I don't particularly,' she said. 'I'm more focused on outlining our policy announcements and vision for the future.' Whether or not Ardern had spent much time thinking about Morgan's comment in private, she was able to limit her involvement in the public discourse. Morgan, on the other hand, would never quite manage to free himself from his ill-advised comment.

On the day Ardern was made leader, she appeared on the news and culture panel show *The Project NZ*. As they moved through the short, live interview, hosts Jesse Mulligan and Kanoa Lloyd had a disagreement over the final question, with Mulligan wondering out loud if he was 'allowed to ask' it. In the end, he did. 'A lot of women in New Zealand feel like they have to make a choice between having babies and having a career, or continuing their career at a certain point in their lives. Is that a decision you feel you have to make or that you feel you've already made today?'

Immediately viewers expressed their opinions on the question through social media. The views were split. Many (mostly women) believed Mulligan had made a rare error in asking an outdated question, while others thought it valid and relevant for the 37-year-old Ardern to address.

Ardern sided with the latter group in her answer. 'I have no problem with you asking me that, Jesse, because

I've been really open about that dilemma because I think probably lots of women face it. For me, my position is no different to the woman who works three jobs or who might be in a position where they're juggling lots of responsibilities. You've just got to take every day as it comes and try and see if you can make the best of the lot you're given. So I'm not predetermining any of that just like most of the women out there who just make their lives work.'

It was the perfect politician's non-answer. But in the hours following the programme, no one really cared about Ardern's answer; they were too busy arguing about Mulligan's question. Mulligan was in fact an old friend of Ardern's (because yes, New Zealand is very small) and if anyone was going to get away with asking a question along that line, it was him.

It came to a head the next morning with ex-cricketer Mark Richardson, who had been on *The Project NZ* panel the night before and was appearing on the second of his seemingly infinite TV spots, *The AM Show*. Ardern was scheduled to appear midway through the breakfast show but, to get conversation going before she arrived, the three hosts discussed whether or not Mulligan's line of questioning was appropriate. Richardson came out strong, arguing that not only was Mulligan correct in asking Ardern about it, all employers had a right to know if the woman they were interviewing for a job was planning to have children anytime soon.

Richardson argued against his co-hosts and when Ardern eventually sat down for her interview, one of them put the idea to her.

Ardern reiterated her comfort with being asked about having a family as it was something she'd discussed on numerous occasions with the media. 'I decided to talk about it. That was my choice. So that means I'm happy to keep responding to those questions.'

'But *you*,' she added, turning to point a finger at Richardson in a frame that would quickly be shared around the world. 'For other women, it is totally unacceptable in 2017 to say that women should have to answer that question in the workplace.'

Richardson countered and they debated for a few moments before Ardern laughed, gave Richardson a thumbs up, and concluded, 'Good debate!'

The debate, but mostly the still image of Ardern pointing and looking disapprovingly at Richardson, went viral. Women all over the world adopted it as the face of 'I've had enough of your sexist shit'.

Ardern had to tread an incredibly fine line in that interview. She couldn't dismiss the question or allow Richardson's view to go unchallenged lest she be seen as being complicit in it. But at the same time, if she got too angry or appeared visibly flustered, she'd be seen as lacking the temperament required to be a leader. By sternly dressing down Richardson while also appearing to be in good spirits about the whole thing, Ardern succeeded in both demoting Richardson to a mere sideshow and making a clear statement about women's rights that would resonate around the world.

Everything about this situation, from the issue of family versus career, to the challenges in behaving 'correctly' when debating on television, was uniquely female. That Ardern spent the first twenty-four hours of her party leadership defending a woman's right to have children while pursuing a career served as a reminder of how much further we have to go, as well as demonstrating that Ardern could handle the 'personality' side of political leadership just fine.

When she announced her pregnancy five months later, some recalled that morning on the *AM Show* and suggested that maybe Richardson had a point. Whether or not votes would have been affected had Ardern stated her intentions before the election will remain a mystery. Her opponent, Bill English, was the father of six children, and his predecessor John Key had two, both young when he began his first term as prime minister. Neither man was asked about the challenges involved in having children while maintaining a political career.

In August 2019, almost four decades after Clark first publicly supported abortion law reform, justice minister Little announced a law to decriminalise abortion. This came as a surprise to many New Zealanders who assumed abortion was already legal. But, as Patrick Gower has noted during the televised leaders' debate, while abortion is technically available for all New Zealanders, it is still in the Crimes Act. For someone to get an abortion, the procedure must be authorised by two doctors. And for those doctors to sign off, they have to believe that there is a real risk to the physical or mental health of the pregnant person. Essentially, this means that the overwhelming majority of people getting abortions bend the truth around their mental state. The bill would remove this step and allow the pregnant person to 'self-refer' to an abortion provider up to twenty weeks into the pregnancy.

The bill was long overdue, and would class abortion as a health issue rather than a crime. 'Abortion is the only medical procedure that is still a crime in New Zealand. It's time for this to change,' said Little. 'Safe abortion should be treated and regulated as a health issue; a woman has the right to choose what happens to her body.'

The Abortion Reform Bill would need to pass three readings in the House, where MPs would vote on it proceeding. It would be a conscience issue, meaning MPs would not have to vote along party lines. Ardern, who was raised Mormon and whose family still practised, said that she would be voting in favour of decriminalising abortion. It was the first time a bill on abortion law reform had made it to a first reading in over forty years.

Ardern's government would rightly receive the credit for pushing the bill through, but the pro-choice seed had been planted years before by Clark and others. Clark and Ardern shared many values and opinions, particularly around women's right to choose; whether it be marriage, careers, or children. But in politics, substance needs style, and from mutual beginnings, the two politicians shaped distinct images.

Where Clark was most effective showcasing brusque efficiency and perceived coldness, Ardern was able to succeed with the opposite approach. Clark's style came naturally to her, but it seems unlikely that Ardern would have succeeded in politics had she been running in the 1980s. Equally, despite the historical successes of leaders like Clark (those viewed as matronly rather than maternal), Ardern has shown both a need and appetite for a new style of leadership. One that puts more emphasis on the day-to-day humanity of a leader, and promotes emotional intelligence and vulnerability alongside steel and resolve.

Clark never saw herself having kids and chose not to. Ardern was vocal for years about her dreams of having a family and chose to do so while holding the highest office in the country. Both women had similar trajectories but vastly different experiences within politics. They also had opposing aspirations outside of it. But most importantly they were both able to exercise their freedom of choice, something all women deserve. On that, at least, they could agree.

***

Addressing the UN General Assembly in 2018, Ardern spoke about climate change, trade, and gender equality. Her speech was universally applauded and, combined with her reputation as a young mother in office, made her one of the success stories of the assembly. During her speech, Ardern passionately stressed the need for gender equality in all areas. 'Me Too must become We Too,' she said, a line that was not included in the version of her speech she submitted to the United Nations.

It would come back to haunt her. Almost one year to the day after delivering those words, Ardern fielded questions about the mishandling of a sexual assault allegation made against a staffer in her own party.

The allegation was serious: a number of complainants alleged that the staffer had sexually harassed and verbally abused them, while one woman detailed an alleged sexual assault by the same man. As the story unfolded, it revealed fundamental failings within the party to address legitimate concerns from younger, mostly female, members. The complainants described being ignored, dismissed and palmed off, while the accused man remained employed and on the Labour premises.

Since the #MeToo movement began in 2016, endless stories had emerged of delinquent, predatory and abusive behaviour by men in power. But what further disappointed people, particular Labour voters, about this story was that the mishandling of complaints happened under Ardern's watch.

She claimed not to have known the seriousness of the complaints, saying that she asked on more than one occasion if they were of a sexual nature and was assured they weren't. Public reaction was split. How could Ardern not have known? There had been news reports and questions about these complaints for weeks. If it turned out she had known and had lied about knowing, she'd have to resign, argued some commentators. But by and large, people believed that Ardern wouldn't lie about that. And, perhaps more crucially, that she wouldn't have allowed such failings to occur if she had known.

There was reason to trust her. The year before, Ardern had responded to multiple allegations of sexual assault at a Young Labour Camp and had acknowledged that the party had handled the complaints poorly. 'The party is taking steps now to ensure it never happens again,' she had said. 'We are bringing in independent advice and assistance to make sure we improve the way we operate in the future, so we create a safe environment.'

Speaking to media the day the 2019 story broke, Ardern had said she was 'incredibly frustrated and deeply disappointed' in how her party had handled the complaints. In the days that followed, as she looked into the details, her responses only became more compassionate. 'Raising an allegation of sexual assault is an incredibly difficult thing to do; for additional distress to be caused through the way those allegations are handled is incredibly upsetting. On behalf of the Labour Party I apologise to the complainants for the way this matter has been dealt with,' she said on 11 September, two days after the story broke.

But as Ardern was apologising for her staff's mishandling of the complaints, her staff were publicly disputing the claims. Members of the investigative panel and party president Nigel Haworth maintained that the allegation of sexual assault was never brought to them – and they stuck to this line even when the complainant provided media with copies of emails sent to the panel members containing the phrase 'sexual assault'. After a meeting with Ardern, Haworth announced his resignation as party president without apology or concession of wrongdoing. Ardern didn't agree. 'I discussed the correspondence with the Labour Party President this morning,' she told media. 'Whilst he stands by the statements he has made on this matter, I believe mistakes were made.'

'There are no excuses for the handling of the complaints by the Labour Party, and I will offer none,' she stated. 'To do so risks minimising the seriousness of the allegations that have been made. We have a duty of care, and we failed in it ... The Labour Party has not dealt with these complaints adequately or appropriately.' She was apologising for a party and panel that had yet to admit any wrongdoing. Ardern was very deliberately not walking the line her party had painted.

Ardern appointed a QC to conduct an independent review of the complaints, with terms of reference agreed upon by the complainants. There would be a second review of the party's process for handling the complaints and an overhaul of the complaints processes, competence training, and culture within the Labour Party. Finally, Ardern would meet with the complainants if they wanted her to, to hear what they wanted from the party going forward. A reporter had already spoken to one, who passed on the group's wishes. They wanted to be able to share their experiences with Ardern, and for her to put in place a number of processes, including sexual harassment training and volunteer code of conduct. These could be addressed. But the complainant also mentioned something that couldn't be

rectified with a code of conduct: the power imbalances that
existed within Labour. 'We [the Labour Party] are not only
male-dominated,' they said, 'but incredibly white.'

Politics has always been a man's game – more specifically, a white man's game – even when there's a woman
in charge. Since Ardern was made leader, she'd had four
chiefs of staff and two chief press secretaries. All six of those
people were men. The overall gender make-up of Ardern's
staff was fairly even, but the top jobs were still overwhelmingly occupied by men. Ardern's closest advisers in cabinet
were also men: Grant Robertson, Phil Twyford (though
he was later demoted), Chris Hipkins, Andrew Little. Not
to mention Winston Peters as deputy prime minister and
Kelvin Davis as deputy Labour leader. Megan Woods was
the highest-ranked woman, but she wasn't in the cabinet.

As Labour's sexual assault scandal unfolded, there were
suggestions that some of the men around Ardern had
known about the claims but not told her of them in an
attempt to protect her (what you don't know can't hurt
you, politically). Once she found out – by reading the news
story like everyone else – she addressed it. She had to, of
course; it was front page news for three consecutive days.

While Ardern responded to the allegations and attempted
to move towards a resolution, those around her kept getting in the way. Labour deputy leader Davis dismissed the
allegations as 'rumours'. He actually used the Māori word
kōhimuhimu, which he later claimed could mean 'rumours'
or 'allegations'. But New Zealand First MP Shane Jones,
himself a te reo speaker, confirmed the word meant 'to
whisper or gossip'. The same day, the staffer at the centre
of the sexual assault claims resigned, but maintained his
innocence, stating 'I adamantly refute the serious allegations
made against me.' Simon Mitchell, chair of the panel that

handled the complaints, issued a statement via his lawyer, reiterating his claim that the panel never received a complaint of sexual assault. Within hours, a lawyer acting on behalf of the complainant responded with a timeline and further evidence of such a complaint. And the next day, after a prolonged absence for an unspecified medical operation, Winston Peters returned to parliament. As he'd done many times before, the deputy prime minister said something that directly contradicted Ardern's message. When asked for his thoughts on recent revelations during a radio interview, Peters called the story and its developments a 'disgraceful orgy of speculation and innuendo'. He went on to defend the accused and described the documents released to the media as 'a plethora of misinformation'.

On 18 December, a summary of Labour's independent review was released, stating that the most serious allegations, of sexual assault and sexual harassment, were 'not established' and that misleading information had been supplied by complainants. The complainants stood by their accounts.

Women who can progress beyond the institutional sexism and misogyny within their industries (something no person should have to deal with) will succeed. But their success should have no bearing on or be considered an endorsement of that organisation's practices. These women most often succeed despite the efforts of the men around them, not because of them.

That Labour had two women elected as leader and then as prime minister suggested a strong female influence and acceptance within the party. What the allegations and mishandling of 2019 revealed was that where Labour purported to be a great party for women, they were simply the chosen party of two exceptional women.

When Helen Clark became an MP in 1981, there were three women in parliament. She succeeded by beating the men at their own game. She spent hours in the smoke-filled billiard rooms of parliament despite despising both activities. Clark didn't so much smash through the glass ceiling as put on a fake moustache and convince it to let her through. And though Ardern had succeeded in a traditionally accepted 'feminine' way, she did so overwhelmingly surrounded by men.

Aside from Clark and King, Ardern's rise through the party ranks was unprecedented. When Ardern announced her government ministers, only one-third of them were women. And when two female ministers were removed from cabinet within a year (women can be bad at their jobs and abusive too), the balance only worsened.

One woman's success, no matter how groundbreaking or progressive, can't shift the institutionalised misogyny and power imbalances of an entire sector. And a single, unprecedented success story does not equal a trend. Ardern and Clark succeeded not by being good, but by being the best.

The two women occupied opposite ends of the 'female politician' scale. Clark was known for her ruthless efficiency, her baritone voice and her intimidating presence. Ardern was known for her empathy, self-deprecating humour and glamorous photoshoots. Both sharpened their strengths into effective political weapons, and both succeeded in a male-dominated arena. But while they both experienced very real instances of sexism, harassment and injustice, they also experienced something that 99 per cent of women don't: they got to the top.

What about the other women? The competent, hard-working but not exceptional ones? These were the kinds of women who had looked up to Clark – and who now looked up to Ardern. They wanted to follow in their footsteps, but found the path blocked by harassment, apathy and, in the case of the Young Labour compainants, alleged assault.

They believed in the party, but they didn't feel safe within it. By persevering through the broken systems, a group of young people had forced the leaders of their party – those whose job it was to protect them, a job they had failed at miserably – to confront their failings. By doing so, they maybe, just maybe, opened the door to progress. Ardern seemed to understand this, and promised a different Labour Party going forward.

'This will be a catalyst for change. Greater insight into what happened here will help us build a different culture. I'm going to lead forward this work, not just for the party, but out of a belief that if we can learn from this, and we can change ourselves, then there is a role for us to play in helping change occur in other places too.'

Ardern pledged to clear the path that she had forged, to make it easier and safer for women to follow in her footsteps. But as the events of 2019 revealed, there was still a lot of old-fashioned rubbish to clean up.

13

Christchurch, 15 March 2019

Naeem Rashid was helping his 21-year-old son Talha plan his wedding. On 15 March, the two men arrived at Masjid Al Noor on Deans Avenue in Christchurch shortly before 1.30 pm for Jumu'ah, Friday prayers. They joined close to 300 of their brothers and sisters from the Muslim community, leaving their shoes at the entrance and entering either barefoot or in socks. Because it was the beginning of autumn and the summer had been long, the air was still warm. Many of the shoes placed at the front door were sandals or jandals. Inside, the carpet was a striking green, with white patterns.

Husna Ahmed and her husband Farid were already there. Farid was wheelchair-bound after a 2013 car accident, so Husna had wheeled him into the men's area (the men prayed in one area and the women and children in another) before rejoining the women in the other room. The minute hand ticked past the six and the brothers and sisters readied themselves for prayer.

At that moment, one street away, a 28-year-old male white supremacist began a Facebook Live video, streaming directly to his personal page. Filming from a camera attached to his helmet, the man drove out of a small side street and made his way to the mosque. While driving, he spoke to his viewers, at first numbering only a handful but eventually thousands. He referenced memes and cultural touchstones for white supremacists from websites like 8chan, where he was an active member. At one point, he turned the camera on himself, revealing a military-style outfit with bulletproof vest. At 1.40, he parked in a small lane beside the mosque. He got out of the car and opened his boot, revealing five guns. Two were semi-automatic weapons and two shotguns. He picked up one of the semi-automatic weapons, closed the boot and walked towards the door of the mosque.

Inside, Haji-Daoud Nabi had heard a car arrive. It wasn't uncommon for someone to arrive late, so Nabi walked to the back door to greet them. He saw a man approaching and greeted him: 'Hello, brother.'

Without saying a word, the man shot Nabi three times, killing him.

The brothers and sisters inside didn't know what the noise was. Most assumed it was a car backfiring, or fireworks.

After killing Nabi, the man entered Masjid Al Noor and opened fire. People fled. For many, there was nowhere to go. He walked through the mosque unloading hundreds of bullets at point blank range, striking dozens within seconds.

While trying to usher others out another back entrance, Talha was hit. His body fell and covered a younger boy on the ground. 'Don't move,' he whispered. They were his last words. The boy beneath him didn't move, and survived.

Naeem saw his son shot, rushed at the gunman, and attempted to wrestle the gun from him. He was shot and killed in his attempts, but was able to buy his fellow worshippers a few more moments to flee.

Men, women and children streamed out of the mosque. A small back door was smashed open and children were instructed to crawl out and run. At first, some of the escapees hid behind and under cars in the parking lot, but when the shooting continued – somehow it continued – they jumped over the fence and hid in a neighbour's yard.

At 1.41 pm someone called emergency services and reported a shooter, mere moments after the gunman fired his first shot. At around 1.43, silence fell. The gunman had unloaded what appeared to be a full ammunition belt. Those who had made it over the fence peeked back over to see the gunman exit the mosque through the same door he'd entered, walk to his car, and swap out his empty weapon for another semi-automatic. He then turned and reentered the building. Seconds later, the gunshots resumed.

When the firing had first started, Husna Ahmed had led women and children to safety. She knew she needed to get them outside so they could scatter. When the shooting stopped, Husna returned to retrieve Farid: in his wheelchair, she knew he was probably unable to get out on his own. She was killed making her way back inside.

The gunman was still live-streaming to Facebook. Anyone watching saw footage from the man's point of view as he re-entered the mosque and shot at piles of bodies on the ground.

He first entered Masjid Al Noor at 1.40 pm and left at 1.46 pm. In those six minutes he killed forty-one people and wounded dozens more.

He then climbed back in his car and drove 5 kilometres to Linwood Avenue. Halfway there his livestream video cut out.

At the Linwood Islamic Centre, about 100 worshippers were in the middle of Friday prayers. They'd finished one rak'at (prayer) and were standing for a second. Latef Alabi was acting as imam at the time. He heard noises outside. It sounded like somebody had dropped something. When he looked out the window, he saw a man holding a large gun and wearing a helmet. His first thought was that it was a police officer. When the man began swearing, Alabi yelled for his congregation to take cover. So rare was such an instruction that everyone paused.

The man outside was yelling because he couldn't find the door. He had planned to enter the second mosque as he had the first, but due to its unusual geography he'd parked on the wrong side of the building. Frustrated, he shot at the windows instead. One bullet passed through a window, hitting a worshipper and killing him instantly. Seeing him fall, everyone scrambled. Everyone except Abdul Aziz.

Aziz was praying with his four sons. Originally from Afghanistan, Aziz had fled as a child refugee and spent over two decades working as a builder in Australia before moving to New Zealand with his family only a couple of years earlier.

As soon as Aziz saw his brother in worship fall, he went after the shooter. As he ran out the door, he scanned the room, looking for something, anything, to use as a weapon. He spied a portable eftpos machine, roughly the size of a brick. Aziz grabbed it and ran out into the parking lot. The gunman was at his car, looking for another weapon.

Aziz ran towards him, past two bodies on the path leading up to the mosque. He didn't stop to check who they were, instead yelling 'Who the hell are you?' at the gunman as he got closer. Realising the man was reaching into his car for another gun, Aziz threw the eftpos machine at him.

The gunman ducked, avoiding it, and stood back up holding another weapon. Walking back towards the mosque, the man shot multiple times at Aziz, who took cover behind a parked car.

Aziz ran around behind the cars and came across another body, this one with a shotgun next to it. He picked up the gun and saw it was empty, but he held onto it anyway. When he heard gunshots again, he knew the man was near the door.

Inside, one of Aziz's sons was calling for him to run. Another, not yet a teenager, was lying on the ground as those running around him were being shot. Another worshipper, Tofazzal Alam, was next to him, holding him while trying to call the police. Alam pleaded for help. 'Someone is killing us, please send ambulance, fire, police service.'

Aziz ran out from behind the cars and tried to distract the shooter.

'Come! I'm over here! Come over here!'

He figured it would buy everyone else some time, even if he got shot himself. When the man didn't come towards him, Aziz went to him, holding the shotgun. When the gunman saw Aziz approaching, he panicked. He dropped his gun and sprinted back to his car. Aziz chased after him.

Aziz didn't know if there were more weapons inside the gunman's car and didn't want to find out. Too far away to tackle him, Aziz threw the shotgun like a spear. It went through the gunman's side window, shattering it completely and giving the impression that he'd been shot at. The man turned to Aziz, yelled 'fuck you all', got into the car and fled. Aziz picked up the fallen shotgun and chased the car on foot. When the gunman slowed down for a nearby traffic light, he saw Aziz chasing him in his rearview mirror and sped through the red light.

Once he was out of sight, Aziz ran back to the mosque to find his sons, and arrived at the same time as the police, some of them in full uniform, some wearing only pants and t-shirts, having scrambled after receiving the call-out. He gave them every detail he could: Subaru station wagon. Gold. Smashed side window. White male.

It was 1.56 and a further seven people had been killed.

Nearby, two cops stationed in rural communities outside of Christchurch were in the city attending a training workshop about dealing with armed offenders, when they received word of a live shooter situation. The two men, with decades of experience in the force between them, jumped in their patrol car and headed towards Linwood. As they drove down Brougham Street, around the corner from the Islamic Centre, they noticed a car driving erratically towards them. It matched the description of the gunman's vehicle.

They did a U-turn and pursued it. In the seconds that followed, the men had to decide whether to allow the man to keep driving or attempt to stop him and risk bystander injury or even death. They quickly decided that he'd caused enough harm.

At 2.02 pm, twenty-one minutes after the first phone call was made to police from Masjid Al Noor, a lone police car rammed into the gunman's vehicle, driving it up the kerb and lifting its front wheels so it couldn't move. Both officers exited their vehicle, guns drawn, and approached the driver's side of the Subaru. They opened the door, dragged the gunman out, wrestled him to the ground and arrested him.

The encounter lasted fifty seconds and was filmed by a member of the public who was driving by on the other side of the road at the time.

Inside the gunman's car, police found two explosive devices and more firearms. The explosives squad arrived shortly after and took care of the devices.

But news of explosives had already got out. Three minutes later, all schools, malls and workplaces in the area were put in lockdown. The lockdown wouldn't be lifted for four hours, until the man was in custody and it was clear he had acted alone.

It took a white supremacist with access to guns and social media eight minutes to set up a Facebook Live video and drive to Masjid Al Noor mosque. It took him six minutes to shoot nearly 100 peaceful worshippers, which would result in the deaths of forty-three. It took him seven minutes to drive to the Linwood Islamic Centre, where in just three minutes he shot and killed eight more innocent New Zealanders. It took the police twenty-one minutes from receiving a call to arresting the man responsible for fifty-one deaths that afternoon.

In just thirty minutes New Zealand changed forever.

★★★

At 1.32 pm, just before the gunman started his live-stream, he emailed Jacinda Ardern, among others, including Simon Bridges, the leader of the opposition. The email contained his manifesto, a racist's creed intending to explain the reasoning – if such a word could be used – for the atrocities he was about to commit. The email went to Ardern's general, public address: a formal auto-reply was sent in response. Eight minutes later he began shooting.

Ardern was in New Plymouth in the North Island that day, for a planned appearance at a local school strike for climate change, and then to open an arts festival that evening.

At 1.50, while Ardern's entourage were in a van on the way to the school strike, her press secretary for the day, Kelly Spring, received a call – there was an 'evolving incident' in Christchurch. She passed the phone to Ardern, who was told there was a shooting happening at a Christchurch mosque. Details were scarce, but there were fatalities. Ardern instructed the van to turn around and go to the police station instead, and handed the phone back to Spring. It was Spring's first day on the job.

Andrew Little stepped in to attend the scheduled events in Ardern's place and the prime minister stayed at the local station, receiving updates and planning how she would address the nation.

This was unprecedented. New Zealand had experienced disasters before. The Christchurch earthquake in 2011 had killed 185 people. And an Aramoana man had shot and killed twelve local residents in 1990. Until now, that was the worst mass shooting in New Zealand history, outside of the New Zealand Wars. As in every country, horrible acts were committed every day. But never had such a monstrous act of terror been unleashed on the country. Ardern knew her words would set the tone of the coverage and be an example to all New Zealanders of how to react.

At 4.20, while victims were still arriving at Christchurch hospital with gunshot wounds, a very small group of media gathered in a nondescript hotel conference room for Ardern's press conference. Two seats were placed behind a small table but Ardern entered and sat down alone.

'Clearly, what has happened here is an extraordinary and unprecedented act of violence,' she said. She spoke into the cameras, knowing the address was, in a sad parallel, being live-streamed to thousands of New Zealanders at desks, in break rooms or at home, across the nation. 'Many of those who will have been directly affected by this shooting may be migrants to New Zealand. They may even be refugees here. They have chosen to make New Zealand their home, and it is their home.'

It was a clear, precise speech. She had a page of notes in front of her, but only glanced at it occasionally before addressing the cameras again. She didn't hesitate in her delivery, though she had little more information than the rest of the country.

Ardern answered questions, put gently to her by an equally shocked reporter. For now, the antagonistic relationship between prime minister and media was absent. Ardern didn't have many specifics about fatalities or injuries. Instead, she repeated, 'This is, and will be, one of New Zealand's darkest days.'

Afterwards, Ardern was flown to Wellington in a defence force plane. On the flight she typed notes into her phone for what would be a much longer address later that night.

At 5.52 pm, Ardern tweeted a message to the world. 'What has happened in Christchurch is an extraordinary act of unprecedented violence. It has no place in New Zealand. Many of those affected will be members of our migrant communities – New Zealand is their home – they are us.' She followed it with another message urging those in Christchurch to stay safe and promising that she would provide another update soon.

Besides a message of condolence in May at the passing of former Australian prime minister Bob Hawke, Ardern's once prolific Twitter account would remain inactive. By the end of 2019, her messages from 15 March were still among her latest tweets, serving as a reminder of the magnitude of what had unfolded.

While Ardern flew to Wellington, a group of chief executives from intelligence agencies, health, civil defence and the police gathered in Wellington to form a joint plan of action in response to the attacks.

When Ardern arrived at the Beehive, armed police stood guard outside, a rare sight for New Zealanders. In Christchurch, dozens of armed police were now stationed outside mosques. Armed officers stood watch outside mosques all around the country for the next three nights.

Shortly after 7 pm, Ardern made an official address to the nation. She wasted no time in defining what had happened. 'It is with extreme sadness that ... we believe that forty people have lost their lives in this act of extreme violence. It is clear that this can only be described as a terrorist attack.'

It was a simple statement. A white supremacist had targeted two places of religious worship: this was clearly a terrorist attack. But while white supremacy was on the rise globally, many dismissed or underestimated the danger. Mass shooters in the United States, almost every single one white and male, were deemed killers and murderers by politicians, but never terrorists. Terrorist was a label most often reserved for acts of violence committed by non-white people. Ardern stating simply and forcefully that a white man had committed an act of terror was sadly new.

Until that point, the number of victims was unclear. Reports had indicated 'multiple fatalities', but everyone had hoped for the best. When Ardern said forty, hearts sank.

'These are people who I would describe as having extremist views that have absolutely no place in New Zealand and in fact have no place in the world,' Ardern continued, her voice steady and calm, again without reading from a prepared statement. Details about what had happened and why were still scarce. How had the man gone undetected by New Zealand intelligence agencies? How did he obtain his firearms? These questions would need to be answered, sooner rather than later. But that night, six hours after the worst act of violence in modern New Zealand history, Ardern spoke to a nation in shock and emphasised the need for love, not vengeance. Kindness, not vitriol. She spoke little of the terrorist, but instead addressed those directly affected by his actions. 'Our thoughts and our prayers are with those who have been impacted today. Christchurch was their home. For many, this may not have been the place they were born, in fact for many, New Zealand was their choice. The place they actively came to and committed to. The place they were raising their families. Where they were parts of communities that they loved and who loved them in return. It was a place that many came to for its safety. A place where they were free to practise their culture and their religion.'

The shooting had attracted worldwide attention. Ardern's words were heard around the globe. But it was heartbroken and confused New Zealanders Ardern addressed next: 'For those of you who are watching at home tonight and questioning how this could have happened here. We, New Zealand, were not a target because we are a safe harbour for those who hate. We were not chosen for this act of violence because we condone racism, because we are an enclave for extremism. We were chosen for the very fact that we are none of those things. Because we represent diversity, kindness, compassion. A home for those who share our values. Refuge for those who need it. And those values will not and cannot be shaken by this attack.'

The language was intuitive and deliberate. She did not allude to retaliation or even call for justice. That was a given: the man was in custody and everyone knew he would never know freedom again. Ardern was determined he would not ignite the hateful response he had sought with his actions. To him, she had only this to say: 'You may have chosen us — we utterly reject and condemn you.'

Immediately after the press conference, Ardern was briefed by Police Commissioner Mike Bush on the latest updates. The man had purchased his firearms legally within New Zealand. It felt inconceivable, despite the very public availability of guns around the country. Inconceivable because, despite guns being very much a part of the national (farming, hunting, sport) culture, gun violence, particularly with semi-automatic weapons, was virtually unheard of in New Zealand. Now it was suddenly, shockingly obvious how available assault weapons were to New Zealanders.

Then and there, Ardern made it clear she wanted this to change. Gun laws would need to be reformed. When she went home to Premier House late that night, she took with her the most recent police report on the Arms Act.

Before most of the country had woken up on 16 March, Winston Peters was called by his chief of staff, who had been at Ardern's briefing the night before. 'Ardern wants gun law reform,' he told Peters. Historically, Peters and New Zealand First had been opposed to gun reform. But that was before. Now, Peters gave his full support.

Ardern spent part of the morning speaking to world leaders, who offered their condolences and messages of support. Her calls included one with US President Donald Trump. Trump, who had enacted an executive order restricting entry into America from certain countries, otherwise known as the 'Muslim' ban, asked if there was anything he or the people of the United States could do. Ardern replied, some would say pointedly, 'Sympathy and love for all Muslim communities.'

Overnight, New Zealanders found themselves at the top of the world news for all the wrong reasons. They were used to seeing mass shootings in America or Europe. On social media, New Zealanders would offer their messages of solidarity to those affected on the other side of the world and listen as international political figures and celebrities again voiced grief and disappointment. They weren't used to it happening in peaceful New Zealand.

By the time Ardern spoke to the nation again at 9 am, the Christchurch terror attack was leading the news all over the world. Overnight updates only reinforced the scale of the crime. The death toll was now confirmed at forty-nine.

A lot of people – at home and abroad – wondered if New Zealand would follow the same script as the United States: terror, grief, assertion that something must change, acceptance that nothing would change, repeat.

Ardern addressed the elephant in the room immediately. 'I want to speak specifically about the firearms used in this terrorist act. I'm advised that there were five guns used by the primary perpetrator. There were two semi-automatic weapons, and two shotguns. The offender was in possession of a gun licence … While work is being done as to the chain of events that led to both the holding of this gun licence and the possession of these weapons, I can tell you one thing right now. Our gun laws will change.'

New Zealand was not the United States.

Overnight, a reporter in Washington, DC, had asked Trump if, in light of the Christchurch attacks, he believed the rise of white supremacy was a problem. He said no. Hours later in Wellington, a local reporter asked if Ardern agreed with Trump. She was equally firm: 'No.'

An hour later, Ardern was wearing black and needed a scarf. There were no scarves at Premier House. As part of their faith, many Muslim women wear headscarves, and Ardern was about to meet with them in their grief. So she asked a friend if she could borrow one of her scarves. She would later say she didn't think much about it, she just knew it was a sign of respect.

At 11 am, Ardern, Peters, Opposition Leader Bridges, and the Greens' Shaw boarded a Boeing Air Force plane and flew to Christchurch.

★★★

Christchurch was quiet, almost silent. On a sunny Saturday morning, the streets downtown were deserted. Weekend sports had been cancelled and the cafes that had chosen to open were empty bar the occasional reporter, fresh off a flight and scribbling notes.

The city had suffered great losses before. In 2011, when a series of earthquakes struck the city, opening up the ground from below, toppling buildings and killing 108 people, the city's residents had banded together and rebuilt. But there was nothing to rebuild in Christchurch on 16 March 2019. There were no bricks to clear, no mud to dig, no practical ways to help the city return to its former state. There was simply an emptiness, and fifty-one fewer lives.

In a private hearing at the district courthouse, a 28-year-old white supremacist stood before a judge, charged with one count of murder. At that time, only one death had been officially confirmed, as only one victim had been formally identified. Many more charges would follow. He entered the courtroom, glared at the media present and formed a white power sign with his cuffed right hand. Armed guards had been stationed at the entrance to the court, in case of public retaliation.

They needn't have worried. The few people who stopped simply did so to ask what the guards were there for. The public didn't care to see the man who'd killed at least forty of their neighbours.

Instead, crowds were slowly gathering one block over. Hagley Park, the busy public grounds across the road from Masjid Al Noor, had been opened again, having been cordoned off by police the night before. Deans Avenue was still blocked with armed officers at each end, but traffic had resumed on the other side, and someone had placed a bouquet of flowers at the far entrance. By mid-morning, a few dozen more had been placed alongside it. By day's end, the whole wall was covered, the first bunch buried beneath hundreds more. Throughout the day residents of Christchurch left flowers, or wrote notes and stuck them along the wall. One woman brought along chalk, felt-tip pens and pieces of coloured card. Kids and adults alike drew pictures and wrote messages on the footpath, or made signs to place among the flowers.

We love you
We grieve with you
This is not New Zealand
Al salam Alaikum

Ardern arrived at noon and met with leaders of the Christchurch Muslim community at the Canterbury Refugee Resettlement and Resources Centre. Media were permitted to film and take photos but were driven in convoy with the prime minister and, for security reasons, were not told where they were going.

Ardern stood before a small group of leaders in her hijab and promised that the man who had done this did not represent New Zealand. In interviews, many survivors of the attacks had expressed that this sort of violence was not the

New Zealand they knew, not the New Zealand they had chosen to move to. Ardern sought to affirm this.

'This act of terror was brought to our shores and rained down upon us here. The only part of the incident and actions that we have seen over the past thirty-six hours that is New Zealand is the support you are seeing now.'

She was standing in a small room, with couches filled on either side, and addressing those standing opposite her, an imam and other leaders.

'I have many roles in my role as prime minister but at the moment I have three incredibly important jobs,' she said. 'One is to bring with me the message of love and support and grief of the people of New Zealand.' She gestured towards Peters, Bridges and Shaw, as well as other MPs who had come with her. 'New Zealand is united in its grief and we are united in our grief.'

'The second job that I have is to ensure your safety, your freedom to worship safely, your freedom to express your culture and religion. The third role I have is … to ensure that you have the space to grieve while we make sure that we take care of those concerns that may not be in the immediate aftermath but will be in the days and weeks to come. There will be questions around how we ensure people's livelihoods, how we ensure that they're able to meet day-to-day needs when they've lost, often, those who will be primary breadwinners.'

This had already become apparent as victims' names and stories were being shared. Of the fifty-one killed, four were women, three were teenage boys, one was a young boy, and forty-three were men. Many had moved to New Zealand to work and support their families in their birth countries. Of those whose families had joined them in Christchurch, many had been the main earners in their homes. Adding to the terror that had already befallen their families was financial uncertainty and questions of visas, residency and burials for those not fully settled in New Zealand. Ardern did her best to reassure those in the room.

'What I want to share with you now is that we do in New Zealand, through ACC [Accident Compensation Co.] have a form of support that ensures that, over weeks, months, and years, individuals who are left with children to care for are provided support on an ongoing basis for the loss of those who provide income to their families. I know that for many this won't be an immediate concern but I need you to know we are thinking about those issues.' It was announced soon after that funeral grants would be given to victims' families, and the government would cover expatriation costs for those whose families wished to bury them in their birth country.

After spending some time answering questions and conversing, Ardern met with victims and their families. Media were not told the details of these meetings and were not permitted to film, but some of those who met with Ardern captured footage on their phones.

In a crowded room on the opposite side of Hagley Park to Masjid Al Noor, Ardern spoke to the friends and families of those killed the day before.

'Al salam Alaikum,' she began, holding a microphone in one hand, and placing her other hand over her heart. 'Peace be upon you, peace be upon all of us.'

'My immediate concerns are twofold. You want your loved ones back, and I know that there are religious considerations with their burial.' Ardern was referring to the Islamic funeral custom of burying a loved one within twenty-four hours of their passing. As she spoke the words, it had been twenty hours since many of the victims had died, and most of the bodies still lay within the mosques. 'One of the issues that we've had in the mosque is that we had to ensure that it was safe to retrieve those who had fallen within it.' She promised that the police were working as quickly as possible, and that updates were imminent.

Phones were raised as Ardern spoke, and faces of family members from overseas could be seen on the screens, watching and listening over FaceTime. She reiterated her government's commitment to providing support 'regardless of the immigration status of those who have lost their lives, and regardless of the immigration status of their families and loved ones'.

She asked the community to be patient and support each other in potential language barriers as they worked with social agencies over the coming days. She ended her short address by speaking on behalf of all New Zealanders. 'You have our love and our support. You have it now, you have it for the coming days, you have it for the coming weeks. You have it because this is your home. Al Salam Aliakum.' Her voice had wavered while announcing the death toll the night before but this time it broke.

A mere 300 metres down the road at Christchurch hospital, doctors and nurses were under pressure. Gunshot wounds were rare cases, and almost always accidental – perhaps someone shot in the foot or the hand. But on Friday afternoon, as one nursing shift was about to end and another begin, two men had walked into the hospital on foot, covered in blood from broken windows. They told emergency staff about the shooting and warned of many more injuries to come. Almost fifty patients would be admitted with traumatic injuries that afternoon. Nurses from all over the hospital were reassigned to cover the influx, and those whose shifts had just ended wouldn't go home until the next morning. Seven operating theatres opened; usually only three were in use at one time.

Ardern visited survivors in hospital on Saturday afternoon, alone, without media or other politicians. She embraced those who could do so and held the hands of those who couldn't.

Across the road at Hagley Park, media were gathering. The local and national outlets had arrived early that morning, and by the afternoon reporters and camera crews from all over the world had set up temporary studios. As families of victims and those injured visited their loved ones, media shared their stories.

Over the course of the weekend, week and months following the attack, New Zealand and the world would learn of the lives and final moments of those who'd perished. Salway Mustafa talked of her sixteen-year-old son Hamza, who called her from Masjid Al Noor as the attack was happening. They spoke for a moment before he stopped answering her questions. Mustafa waited on the line for twenty-two minutes before someone, not Hamza, spoke into it from the other end. 'Sorry, your son can't breathe. I think he's dead.'

A large portion of the New Zealand futsal community gathered on Deans Avenue to remember Atta Elayyan, twenty-four, the national goalkeeper. One man recounted how Elayyan had tried to chase down the gunman but was shot. He got up and was shot again.

Mucad Ibrahim, just three years old, was the youngest victim. He was at Al Noor with his father and older brother. Mucad would become the face of the tragedy. A pure embodiment of innocence and life snatched away.

At each end of Deans Avenue, orange road cones became centrepieces in floral displays as mourners used the cordons as settings for their tributes. Thousands were left and hundreds of locals gathered in silence throughout the day. The local chapter of the Mongrel Mob, New Zealand's most notorious gang, offered to act as security outside mosques in the area if any worshippers wished to pray. Neighbours who lived on Deans Avenue, within the cordon, made coffee and baked biscuits for the officers on duty.

Ardern flew back to Wellington that evening, where Robertson was still at the Beehive, having begun the process of drafting materials for gun law reform proposals.

Overnight, when the city of Christchurch was quiet again, road crews came out to adjust cordons and cones around Deans Avenue. Thousands more flowers had been placed right across the road, but with bodies expected to be removed the next day the path needed to be cleared. On a shift that night, Jay Waaka picked up the nearest bunch of flowers and moved it to the side of the road, being careful to place it upright against the fence. He went back and picked up another, relocating it to the fence line. Over the next hour, he and his crew delicately moved thousands of flowers, teddies and tributes so that they lined the road rather than blocked it. Any messages of support were positioned facing out so they could be read easily by mourners.

Road crews would complete the same ritual every night for the rest of the week.

On Sunday, forty-eight hours after the shooting began, Ardern, Robertson and Gayford visited a mosque in Kilbirnie, Wellington. As she had the day before, Ardern dressed in black and wore hijab. The front steps were filled with floral tributes and the parking lot crowded with locals paying their respects. Ardern added a wreath to the flowers and spoke with many Muslim women who were present and grieving. One woman gripped her tightly, her

son in her other arm, and wept into her shoulder. Ardern
held her. In the background the words of Leonard Cohen's
'Hallelujah' could be heard, sung in te reo Māori by a group
of schoolgirls.

The embrace was filmed by an Associated Press camera-
man, and the footage made its way around the world. The
group then walked by Naima Abdi, who was greeting people
as they arrived. Abdi hugged Ardern, who told her 'we
will get through this together'. The moment was captured
by photographer Hagen Hopkins, and the resulting photo
would become one of the most recognisable images of the
year. Ardern, eyes closed, arms wrapped tightly around Abdi,
who was still holding a box of tissues she'd been offering to
crying mourners.

Islamophobia has been increasing in the Western world
since the events of 11 September, 2001. Experiencing anti-
Muslim sentiment was nothing new for immigrants and
refugees, including those who called New Zealand home.
But only a slim few reacted to the events of 15 March with
racist, dangerous rhetoric; overwhelmingly New Zealanders
had followed Ardern's lead and wholeheartedly embraced
the Muslim community. In literally embracing them,
Ardern showed, very simply, how a small act of compassion
from a leader can affect a community.

The image seemed to embody the words Ardern had
been saying for the past forty-eight hours. Those living
overseas in countries that had experienced similar attacks,
shared the photo and video from Kilbirnie as an indictment on their own leaders whom they believed had failed
in their responses.

One week later in Dubai, the world's tallest building
would be illuminated with the image. The Burj Khalifa,
829 metres tall, was lit in full with the image of Ardern and

Abdi. Above them, the Arabic word 'salam' and its English translation, 'peace'. Sheikh Mohammed, the prime minister and Vice President of the United Arab Emirates, tweeted a photo of the illuminated Burj Khalifa, with a message of gratitude. 'Thank you PM @jacindaardern and New Zealand for your sincere empathy and support that has won the respect of 1.5 billion Muslims after the terrorist attack that shook the Muslim community around the world.'

As support poured in from around the globe, conservative Australian senator Fraser Anning shared his thoughts on the attacks. Thoughts that included suggestions the Muslim community was to blame. During her fifth press conference since Friday, Ardern was asked about Anning's comments. She refused to discuss them, except to say that 'they were a disgrace'. Anning was censured by the Australian senate and roundly condemned by leaders around the world. But someone felt the senator deserved a little more. When Anning spoke to press in Melbourne a few days later, Will Connolly was there. Connolly, seventeen, stood behind Anning and ever so calmly smashed a raw egg over his head. Anning struck Connolly across the face before his security tackled the teenager to the ground. A GoFundMe page raised just shy of $100,000 to help with 'Egg Boy's legal fees, all of which Connolly subsequently donated to the Christchurch Foundation and Victim Support Fund. The Victim Support Fund had been set up via GiveALittle, a local crowdfunding platform. The fund received over $10 million in donations.

On Monday, as New Zealanders returned to work and school, more bodies were being removed from the mosques. They still needed to be identified; some families were holding out hopes that their missing loved ones were okay.

When Ardern addressed media once again from the Beehive theatrette in Wellington, she announced that 'in principle decisions' had been made by cabinet around gun law reforms. Although she'd already said gun laws would change, confirmation of a practical step in that direction was welcomed by everyone.

At 2 pm on Tuesday, parliament rose for the first time since the mosque attacks. Usually Speaker Trevor Mallard entered the House alone, but this time he was joined by a group of religious leaders from all the major denominations. He held the hand of Imam Nizam ul haq Thanvi before they entered the chambers together. Thanvi said an Islamic prayer, which was then repeated in English, and followed by the parliamentary prayer in te reo.

Following the prayers, Ardern stood to give an address. She spoke about the collective responsibility of social media platforms not to broadcast hate: 'They are the publisher. Not just the postman. There cannot be a case of all profit no responsibility.' She spoke of the nation's aspirations: 'We wish for every member of our communities to also feel safe. Safety means being free from the fear of violence. But it also means being free from the fear of those sentiments of racism and hate, that create a place where violence can flourish. And every single one of us has the power to change that.'

She spoke of many things, but she did not speak the terrorist's name. 'There is one person at the centre of this act of terror against our Muslim community in New Zealand. A 28-year-old man – an Australian citizen – has been charged with one count of murder. Other charges will follow. He will face the full force of the law in New Zealand. The families of the fallen will have justice. He sought many things from his act of terror, but one was notoriety. And that is why you will never hear me mention his name. He is a terrorist. He is a criminal. He is an extremist. But he will, when I speak, be nameless. And to others I implore you: speak the names of those who were lost, rather than the name of the man who took them. He may have sought notoriety, but we in New Zealand will give him nothing. Not even his name.'

If anyone hadn't picked up on the mood of the nation in the past four days, it had been set by Ardern throughout the week and was laid out clearly and emphatically in her speech that day.

Later that evening, the first bodies of victims were released back to their families, four days and four hours after the first shot was fired.

Ardern returned to Christchurch on Wednesday morning as burials began. Bodies had been washed and shrouded according to Islamic custom, and were buried, often in groups, with heads turned to forever face Mecca – the same direction they had faced during their last karat at Friday prayers.

At Cashmere High School, Ardern spoke to students who had just lost two of their friends, Sayyad Milne and Hamza Mustafa. Ardern had spoken a lot since Friday, mostly to the media, but also to the Muslim community and those mourning with them. She hadn't spoken much to kids, and these teenagers were kids.

She was welcomed by a whole-school haka. There had been many haka performed outside mosques all around the country and even overseas. Often impromptu, haka around Deans Avenue would begin with a handful of people and end with dozens lending their bodies and voices to the cry of solidarity. But of them all, it was those started by young people that seemed to resonate the most. A video showing a small group of students performing a haka on Deans Avenue was viewed millions of times around the world. When the students of Cashmere High School welcomed Ardern, they did so with pride and in grief.

When Ardern spoke, she got straight to the point. 'In these times it's hard to know sometimes how to express how you're feeling,' she told the packed gymnasium. 'One of the messages that I want to share to our young people in particular is that it is okay to grieve. It is okay to ask for help even if you weren't directly affected.'

She asked them to continue to show love, and to drive out hate, to 'let New Zealand be a place where there is no tolerance for racism, ever'.

When she opened up the floor for questions, it was with the intention of giving the young people information around the attacks in a digestible way. She explained the legal reasoning behind the man being charged with just one murder so far, and assured them that 'many more charges' would follow. She gave sparse details about the terrorist, and instead walked them through what was happening with gun laws.

She was prepared for all their questions, except one.

'How are you?'

'How am I?' Ardern paused. 'Thank you for asking,' she said.

Unsurprisingly, she hadn't been asked that during her press interviews so far. But during one question round, in the halls of the Beehive, a veteran reporter grumbled at her, in a moment that seemed straight from an episode of *Veep*, 'Do you ever cry at night when you go home?' Then, Ardern hadn't given him an answer, saying instead that those were private details. Now, however, she answered honestly. 'I'm very sad.'

As Ardern stood with her team to leave, the school stood too. She noticed someone in the crowd was trying to get her attention and motioned for them to come towards her. A young girl, thirteen years old, emerged and greeted her. They hugged, and Ardern left.

Ardern had assured the students, as she'd assured the House the day before, that gun law reforms would be confirmed by the end of the week. But she didn't wait that long. On Thursday, six days after the attack, she announced a national ban on all military style semi-automatics and assault rifles. The sale of these weapons was now illegal. An amnesty was put in place to allow gun owners to surrender any now-prohibited firearms, but the legislation was moving under urgency.

On Friday in Christchurch it was sunny again: the perfect time to visit Hagley Park. Thousands of people gathered, after Ardern announced that a nationwide call to prayer would be broadcast at 1.30 pm on national radio and live-streamed on all major news sites. It would be the first Friday prayers since the attacks, and Ardern called on the people of New Zealand to observe it and show their support for the Muslim community. Her invitation, given at the behest of the community itself, was consistent with her actions throughout the week. Those who took issue with it were largely ignored, while international outlets expressed disbelief that the nation would so readily support such a notion.

The call itself would come from Hagley Park, where hundreds of Muslim men had formed lines in preparation, with the women and children behind them. Mongrel Mob gang members stood at the ends of each row of men, on guard. Behind the women and children were thousands of non-Muslim New Zealanders, there in solidarity. Some women covered their heads with scarves and some didn't. As the words rang out, vocalised by a young man on a makeshift stage, across the country, everything slowed down. Schools, offices, even airports, stopped to acknowledge what was happening in Christchurch.

Al Noor's Imam Gamal Fouda spoke after the prayers had been observed. His speech on behalf of the Christchurch Muslim community was heartfelt, full of love and forgiveness.

'The terrorist tried to tear the nation apart with evil ideology. Instead we have shown that New Zealand is unbreakable,' he said to the thousands gathered, and many more around the country. 'We are brokenhearted but we are not broken.

'To the people of New Zealand, thank you for your peace. Thank you for your haka. Thank you for your flowers. Thank you for your love and compassion.

'To our prime minister, thank you. Thank you for your leadership. It has been a lesson for the world's leaders. Thank you for holding our families close, and honouring us with a simple scarf. Thank you for your words and deeds of compassion. Thank you for being one with us.'

Ardern was there, along with a number of MPs. They sat at the front, near the stage. Ardern had spoken more to the country that week than she ever had before. She had held almost a dozen press conferences and answered over 300 questions from reporters. This time, she did not speak.

On Friday, 22 March, exactly one week to the minute after the worst act of terrorism New Zealand had ever experienced, Ardern returned to Christchurch and Hagley Park, just across the road from Masjid Al Noor. She stood alongside the Muslim community and New Zealanders around the country, and there was silence.

14

Highs and Lows

Although the first terrorist attack on New Zealand soil had united the nation in shock that such a thing could happen in their country, some within the Muslim community weren't so surprised. Anjum Rahman of the Islamic Women's Council wrote an op-ed arguing that for years Muslim representatives had sought to bring attention to the rising level of hate speech and alt-right sentiments in New Zealand. Rahman was angry. Why was so much money being spent on surveilling the Muslim community, and yet somehow an openly racist, extremist white man was able to pass under the radar? She argued that had the shooter been an extremist Muslim and had the victims been non-Muslim New Zealanders, the reaction from the country towards her community would have been drastically different. 'This is not New Zealand' had been the rhetoric in the immediate aftermath of the attacks. Actually, said Rahman and many others, it is.

Ardern had called for an inquiry to explain why the terrorist had not appeared on any watchlists, despite spreading dangerous rhetoric on social media and having recently purchased a number of firearms. That inquiry would be long and intensive, but she had two other concerns: guns and social media. Gun law reform was actioned swiftly. Social media was harder to tackle.

When the terrorist began his live-stream, it was on Facebook. Somebody shared the stream to 8chan, an online forum with next to no moderation that's become filled with the worst depravities anyone can imagine. Anonymous members of a message board for racist, extremist hate speech watched the stream, gleefully commenting as the man killed innocent worshipper after innocent worshipper. They then shared the video as widely as they could. It was later revealed that the video of the mass murder had been shared online over 300,000 times. YouTube recorded one upload per second in the first twenty-four hours after the attacks. Moderators of platforms such as Facebook and Twitter were unable, or simply didn't try hard enough, to remove all traces of it.

News outlets had to decide what was appropriate to show and what wasn't as the story was unfolding. Some drew a hard line and refused to show any frame from the video, quote any lines of the shooter's manifesto, or mention the man's name. Others showed stills from the live-stream of the shooter in his car, and quoted lines from his manifesto. One outlet uploaded a portion of the video, which autoplayed when the news article was clicked on. The video showed the man parking at Masjid Al Noor, retrieving his guns and walking towards the entrance. It also showed him shooting and killing Nabi before the footage abruptly ended. Mere seconds after that video was published, the outlet was flooded with complaints, demanding they remove the clip. They eventually did.

It was soon made clear by Ardern and Police Commissioner Bush that it was a crime to view the footage of the attack. To do so, or to attempt to do so, was illegal. A white supremacist in Christchurch was arrested and charged with distributing objectionable material. He admitted to the charges and was sentenced to twenty-one months in jail. His appeal was thrown out.

A lot of anger after the attacks was directed at Facebook founder Mark Zuckerberg and his continued apathy about the harm his website was enabling. The Christchurch terror attack was the first time a horrific crime of that scale and that motivation had been live-streamed. Social media had been seen as a tool for good, but now it was a tool for spreading hate and violence. People asked Ardern what the government planned to do about it. In May, she set up the 'Christchurch Call to Action Summit' in Paris. She chaired it with French President Emmanuel Macron with the aim to 'bring together countries and tech companies in an attempt to bring to an end the ability to use social media to organise and promote terrorism and violent extremism'. Leaders from around the world, as well as tech CEOs, met together and drafted an action plan. Mark Zuckerberg did not attend.

Those who signed the Christchurch Call pledged to undertake changes (such as greater transparency and a review of algorithms) that would reduce the spread of extremist materials on their websites or in their countries. The United States did not sign, citing freedom of speech concerns. Ardern personally developed the Christchurch Call and said that it would be an ongoing mission for her while she was in office. In August, Spark, one of New Zealand's largest telecommunications providers, blocked access to 8chan, the site that had spread the terrorist's footage and manifesto. Chief Censor Brian Shanks stated that he would back any internet service providers that chose to block the site. There were a few objections and calls of state censorship (despite Spark being a private company) but the overwhelming majority of New Zealanders were happy never to see the site again.

The Christchurch Call had widespread support in New Zealand and around the world. Even if some were cynical about how much change would happen in the short term, there was consensus that it was moving things in the right direction. Bridges attempted to criticise the effort by suggesting that 'ordinary New Zealanders' didn't care about online extremism as much as they cared about housing and education. His comments were met with swift backlash from a lot of ordinary New Zealanders.

Bridges made his comments at the start of September, and at the end of September, Ardern travelled once again to New York for the UN General Assembly. Twelve months earlier, she had attended as the world leader known for having a baby while in office. This time she attended as the leader of a country that had experienced one of the year's worst hate crimes.

While there, she met with Facebook's Chief Operating Officer Sheryl Sandberg to discuss the Christchurch Call. Ardern also hosted a meeting on the issue, where she announced that the Call pledge had thirty-three additional signatories since Paris (thirty-one countries and two organisations, one of which was Facebook). One of the major announcements was the 'crisis response protocol', a set of guidelines to follow in the event of another terror attack being posted online. Ardern reiterated that she wanted countries and companies to learn from what happened after the Christchurch terror attack, where the initial live-stream was taken down but more than 1.5 million attempts were made to re-upload it to Facebook in the following weeks.

Nothing was enforceable. The whole operation relied on leaders truly committing to the cause and making their own moves to change. Understandably, there was much cynicism about Facebook's statement that they intended to clean up their platform and make it a safer online space. For years, Facebook had run circles around US authorities and legislation, seemingly able to do as they pleased. There was no reason to believe they would change so much of their operation simply because Ardern asked them to. But they had shown up and signed the pledge – this was more than the indignant company had ever committed to before.

Getting leaders of nearly seventy countries, as well as the CEOs of major tech companies, to agree on a joint objective was a diplomatic feat unmatched by past prime ministers. It was something only someone like Ardern could execute. Forming relationships and building connections one-on-one was always Ardern's greatest strength. The photo of so many powerful leaders around the world in one room, answering the Christchurch Call, was possibly a glimpse into Ardern's future. Some of her most impressive moments had unfolded during general assemblies and there were already murmurings that Ardern's style of leadership was destined for the United Nations. Ardern fervently denied any temptation to take her talents overseas, saying she planned to lead Labour for at least another couple of terms. But at only thirty-nine, two more terms would see Ardern to age forty-six. There would still be a lot of life left after that.

★★★

For decades, the health of New Zealand's economy, like those of other nations, had been measured by Growth Domestic Product (GDP). In other words, on the goods and services it provided. Historically, New Zealand's budgets had strived to improve the economy by raising the GDP. Finance Minister Robertson argued in 2019 that limiting measurements to economic indicators ignored the very real lives of New Zealanders.

'Rather than just focus on the finances and economic indicators, we're adding to that by having indicators of the wellbeing of our people,' he told the *Two Cents Worth* podcast, shortly before the year's budget announcement. 'How educated are we? How healthy are we? How secure do we feel? Indicators of our environment: air quality, water quality. How much trust do people have in government institutions? How connected do we feel to each other?'

Labour was about to roll out their Wellbeing Budget. For what was believed to be the first time in the Western world, a country's economic health would be judged by health, wellbeing and community indicators.

The Wellbeing Budget laid out five key areas: taking mental health seriously, improving child wellbeing, supporting Māori and Pasifika aspirations, building a productive nation, and transforming the economy.

Ardern introduced the Budget by highlighting the fundamental reason for it. 'New Zealand has had strong growth for a number of years, all the while experiencing some of the highest rates of suicide, unacceptable homelessness and shameful rates of family violence and child poverty.' It was true: from June 2018 to June 2019, more New Zealanders committed suicide than any year before. She continued: 'Growth alone does not lead to a great country. So it's time to focus on those things that do.' Finance Minister

Robertson added, 'We do not claim perfection in this first Wellbeing Budget, and we will not fix everything in one go. This is just the start of a programme of change.'

Other countries had acknowledged the importance of measuring success outside of economic growth, with the Kingdom of Bhutan introducing the Gross National Happiness Index in 2008 and the United Kingdom measuring wellbeing as early as 2013. But no country had embedded it throughout all government budgeting decisions. The first and most lauded component was a $1.9 billion five-year investment package into mental health services. Nearly half a billion of it would go to frontline mental health services around the country, at GPs, Kaupapa Māori providers, Pasifika providers, community organisations, universities and youth centres. All in an effort to provide accessible mental health care to New Zealanders with 'mild to moderate' issues.

The announcement was met with widespread support, including internationally. But like Kiwibuild, questions were raised around implementation. The mental health sector would have to grow exponentially to provide for the over 300,000 New Zealanders expected to access frontline mental health care by 2024.

The details of the rollout weren't clear but in September, Ardern announced that twenty-two general practices around the country would receive a $6 million funding boost. It was the first step in implementing the objectives of the Wellbeing Budget. It was expected that, given the increased need for trained health professionals, the services would be expanded over a number of years in order to reach everyone.

Mental health had long been a growing issue for New Zealanders and whichever party formed a government would have invested in it, but the size of the Labour government's commitment made headlines around the world. *The New York Times*, *The Guardian* and Bloomberg all applauded the Wellbeing Budget and suggested other countries follow New Zealand's lead.

Though Ardern announced a \$320 million package for support services, perhaps the bolder move was in cementing the Family Violence and Sexual Violence Joint Venture. Having identified that all wellbeing factors are linked in some way, Fiona Ross, former COO at Treasury, was appointed to direct a whole-of-government response to family and sexual violence. Ross would work with a board made up of the CEOs of ten government agencies, including social development, education, justice and police.

The venture began in an effort to end the era of fragmented assistance in dealing with violence and trauma victims. Violence, particularly violence against children, had rippling effects across all sectors. The joint venture aimed to bring those sectors together in preventing and/or assisting victims of violence.

The agencies would work together and report back with shared accountability. The venture was an acknowledgement that no social issue exists on its own, and a synergised approach would be beneficial for everyone. If implemented correctly, the joint venture would change how government agencies helped victims of abuse: as one entity with a common goal, not ten independent agencies. There would be many questions requiring answers as the budget was put into practice throughout the year, but the messaging was clear, and it was a message almost universally agreed upon. The people of a country should always come first.

The budget provided more support in a number of areas, but unsurprisingly didn't hit all of them. And the most

telling area was climate. While there was widespread agreement that the budget was good for mental health, there was
equally widespread disgruntlement around the lack of transformative action on the climate emergency.

During her election campaign launch, Ardern had called
climate change 'my generation's nuclear-free moment'. In
doing so, she put a stake in the ground, one that would be
frequently pointed out to her as her coalition government
struggled to agree on the terms of their Zero Carbon Bill.
In an interview one year into her first term, Ardern was
asked to reflect on her claim and whether she still believed
it. Not entirely, was her answer, because New Zealand was
united in its anti-nuclear stance, and the same wasn't true
for climate change. But, as ever, she was hopeful. 'I feel at
least positive that we've moved significantly from a debate
that ten years ago was whether or not climate change was
real, now to a debate about how much we need to do and
how quickly. Ten years ago I got booed at a public meeting
for talking about climate change. When I first came in to
parliament, a select committee was established to look at
the science of climate change. So now to have moved to
where I'm still hopeful that we'll get political support from
across the House for a Zero Carbon Bill – I hope – that's a
big shift. So let's feel positive about that.'

Ardern had maintained her vocal stance on climate
since her campaign launch. Speaking at the UN General
Assembly in 2018, she highlighted the fact that New
Zealand's Pacific neighbours were living on the frontline. It
was a stance apparently not shared by New Zealand's largest
Pacific neighbour, Australia. A year later, after fraught discussions at the Pacific Islands forum about climate change,
Ardern suggested that Australia would need to 'answer to
the Pacific', suggesting a disappointment in Prime Minister

Morrison's contributions during talks. As one of the biggest emitters of greenhouse gases, Australia had the opportunity to lead the Pacific on emissions reductions. After hesitating to commit to an agreement on urgent climate action, it was clear they would not.

But in New York in 2018, Ardern remained hopeful of a collective approach. 'Of all of the challenges we debate and discuss, rising sea levels present the single biggest threat to our region,' she told the world leaders who had gathered. 'For those who live in the South Pacific, the impacts of climate change are not academic, or even arguable.

'That's why, as a global community, not since the inception of the United Nations has there been a greater example of the importance of collective action and multi-lateralism, than climate change. It should be a rallying cry to all of us.' Ardern didn't expand on this notion, instead moving on to other subjects. But the following year, speaking at the same assembly, she presented a more pragmatic approach to the UN Secretary-General's Climate Action Summit Private Sector Forum. 'New Zealand is pretty good at hydro, geothermal and wind generation, as well as producing low-emissions food. Other countries are better at making electric cars and mass rapid transit systems. Let's trade. For too long, our trade deals have run counter to the environmental outcomes we want to achieve. Let's start by putting climate change at the heart of our trade relationships.'

That week, as Donald Trump was threatened with impeachment and Boris Johnson had to urgently fly home after a Supreme Court ruled against him, Ardern met with the leaders of four small countries – Iceland, Norway, Costa Rica and Fiji – to discuss a climate trade deal, the Agreement on Climate Change, Trade and Sustainability

(ACCTS). The grouping hardly amounted to a global superpower, but the agreement had potential. Its main purpose was to remove tariffs on environmental goods, such as LED lights and solar parts.

Given the size of the countries involved, the immediate global impact would be minimal. But Ardern believed that if they led the way and established a clear set of terms for such an agreement, more countries would sign up. She was being ambitious. New Zealand is a tiny country and had never been considered a power player in international trade agreements. Maybe that was about to change.

★★★

Until Jacinda Ardern became prime minister, mentions of New Zealand politics on American television were usually accompanied by laughter at its insignificance.

It happened rarely enough that New Zealanders felt an impulsive sense of pride every time New Zealand got a mention. But frequently the only reason local politics made news overseas was when it was being mocked.

When the production company behind Eminem's 'Lose Yourself' took the National Party to court for using an eerily similar tune in their 2014 campaign video, the scuffle made great fodder for John Oliver from *Last Week Tonight with John Oliver*, who dissected, with glee, the ridiculousness of New Zealand politics.

And in 2016, then minister of economic development Steven Joyce was speaking to media outside his motel when a young woman approached. Within seconds, she threw what looked to be a dildo in his direction. It struck Joyce across the face, before landing on the carpark concrete. The woman was led away by police, but no charges were laid. The dildo was later revealed to be a penis-shaped dog toy.

This incident was, again, perfect fodder for John Oliver. Even Joyce accepted this, tweeting that night, 'Someone send the gif over to John Oliver so we can get it over with.' Oliver didn't disappoint. He featured the incident as an extravagant ending to his show's episode the week after, complete with a choir singing about dildos, two people wearing dildo costumes dancing together, and Peter Jackson waving a prototype New Zealand flag with a still of Joyce and the dildo on it.

New Zealand politics had become a joke well for Oliver, who visited it over, and over, and over again.

When Prime Minister John Key appeared on *The Late Show with David Letterman* in 2010, it was the first time a New Zealand prime minister had ever been invited onto a US late-night television show. Key appeared as part of a Top Ten segment of 'Reasons to visit New Zealand'. He delivered the lines, pretty run of the mill jokes, followed by the traditional badum-tss. But first he, and the studio audience, and every viewer at home, endured a mildly excruciating exchange of small talk with Letterman about flight times between New Zealand and Los Angeles. It was a fine enough appearance, and millions of viewers remembered, just for a moment, that New Zealand was a thing that existed. But Key wasn't delivering the joke, he was part of it.

It was still better than the eventual treatment Key would receive on American television. He featured on *Last Week Tonight* a number of times between 2015 and 2017, all of them at his expense, with Oliver taking particular delight in unpicking every one of Key's gaffes. By the time Oliver got to dildogate, Key was simply referred to as New Zealand's 'ridiculous prime minister'.

Unlike Key and English, Ardern has yet to give John Oliver a reason to mock New Zealand again. He hasn't spoken in jest about the country on his show since May 2017.

When Ardern was elected, she didn't take over English as leader of a country that was sometimes part of the story. No, quite the opposite. New Zealand became the country with the leader that was the whole story. International media didn't want to speak to the Prime Minister of New Zealand, they wanted to speak to Jacinda Ardern.

Ardern wasn't new in the world of New Zealand politics. She was, after all, that dreaded thing, a career politician. But she was new to the rest of the world. A world desperately grasping for any semblance of hope in a reality that had so recently seen the election of a man who bragged about committing sexual assault.

Outlets reserved for actors and models wanted to feature Ardern. A *Vogue* profile and photoshoot had her looking like she was about to star in a Scandi-noir mini-series about an overworked detective in a small coastal town. A young, conventionally attractive woman succeeding in politics. What a novelty! The profile, published online on Valentine's Day 2018, was headlined 'New Zealand's Prime Minister, Jacinda Ardern, Is Young, Forward-Looking, and Unabashedly Liberal—Call Her the Anti-Trump'.

Anti-Trump. She-Trudeau. The world needed alternatives and they desperately wanted Ardern to be as likeable as she appeared to be in the glossy magazines. She offered up a promising anecdote shortly after the election, from her first overseas trip as prime minister, attending the APEC and East Asia summits in Vietnam. On her return she spoke to media and revealed that she'd had a back and forth with

President Trump while they both waited to be introduced at a gala dinner.

Trump had pointed to Ardern and addressed the person standing next to him. 'This lady caused a lot of upset in her country,' he said, referring to her surprise election win.

She was quick to respond. 'Well, you know, only maybe 40 per cent.'

When he repeated his joke, Ardern quipped, 'No one marched when I was elected.'

It was an objectively impressive comeback, dripping in more than a little disdain. Ardern had made known her feelings about Trump's election win at the time. She attended the Women's March in Auckland in January, one of hundreds held around the world the day after Trump's inauguration ceremony. At the Auckland event, she addressed the crowd of about 1000 marchers. 'We know the power of the collective,' she said.

Two months earlier, on the night of the US election, Ardern had tweeted, 'I've never really pretended to understand the quirks of other countries – even mine surprises me sometimes. But I thought I understood humanity'.

Although only a single year had passed between that tweet and her meeting Trump, when Ardern tweeted and marched she was simply an opposition MP in a party that didn't seem in any danger of being voted into power. But mere months later, she wasn't allowed to be so transparent with her opinions on the President of the United States. 'No one marched when I was elected' was about the most diplomatic way the new leader of a relatively insignificant country could tell Trump where to go, and it took off.

The quote was shared around the world, confirming that the bright new hope of New Zealand was also funny.

Many politicians aspire to be 'someone you could have a beer with'. Trying to be relatable to the average voter while not alienating the wealthy voters has led to cringeworthy photos from politicians everywhere.

Ardern wasn't 'someone you could have a beer with'. She didn't even drink beer. But she could deliver a snarky joke without it feeling facetious, a skill arguably more valuable in the age of social media.

Just as the novelty of Ardern's rapid rise to leadership was dying away, her pregnancy was announced. This kept the world's attention on New Zealand and its leader for another seven months (at least). Every magazine and radio station and website now had a new reason to want to speak to Ardern. The pregnant leader.

Gushing profiles from large international outlets popped up with a regularity that made it feel scheduled. Where initially New Zealand readers chuckled at the outsized affection for their new prime minister, the profiles began to repeat themselves. In fact, I myself wrote an article mocking international media for all hitting the same story beats and publishing features on Ardern that were starting to look like profile-by-numbers.

When Ardern gave birth in June of 2018, close to 800 media outlets around the world reported on it. It felt more like personal news than news about the country as a whole, but it would be naive to believe that New Zealand as a nation was ignored in all the positive press for Ardern. It was, after all, the people of New Zealand who had (kind of) voted Ardern into power and (mostly) been chill and normal about her making history as a pregnant prime minister. Any good press for Ardern was good press for New Zealand. And there's nothing New Zealand loves more than a bit of good international press.

But try complimenting a parent on how well behaved their child is. They'll inevitably scoff and mutter something about how they're never that good at home and you should see them when they're tired. Those who only flew in for a moment or saw the trending tweets saw only the best parts: the speeches, the interview clapbacks, the empathy. But the commentators back home were harbouring doubts and questioned the follow-through of the good optics.

Ardern could never live up to the angelicising labels thrust on her by international outlets, but as time went on, each perceived failure of her government would be juxtaposed against a gushing *Vogue* profile or *New York Times* feature.

By November, Ardern's name had cemented itself among the most recognised in the world. Where New Zealanders on holiday overseas would once be asked about *The Lord of the Rings*, Flight of the Conchords and Lorde (in that order) they were now only being asked about 'Jacinda'.

So when Ardern landed in New York for the UN General Assembly, with Gayford and Neve in tow, she was one of the most sought after figures among the world leaders.

In an unprecedented show of international interest, Ardern had fielded requests from an overwhelming number of American media outlets prior to her arrival. Her schedule for the week was packed.

On Monday there was *The Today Show*, talking to Hoda Kotb about being a world leader and a new mother. On Tuesday there was a sit-down interview with CNN's Christiane Amanpour and a publicised meeting with Anne Hathaway, UN Women Goodwill Ambassador, at Hathaway's request. On Wednesday there was an interview on *The Late Show with Stephen Colbert*, the first time a New Zealand prime minister had been interviewed on late night television. All of Ardern's appearances went well. It was soft media, but even soft media can be done poorly. Her conversation with Amanpour felt natural and her jokes with Colbert landed. Few politicians, no matter how seasoned or trained, can exit a high-profile interview looking more like a nice celebrity than a politician. Barack and Michelle Obama could deliver a good joke, and so could Ardern. It was an exclusive club.

Back home, New Zealanders were proud of their new, not embarrassing leader, while at the same time unsure about the level of attention they were receiving. It wasn't that American media had never been interested in a New Zealand prime minister before. It was that American media had never been unironically interested in a New Zealand prime minister, full stop. If you squinted, you could see Ardern's trip as a PR holiday, spent conducting feel-good interviews and not much else.

It was classic New Zealand. To cringe at the thought of representatives embarrassing everyone on the world stage, but almost hate it more when they don't. New Zealanders didn't know how to feel about the prime minister, a position almost exclusively occupied by either boring or cringey figures, suddenly being lauded as a personality around the world. It was ostensibly great exposure for New Zealand. And part of a prime minister's job is to present their country in a positive light and foster productive connections. But how much of the positive exposure was for the nation and how much of it for Ardern? The answer varied drastically, depending on who you asked.

On Tuesday the 25th, the first day of the general debate, United States President Donald Trump spoke for thirty-four minutes. When he said that his administration had 'accomplished more than almost any administration in the history of our country', the assembly laughed. Stephen Colbert would ask Ardern about the laughter the next night during their interview, and she'd offer a diplomatic but damning response. She was very good at soft media.

★★★

In September 2018, one year on from the election, Ardern hadn't yet hit any major hurdles. Sure, some of her ministers had tripped into demotions and she'd had to tidy it up. Sure, Peters and New Zealand First threw their weight around by derailing a few minor policy announcements. But no big missteps in the honeymoon phase of Ardern's government. She'd only done everything once. It would be the next time around that would prove crucial.

Then a terrorist targeted the Christchurch Muslim community and all 'normal' politics was cast aside. Even the most partisan of critics would struggle to find fault in how Ardern and her team handled the immediate aftermath of 15 March. Never before had a New Zealand prime minister been required to deal with such a violent fracturing of humanity, but in the days following the attacks, people were so relieved that the first, and hopefully last, to do it would be Ardern. Unsurprisingly, she was praised all over the world for it. So much so that she began feeling uncomfortable about it.

In the first poll released after the attacks, Ardern's popularity was at a record high. Commentators around the country remarked that never had a prime minister had such political capital before.

But as always in politics, it didn't last long. In April 2019, Ardern ruled out a capital gains tax – which had been touted as a tangible step in relieving the national housing crisis – not just for one term but for her entire time in office, however long that may be. The announcement shocked many, and disillusioned a lot of her vocal, young supporters.

Ardern had been a vocal supporter of CGT for years, even before the housing market exploded.

And in February the tax working group had concluded that 'there should be an extension of the taxation of capital gains from residential rental investment properties.' It should have been a victory for Labour. They had wanted to push through CGT and now they had an official recommendation from tax experts to back them up. But their coalition partners, New Zealand First, had never supported a CGT. They catered to the older vote, and the older vote owned a lot of property. Peters was probably never going to budge on this issue, and Labour may not have been able to get it over the line before the next election. But Ardern didn't just put off implementing one in her first term. She ruled it out for good. When she presented her decision in April 2019, she shut the door on a capital gains tax for a whole generation.

'While I still believe capital gains tax would have made a difference, the Labour Party has now campaigned on this for three elections. We have tried to build a mandate but ultimately have been unsuccessful. For that reason I am today setting out for certainty's sake, that under my leadership we will no longer campaign for or implement a capital gains tax.'

It was April, one month after the Christchurch terror attack and her uniting of a nation in its aftermath. Ardern's political capital had never, and probably would never, be greater than in that moment. If there was something she wanted to use it on, it clearly wasn't a CGT.

Why not? Winston Peters. The coalition between Labour, New Zealand First and the Greens, while largely diplomatic on the face of it, was fraught. Predictably, Peters kept everyone on a knife's edge. While he wasn't openly at war with his coalition partners as he had been in past governments, Peters was never short of a comment or two, particularly about policies he disagreed with, even after they'd already been announced. Peters was the classic successful businessman uncle everyone seems to have. He comes over for dinner and can charm the room, but the whole time you're nervous because he might decide to say something racist. In 2012, when asked in an interview why Labour continued to 'treat Peters like some likeable, irascible uncle', Ardern had been diplomatically distant in response. 'You can treat someone like an uncle in that way but it doesn't mean that you want them to lead the family dinner, does it?' The problem was, in many ways Peters was very much leading the family dinner. He may have chosen Labour over National but he still held the balance of power in coalition and if he didn't want something to happen, he was very good at preventing it from happening.

After Ardern's tax announcement, somebody asked Green co-leader James Shaw on Twitter what he thought of it. At the start of the year, Shaw had spoken in the debating chambers strongly in favour of the tax. 'The last question we should be asking ourselves is, "Can we be re-elected if we do this?" The only question we should be asking ourselves is, "Do we deserve to be re-elected if we don't?"' Shaw replied to the tweet with no text, just a gif of actor Kevin Sorbo as Hercules, yelling 'disappointed!'

Meanwhile, New Zealand First openly celebrated. Peters tweeted an image of himself with a text overlay reading: 'We've heard, listened, and acted: No capital gains tax.'

Fellow MP Shane Jones, speaking at a business luncheon in May, jokingly chastised the crowd, saying, 'None of you rung to thank me for New Zealand First killing off the capital gains tax'. His remark garnered a round of applause from business leaders.

So when Ardern vowed never to campaign on or implement a tax she wholeheartedly supported, she did so with her mind on the future. More specifically, a future without New Zealand First. By taking capital gains tax off the table, Ardern took an election weapon out of the pockets of National and New Zealand First. Labour wanted to govern without New Zealand First, and believed that by completely removing a policy New Zealand First opposed, they might poach some of their voters in the next election. Once again, Ardern was the pragmatic idealist. It was smart, but many commentators believed the move wasn't necessary, especially considering Ardern's popularity at the time.

Young supporters of Ardern were, across the board, disappointed. After climate change, housing was the next biggest concern for millennials and Labour had promised to act on both. With a capital gains tax gone for the foreseeable future, the young voters of New Zealand got a taste of the cynical nature of politics. Housing was going to continue to be unaffordable for the vast majority of millennials. But they still had one last hope: maybe, just maybe, Kiwibuild would save them. Four months later, Kiwibuild collapsed.

It was supposed to solve the housing crisis. In the distant Labour past of November 2012, David Shearer had made the big announcement. Kiwibuild (following the Labour naming trend – KiwiSaver, KiwiRail and Kiwibank) aimed to add 100,000 homes to the market over ten years.

The concept was reasonably straightforward. Labour, if in government, would build affordable houses for less than $300,000 then sell them to first home buyers for just a little more. The profit from the first round of sales would go towards building the next round, and so on. At the time, the announcement was met with muted approval. It sounded too simple to not have been done already, which made people sceptical. But after a less than desirable 2011 election result, it gave Labour a flagship policy around which to base its 2014 campaign. It was something.

Then prime minister John Key didn't like it. In January 2013 he spoke at a business event and came down hard on Kiwibuild. 'It will either fail miserably, deliver dwellings that people don't want to live in, or require massive tax-payer subsidies,' he said. The public didn't seem to agree: they came out overwhelmingly in favour of the Labour policy, despite David Cunliffe busily organising a coup to overthrow Shearer behind closed doors.

By the 2014 election, Shearer was out and Cunliffe was in, but Kiwibuild remained. However, the offering had been downgraded from three-bedroom homes for $300,000 to two-bedroom homes for $360,000. By the 2017 election, Cunliffe was out and Little was in. Then Little was out and Ardern was in – but Kiwibuild remained. In a perfect model of the housing crisis in motion, the offering had been further downgraded to three-bedroom homes for $579,000. Housing spokesperson Phil Twyford had been a standout in opposition as the National government struggled to handle the worsening housing crisis. Kiwibuild would be his project if Labour formed government, and they did. After five years of attacking National's meagre efforts and talking up Kiwibuild, it was up to Twyford to actually deliver: 100,000 homes in ten years.

During the campaign, Ardern had promised that Labour would begin Kiwibuild within their first 100 days in government, as well as tightening restrictions on overseas buyers. Twyford was made housing minister and presented a plan with a modest starting point: around a thousand houses in the first year. 'It's not going to happen in the first week,' he said. 'We've always said we'll step it up over three years to hit the 10,000-a-year target.'

One of the earliest criticisms of Kiwibuild was that it overestimated the size and scope of New Zealand's construction industry. There simply weren't enough builders. Labour had addressed the issue in part by offering fee-free tertiary education, but the scope was too broad. It didn't target the relevant trades specifically. Besides, trade school doesn't happen overnight, and Twyford had homes to build immediately. But two weeks before 1 July 2019, nearly two years since the election, only 122 had been completed. Despite its abject failure, Labour stuck by their 100,000 home target, insisting they could make up for lost progress in coming years. But at the start of September, Ardern threw in the towel and scrapped the original target, although she insisted Kiwibuild would continue in some form. It wasn't a huge surprise. Twyford had already been shuffled out of his housing minister role, and Megan Woods (the highest ranked female minister behind Ardern) shuffled in.

Having the capital gains tax and Kiwibuild scrapped within six months of each other felt like the Labour government admitting defeat to the housing crisis. Nothing would change, at least nothing as transformative as was promised. Young renters would continue renting, long after they'd stopped being young.

★★★

Ardern spoke of climate change as being the most pressing issue of her generation, while in National there were MPs who denied the very existence of a climate crisis. The government's Zero Carbon Bill, while watered down from its originally ambitious targets, received cross-party support late in 2019 and would be put into action, with emissions targets set in law. It was a step in the right direction.

Ardern's wellbeing budget was universally applauded for its overarching message of placing the people's wellbeing at the core of the economy. But some in the local mental health and social development sectors questioned the delivery methods and investment choices. Regardless, it was a step in the right direction.

Fiona Ross was appointed in April 2019 to oversee the joint venture of a whole-of-government response to family violence, by connecting agencies across the sector (health, education, justice, police, ACC, corrections) to better serve families and victims. It was another step in the right direction, and put action to the rhetoric, but would be hard to quantify. What it would almost certainly do is create the foundation for the next leaders to continue implementing change.

It was all good stuff. And while New Zealanders justifiably asked for more ambition in action, people overseas couldn't help but be envious. Because what Ardern was unintentionally doing by showing a bit of humanity and good intentions was highlighting the complete lack of these things in other countries' leaders. While comparison may be the thief of all joy, those disillusioned by their own leaders' actions found hope in an alternative all the way over in little New Zealand. Celebrities and politicians in America like Oprah, Julianne Moore and Bernie Sanders led a chorus of praise for Ardern after New Zealand's swift action on gun laws.

After two national tragedies in one year, Ardern demonstrated the weight of human response from leaders. At the same time that New Zealand was dealing with the tragic, fatal eruption of Whakaari in December 2019, Australia was in the midst of its own emergency: the New South Wales fires. The contrast in both the prime ministers' actions, as well as the response, could not have been sharper. While hundreds of homes were burning and skies all over the state filled with smoke, Morrison left the country for a family holiday. The outcry at his decision forced him to cut his holiday short, but little was done on his return. Numerous videos surfaced showing locals in destroyed towns refusing to shake his hand during a cursory visit. It became increasingly apparent why Ardern's actions after the Christchurch attacks were so applauded. Turns out a lot of leaders struggle to display humanity in times of struggle. Regardless of how strong their political views, it feels almost unfathomable that a New Zealander would ever feel compelled to yell 'tell the prime minister to get fucked' on the news, as one Australian firefighter did on his way to work.

In New Zealand, even those who found plenty of good reasons to complain about the government throughout the year couldn't help but think 'thank god we don't have that'.

★★★

The day after her capital gains tax announcement, while outlets all over New Zealand featured expressions of disappointment in the decision, Ardern was named by *Fortune* magazine as the world's second greatest leader, behind only Bill and Melinda Gates.

Perhaps the most striking juxtaposition of local and international reception was also the most recent.

In September 2019, while more than one columnist speculated Ardern may have to resign over the mishandling of a sexual assault allegation within the Labour Party, on the other side of the world talk was getting louder that she was a frontrunner for a Nobel Peace Prize. In general, but in that moment in particular, perhaps the last person who wanted Jacinda Ardern to receive a Nobel Peace Prize was Jacinda Ardern.

Ardern herself disputed any accusations of international pandering or a soft media focus. When asked in early 2019 what she thought of all the overseas media attention, she was pragmatic. 'I know that for a New Zealand audience and for New Zealand voters, that stuff's not material, and so for me my focus is always going to be on what we're doing here domestically. Because, you know, ultimately, I'll be judged on my performance here, rather than anything that happens anywhere else – and my performance on behalf of New Zealanders.'

She addressed it again later in the year, and gave a stronger response to those criticising her for accommodating so much international media. 'I get very uncomfortable, very uncomfortable when I hear any suggestion around that. That makes me very uncomfortable because I am only there because of this job and this role and that means my duty is to New Zealand,' she told the *NZ Herald*. 'I'm even very cautious about anything that may give a vague whiff about it being anything other than representing New Zealand.'

The bristly relationship between Ardern and the press gallery was perhaps more pronounced given her global popularity. Past prime ministers weren't fielding dozens of international media requests every day like Ardern's office was. And to see a glitzy profile appear in an international publication at the same time as domestic issues demanded attention and answers could be jarring.

Ardern's popularity among her constituents would never match that of her distant admirers. Ardern had set herself very high expectations – voters expected her to bring about transformative change and prosperity, and there was plenty to criticise. When Ardern proudly stated at the beginning of her first term that she would lead a 'transformative' government, she set a high standard for herself. And New Zealanders would hold her to it. In not spearheading major (and immediate) policy changes within housing and climate change, Ardern failed to reach that high standard. Her reception domestically would never match her reception internationally, but as a representative of New Zealand on the world stage, there was no one better.

15

A New Kind of Leader

Jacinda Ardern never wanted to be prime minister. She didn't consider until the possibility was only seven weeks away. It's widely believed by political writers in New Zealand that everyone in parliament wants to be prime minister and if they say they don't, they're lying. But when Ardern said, over and over, that she didn't want the top job, people believed her. Not only did she not want to be prime minister, she appeared to not want a promotion either. From the surprise IUSY presidency to becoming a Labour candidate to the deputy leadership and then the leadership, Ardern was always asked to step up, often more than once before accepting. Apparently others wanted her to lead before she wanted to. It would be tempting to label her a reluctant leader, but the swiftness with which Ardern adopted the role of prime minister, as if she were meant for the job, shows she wasn't reluctant, she was simply waiting for the right time.

Ardern has succeeded where so many Labour politicians have failed. She did so by being a mirror. Embodying empathy, Ardern invited those she encountered to project their worries and struggles onto her, and in return she projected understanding and support.

Ask the average voter what Ardern did before becoming a Labour MP or what her greatest challenges were as a young person and very few would know the answer. Because Ardern's personal experiences have never driven her political actions.

Even as a teenager, Ardern acted on behalf of others rather than from self-interest. One does not run for student representative two years in a row for the social clout. As a Mormon, Ardern didn't want to wear shorts at school, but her schoolmates did – and she wanted to help them. Similarly, Ardern wasn't a member of the LGBTQIA+ community fighting for equal rights in Wellington, but she saw they needed support and she gave it. She was so generous in that support that she became a well-known political ally to the community.

Her driving focus in politics was always children. She wanted to be Minister for Children and, once she became prime minister, she gave herself the role and pledged to make New Zealand 'the best country in the world to be a child'. Wanting to make the country a better place for children was hardly a revolutionary idea, but Ardern's drive didn't come from growing up in a struggling household in Murupara it came from growing up next door to struggling households.

Ardern pushed for extended paid parental leave long before she had a child, in support of working mothers. Once she had her own, she took a bare minimum of six weeks.

Politicians acting in the best interests of others, rather than themselves, should be the norm, but unfortunately it's not. By doing so, Ardern has become a global icon of empathetic leadership, both a credit to her and an indictment on her international peers.

Ardern's strength is her ability to speak on behalf of those without a voice. But in doing so, she has perhaps limited her ability to speak candidly for herself. At a time when it was almost a political asset to admit to smoking weed at some point in the past, Ardern could never quite bring herself to admit she had, saying instead when she was asked: 'I was raised Mormon and then I was not Mormon – I let other people determine what that means.' It was a clever answer, and made people laugh, but it was also typical of Ardern. She never reveals anything too personal, no matter how inconsequential. Or if she does, it's artfully deployed. Those in favour of legalising cannabis could interpret her answer as being one of understanding and experience. Those against could read it as a roundabout way of saying she did it once a long time ago and never again. Everything and nothing.

When Ardern rebutted Mark Richardson's terrible questions about working women having children, she perfectly exemplified her political approach. I'm not personally offended by what you said about me, she told him with her point, but I am offended on behalf of others. She was one of them, even though she wasn't.

After Christchurch, Ardern's instincts were better than anyone's and the way she carried herself was an exemplary way to lead a nation in mourning. Internationally, Ardern was held up as the embodiment of compassionate leadership. And rightly so. But no one in New Zealand was surprised. Ardern's strength had always been embracing communities – ones she was not personally a member of – wholeheartedly.

In enacting gun law reform, Ardern led the way but received unanimous support. It was not a controversial decision. In fact, the loudest cries were from those wanting tighter restrictions (some of which were added six months later). Ardern was acting on the immediate desires of the country, and the country was grateful.

In many ways, Ardern is the perfect politician. Who better to represent the people than someone who puts aside personal views and works to fulfil the needs of others? The alternative is leaders like Trump or Johnson, who in governing are driven almost exclusively by self-interest. But how much should a leader be guided by voters' often contradictory desires, and how much should they be able to make decisions *on behalf of* those same voters. New Zealanders (and millions of people around the world) trust Ardern to do the right thing. Unlike other leaders, Ardern making decisions based solely on what she believed in would be a good thing.

Which is perhaps why it stung New Zealand voters so much when, mere weeks after uniting the country in mourning, Ardern made a decision that she herself was personally against. When she chose not to use her political capital to push through a capital gains tax, despite it being recommended and her being vocally in support of one, Ardern gave her supporters reason for pause. It made them wonder: what do you actually want? Not 'the New Zealand public', but *you*?

It's hard to gauge. Even in personal, candid conversations, Ardern has an uncanny ability to shift focus. Having a conversation with the most famous person in the country is somehow never about the most famous person in the country. Getting a firm, tangible statement on what she wants can be infuriating because, as she'll tell you, being prime minister is not about her, it's about New Zealand.

Which makes it all the more ironic that after a life spent deliberately promoting others' stories and causes, Ardern herself has become the centre of the world's attention.

Recently political commentators have pondered whether Ardern would be best suited in a diplomacy role, or working in the public or charity sectors, and many have predicted that she will work within the UN once she leaves New Zealand politics. It's these sectors that would allow her to best utilise her skillset without the public scrutiny and weight bearing of leading a government, particularly a coalition government. She herself has said she'd prefer to be a minister, rather than a prime minister, because there's far less scrutiny and relationship management involved. But at the same time, it's hard to imagine any other politician navigating such a precarious coalition half as well as she has, stumbles and all.

Perhaps rather than potentially being in the wrong job, she's simply early.

In 1972, Labour's Norman Kirk took office as the twenty-ninth Prime Minister of New Zealand. Kirk was an orator. He spoke passionately and eloquently on social issues and foreign policy. He is known for preventing the South African rugby team from touring in 1973 during the apartheid era and pulling troops out of Vietnam. But he was also considered too socially conservative by younger members of his party. They wanted more freedoms for the LGBTQIA+ community, women and Māori, and they pushed for Kirk to make it so. He didn't. In fact, his government introduced the early morning police raids (known as Dawn Raids) on Pacific Island immigrant families, looking for overstayers to deport.

But what Kirk did do was set the stage through the speeches he made and the small personal actions he took. He spoke at the first Waitangi Day commemoration about the need to recognise New Zealand as a bicultural country, and a photo appeared on the front page of the paper showing Kirk walking hand in hand with a young Māori boy. The symbols and rhetoric were important, but the practical steps his government took to put his words into action were small. It wasn't until the mid-1980s, a decade after Kirk's death, when the young members of his past government were in charge, that big changes were made.

Ardern has frequently listed Kirk as one of her inspirations. They certainly share a governing style. One of the oft-repeated critiques of Ardern is that her government's actions don't live up to the power of her rhetoric. 'All stardust, no substance,' as English remarked during one of their election debates. Or she's accused of virtue signalling, which has now become an insult. Had Twitter existed in 1973, Kirk would have been accused many times of virtue signalling.

Ardern's government has made undeniable improvements. Extending paid parental leave, introducing winter payments for beneficiaries, introducing free lunches for schoolkids in low socio-economic areas, ending new bids on offshore oil and gas exploration, banning single-use plastic bags nationwide, small weekly payments for new parents, banning overseas speculators, compulsory New Zealand history in schools, prisoner voting rights (for those with sentences shorter than three years) restored. These are all positive actions from a progressive government, but they're not transformational. And those who voted for Ardern were promised transformation. Even the wellbeing budget was about improving, rather than changing. About heading in the right direction, not grabbing everyone and leaping there.

As an opposition MP, Ardern was positioned as a bright, future leader, although her approach to governing was always conservative (in delivery rather than sentiment). Ardern's rhetoric has always been hopeful, optimistic and inspiring, but her political decisions lean more to the pragmatic. And in government she has learned, as many leaders on the left do, that it's hard to remain a figure of inspiration within your own country when you're in government.

But it's not all empty rhetoric. A lot happened, planned and otherwise, in Ardern's first two years as prime minister. Labour's wellbeing budget was a world first, and will undoubtedly be improved upon both in New Zealand and around the world. New Zealand has also adopted a Zero Carbon Bill, setting climate change targets into law. And dangerous assault weapons have been banned.

If re-elected, Ardern will likely see out a generation of climate change sceptics populating the opposition. Those MPs, currently in their mid and late fifties, previously figured they'd have a chance to lead after John Key. Instead, a woman in her thirties is running things. Ardern may well serve as the accelerant taking the country from baby boomer New Zealand to millennial New Zealand. In seven years, today's young MPs, particularly those in the Greens like Chlöe Swarbrick, who are angry at what they deem inaction now, won't be so young. Members of the public, including a massive rise in women representation, who have been inspired by Ardern's rhetoric to enter politics will have experience. There were more women elected to local boards and councils around the country in 2019 than in previous years (though still not enough). They will be the people in charge, and they'll be ready to make all the changes they heard talk of and saw the very beginnings of in 2019.

It's these people that Ardern has inspired. People who have lived their whole lives knowing, without need for debate, that climate change is the world's biggest threat. It may be largely government rhetoric for the moment, but moving beyond the need to justify climate action is the first crucial step. A step few countries in the world have taken.

From her very first year as an MP in 2008, Ardern expressed a desire to promote democracy and equality, and encourage young people to engage in decisions concerning their welfare. In that, she's succeeded. And in succeeding, she's invited scrutiny from those same young people who are wanting more progress, more transformation from their inspiring young leader.

Where Ardern *has* been transformative has been in her own personal, often instinctive, conduct. While the world watched as volatile men rose to power in some of the world's most powerful nations, along came Ardern, a handbrake on the global identity car careening into the abyss. New Zealand has always prided itself on being ahead of the curve, particularly with regards to women in politics. A prime minister giving birth while in office was largely accepted without a fuss. But overseas, in countries where women are still struggling for basic human rights, to see a woman have a baby while leading a country felt monumental. Babies are now frequent guests in the debating chambers of New Zealand parliament, but the image of Neve with Ardern and Gayford at the UN General Assembly marked a turning point in the global body's approach to women in power.

The simple act of wearing hijab in Christchurch united communities both in New Zealand and around the world after a terror attack. It sent a signal to leaders everywhere that even the smallest acts of kindness in positions of power make a difference. The impact of such a simple gesture, as detached from policy-making as it was, cannot be overstated.

When Ardern spoke at the Islamic Women's Council conference in August of 2019, six months after the attack, she was greeted like a member of the family. Her words, hugs and presence during that time were not forgotten.

New Zealanders believed terror would never find a home in their country and it did. In the days following the country tilting off its axis, Ardern held it steady. And in the same year, she would have to do it all over again after a volcanic eruption tragically killed twenty-one people at Whakaari / White Island off the east coast of the North Island. Regardless of anything else, the actions by Ardern in these two moments have cemented her in history. That she acted as she did in a global climate of conflict and vitriol cannot be forgotten.

But there's always more that could be done. One can't help but wonder if the country's progress would be different were Ardern and Labour governing without Peters and New Zealand First. Detractors say no. That New Zealand First has simply been proffered as an excuse for conservative action. Supporters say of course the country would be different. Ardern has done as much as she possibly could given the restraints of a coalition government.

In the second half of 2020, New Zealand will vote again for a leader. If the 2019 elections in Australia and the UK have taught the world anything, it's that there's no such thing as a predictable vote. Maybe Ardern and Labour will win in a landslide and be able to govern alone, or with only the Greens. Maybe the seemingly immortal Winston Peters will once again hold the balance of power. Or maybe, as Australia and the UK did, New Zealand will swing back to the right and elect National into government alone. The steps in the right direction may be built upon or they may be undone. It's up to the people of New Zealand now.

There are many kinds of leaders in the world. Some will go down in history as being only a force for evil. Others will be remembered for one or two things they did exceptionally well. Most will be forgotten entirely.

Whatever unfolds, Jacinda Ardern will forever be known as the second world leader to give birth while in office, the first leader to take maternity leave from office, and the first mother to speak at the UN General Assembly with her child present. And she will be remembered for her humanity and empathy after the horrific Christchurch terror attack.

But Ardern wants her legacy to be more than being a working mother in office, or a 'kind' leader, and plans to make it so.

Whatever she does, she'll have the whole world watching.

Postscript

'Evening, everyone. I thought that I would jump online quickly and just check in with everyone, really, as we all prepare to hunker down for a few weeks.'

It was the evening of 25 March 2020 and New Zealand was only three hours away from entering a nationwide lockdown. Jacinda Ardern was back on Facebook, broadcasting live from her home. The format wasn't new; in fact it was expected given 2020 was an election year and campaigning was on the horizon. Live videos had been Ardern's strong suit in 2017 and would likely be deployed again. However, instead of announcing a policy in her work clothes, Ardern was answering questions about a global pandemic while wearing a jumper.

Ardern had been in contact with scientists and health advisers since January as they tracked the spread of COVID-19. To most people, the virus felt very far away from little old New Zealand at the bottom of the world. But as it spread across continents, it was only a matter of time before it crossed the Pacific Ocean. On 28 February,

New Zealand reported its first case of COVID-19 – a passenger on a flight from Iran. It was just one case, but there would inevitably be more, and the government was making response plans all the while.

By mid-March, the World Health Organization had yet to advise countries to close their borders. New Zealand, along with many other countries, had put restrictions in place for those travelling through and from mainland China, then Iran, Italy and South Korea. On 14 March, Ardern announced that all tourists entering the country must self-isolate for fourteen days except those travelling from the Pacific (where no COVID-19 cases had been reported). It was the first move to indicate a serious reaction to the virus reaching New Zealand's shores.

The very next day, tourists from Europe arrived in the country and calmly told waiting reporters that they would not be self-isolating. It was in clear defiance of the rules and a test of just how serious the government was in its response. Ardern was asked about it hours later and was unequivocal: 'We have the ability to quarantine them – put them in a facility, quarantine them, have a police officer stand outside the door and make sure they don't leave. But I've also asked the question whether I have the power to deport as well.'

Three days later, for the first time in its history, New Zealand closed its borders to everyone but returning citizens and permanent residents. It was the first move in a week of strategically staggered announcements that would culminate in a complete lockdown of the country. On Thursday, the borders closed. On Saturday, Ardern gave an official address to the nation from her office. She spoke alone and directly to the camera, introducing a four-level alert system for New Zealand's COVID-19 response. Level four would involve all non-essential citizens quarantined at home. During her address, Ardern announced that the country was currently at level two. It was deeply serious and strangely reassuring at the same time.

On Monday, Ardern announced that the nationwide alert had been raised to level three and New Zealand would move to a level four lockdown at midnight on 25 March, only two days away. 'These decisions will place the most significant restrictions on New Zealanders' movements in modern history,' she said. 'But it is our best chance to slow the virus and to save lives.' Seemingly overnight, bus stops, billboards, television ads, radio ads, and even road signs all over the country advertised the same message. Stay home. Save lives.

Ardern's messaging had been deliberately simple, with catchphrases repeated over and over throughout her press conferences. Go hard, go early. Stay in your bubble. Team of five million. Be strong but be kind.

Incredibly, there was virtually no opposition to the lockdown. There were valid concerns about the economy and what a lockdown would do to businesses, but the lockdown was announced with measures in place to limit hardship. A twelve-week wage subsidy scheme (which would later be extended) was established, with employers able to apply on behalf of their workers. Self-employed contractors could apply in 60 seconds and receive a lump sum in their bank account within 48 hours. A rental freeze was announced on residential properties. New Zealanders were given the impression that the government was taking the situation very seriously, and so should they.

By the time every cellphone in the country lit up and screeched with a civil defence emergency alert on 25 March reminding everyone of the lockdown, the expectations were widely understood. The alert read:

'This message is for all of New Zealand. We are depending on you. Follow the rules and STAY HOME. Act as if you have Covid-19. This will save lives. Remember: Where you stay tonight is where YOU MUST stay from now on. You must only be in physical contact with those you are living with. It is likely level 4 measures will stay in place for a number of weeks. Let's all do our bit to unite against Covid-19. Kia Kaha.'

For the next four weeks, New Zealand froze. Essential workers such as hospital, government and supermarket staff went to work while everyone else stayed home in their bubbles. A walk or run was allowed, but police patrolled the motorways, stopping anyone trying to drive too far from home. One man who filmed himself coughing on strangers at the supermarket was universally condemned and swiftly arrested. An online form was set up for members of the public to report potential lockdown breaches. Within two days, over 10,000 reports were filed, revealing New Zealanders to be both deeply concerned about their collective health and also huge narks.

Every day at 1 pm, Ardern and the director general of health Dr Ashley Bloomfield (or Bloomfield alone) provided updates on new cases, deaths and total active case numbers. They also provided regular guidance on distancing, hand washing and what to do if you felt unwell. Bloomfield proved an equal match for Ardern, and the perfect partner to front the pandemic response alongside her. His dry delivery of the case updates and health guidance complemented Ardern's more personal style of communication well. So well that, with little else to do during lockdown, New Zealanders quickly deified him, dubbing the 1 pm briefings 'The Ashley Bloomfield Show' and making 'ashley bloomfield wife' a top auto-fill response on Google.

Meanwhile, Ardern was back in the global headlines. First there was news of the comprehensive lockdown, applauded by those in countries where the virus had already taken hold. Then Ardern announced that all government ministers, including herself, would take a 20 per cent pay cut for six months as an act of solidarity with New Zealanders whose livelihoods were impacted by the lockdown. Soon after, Bloomfield and opposition leader Bridges announced that they too would take a pay cut.

The pay cut wasn't material for most, if not all, of the ministers. Eighty percent of (at least) $160,000 is still a large salary. But it was a gesture that resonated around the world and Ardern once again proved that acts of solidarity and empathy are more powerful than most politicians have been led to believe.

Then Ardern declared the Easter bunny an essential worker. During her daily press briefing in the lead up to Easter, a reporter passed on a child's concern about the safety of the Easter bunny's work: 'Have you considered an exemption for the Easter bunny? Because, of course, he would be breaking the bubbles of many families.'

Ardern smiled as she answered: 'You'll be pleased to know that we do consider both the tooth fairy and the Easter bunny to be essential workers.' She went on to explain that given the current situation, the bunny may find it hard to reach every house, but she encouraged children to draw their own Easter eggs and place them in their windows for other children to spot on their walks. Ardern spoke directly to the children at home who were watching. It was most likely the first and last time a politician would be able to address the camera at a midday parliamentary press briefing and know that children would be watching and listening.

Ardern and Bloomfield set the standard high for all New Zealanders, in a way that encouraged each citizen to play their part. And they did. Nobody wanted to let down the team of five million. It took ten days of lockdown for the daily case numbers to reach their peak (eighty-nine new cases on 2 April and 5 April), and once they started to fall, they fell fast. Each improvement was celebrated nationwide, with Ardern quick to give credit to each individual watching at home. 'In the face of the greatest threat to human health that we have faced in over a century, Kiwis have quietly and collectively implemented a nationwide wall of defence,' she said on 9 April. 'You are breaking the chain of transmission and you did it for each other.'

On 20 April, two days before the scheduled end to the level-four lockdown, Ardern announced that New Zealand wouldn't move down to level three until 27 April, despite daily case numbers dropping into the single digits. Yet few complained. In fact, a poll asking for responses to the announcement found that 66 per cent of respondents thought the timing was 'about right' and 22 per cent thought it was too early. While Ardern and Bloomfield's leadership played a major part in the nationwide buy-in to the lockdown, the contrast with other countries' responses didn't hurt.

From the safety and comfort of their homes, New Zealanders watched as UK PM Boris Johnson refused to limit his contact with strangers and was subsequently hospitalised after testing positive for the virus. They watched as case numbers in the US rose by the thousands every day and President Trump publicly dismissed the severity of the virus. If anything, world leaders claiming to know better and being comprehensively proven wrong served as great reassurance to New Zealanders that they were doing the right thing.

On 4 May, there were no new confirmed cases. It was the first day of no new cases since mid-March, and it wouldn't be the last. Thanks to the quarantine system at the border and the compliance of New Zealanders during lockdown, the zero-case days began to add up. By 9 June, New Zealand was on a seventeen-day streak of no new COVID-19 cases. Ardern stood in the Beehive theatrette and made two announcements. The first was that there were now no active cases of COVID-19 in New Zealand. The second was that, as a result, the country would fully reopen its economy and all restrictions would be lifted. Only the border restrictions would remain. It was huge news, and a result better than even the most optimistic of scientists had predicted back in March. New Zealand had successfully eliminated COVID-19. How did Ardern react to the news? 'I did a little dance.'

Just shy of three months since community transmission was declared and the lockdown was announced, New Zealand returned to business as usual. People returned to school and work, went back to hugging loved ones and gathering in crowds. The 1 pm daily press briefings ended and politics returned to its regularly scheduled programming. Which is to say, politicians went back to disgracing themselves, turning on each other and preparing for the upcoming election.

During an ordinary term in ordinary times, a communications degree may have been the second or third most relevant qualification for a leader to hold. In fact, Ardern's field of expertise had been used in the past to discredit her, or to suggest she lacked any 'real' qualifications. However, for reasons beyond her control, Ardern's first term had been anything but ordinary. As most New

Zealanders struggled with terror in their backyard for the first time after the Christchurch mosque attacks, it was Ardern's communication skills that allowed her to show empathy and solidarity, uniting the country in grief. When a natural disaster struck and families waited anxiously for news of their loved ones, it was Ardern who communicated updates sensitively. And now, as leaders around the globe struggled to unite their people against a deadly pandemic, it was Ardern and her team's mastery in communication that ultimately powered one of the most successful COVID-19 responses in the world.

As a result, Ardern's popularity soared once again. Throughout the crisis she could do no wrong, and Simon Bridges could do no right. On 18 May, after shocking poll results for National, Todd Muller made a bid for the leadership. Until then, Muller was largely unknown, as illustrated by his not being mentioned in this book until now. But he was something different, and with Nikki Kaye as his deputy, it was enough to take Bridges' job.

Fifty-three days later, Muller stepped down as leader and veteran MP Judith Collins stepped up. Three leaders in three months. National were looking a lot like 2014 Labour and the saga of the many Davids. Then Nikki Kaye, the only MP to twice defeat Ardern in an election, announced that she would be retiring from politics at the end of the term. National MPs were dropping like flies and it soon became apparent that something would have to go horribly wrong for Ardern and Labour to not return for a second term. With fifty-five days until the election, Labour were polling at 60 per cent, with National on just 25 per cent. If Labour maintained those numbers until election night, they could govern alone, without New Zealand First or the Greens.

Labour governing alone had never happened, and it would allow Ardern the freedom to implement policies without needing to compromise with coalition partners. However, it would also mean there would be no more excuses for not following through on every speech, promise and pledge Ardern had made in the past three years.

In July 2020, the global number of COVID-19 cases surpassed sixteen million. There had been over 640,000 recorded deaths. Cities around the world were entering their second lockdown phases as cases surged again. People protested against wearing masks.

In New Zealand, the death count was at twenty-two. It had been at twenty-two since 28 May. There was no community transmission and no new cases that day. Jacinda Ardern was campaigning in central Auckland, attending a local fair. She stopped and spoke to vendors as she made her way through the crowds. She complimented each of them, shaking their hands and lingering for a chat. She looked genuinely happy to see everyone, and everyone was happy to see her.

OVER AND OVER AGAIN, it was reiterated that New Zealand could never truly eliminate COVID-19 until a vaccine was developed and distributed. The plan was just to put measures in place so that as each wave came, the health system would not be overwhelmed. A nationwide lockdown successfully eliminated the first wave, but it was only a matter of time before the second wave arrived.

On the evening of 11 August, the prime minister's office announced that Ardern and Dr Bloomfield would be holding an urgent press briefing at 9.15 pm. At such a late hour, the news couldn't possibly be good, and Ardern got straight to the point. 'After 102 days, we have our first cases of

COVID-19 outside of a managed isolation or quarantine facility in New Zealand.' Four members of an Auckland family had tested positive for COVID-19 with no known links to the border or other known cases. 'While we have all worked incredibly hard to prevent this scenario, we have also planned and prepared for it,' said Ardern. She went on to announce that while health officials traced contacts and conducted a testing blitz in the region, Auckland would move into level-three lockdown (effective from noon the following day), meaning a stay-at-home order for all but essential movements such as going to the supermarket or exercising, as well as contactless food deliveries. The lockdown would last three days, but if case numbers rose it might be extended. Auckland held its breath. Sure enough, two days later, Ardern was back behind the lectern to inform the residents of New Zealand's largest city that after 48,000 tests in forty-eight hours, twenty-nine new cases had been detected in the community, and there was still no confirmed origin for the outbreak. Auckland would remain in lockdown for an additional twelve days, or two weeks total. While Aucklanders grumbled, the rest of the country wondered what would happen if Auckland's lockdown extended until election day on 19 September. The election was just four weeks away and opposition parties had been pushing for it to be delayed, as restrictions had been placed on campaigning in light of the new outbreak. On 17 August, Ardern once again addressed the nation: 'I have decided, on balance, to move the election by four weeks to the 17th of October.' The country let out a collective groan. Having to stay home was bad enough; an extra four weeks of election campaigning made it even worse.

Nonetheless, polls conducted during the second lockdown showed the majority of New Zealanders still rated the government's response to COVID-19 as 'excellent'. Swift action and clear communication had reassured New Zealanders. Auckland's second lockdown passed much like the first: the case numbers rose for a few days then steadily flattened, allowing for restrictions to be slowly eased throughout September. After briefly returning to her role as co-star of the daily 1 pm briefing, Ardern turned her attention back to the campaign trail. Despite the government's popularity in its pandemic response, Labour weren't taking any chances. Or, apparently, any risks.

Labour were the clear favourites. When Ardern officially launched their campaign in early August (just two days before the new outbreak began), Labour were polling at 53 per cent to National's 32 per cent. Only a week earlier, on Ardern's fortieth birthday, Labour had polled at a whopping 61 per cent. With that sort of support, younger Labour voters hoped that Ardern would use the opportunity to propose more progressive policies this time around. The government had spared no cost in extending wage subsidies and small business loans, and leftie Labour voters crossed their fingers that Labour's plan to repay the huge debt would include taxing the rich. Instead, Labour shifted decidedly closer to the centre in an attempt to entice disgruntled National voters across the aisle. Their much-hyped tax plan was a new tax rate for income earned over $180,000, which would only affect about 2 per cent of New Zealanders. The word 'transformational' was removed from their campaign. Instead, the general message was 'strong and stable'. In other words, a vote for Labour was a vote for nothing too drastic. And in a year when everything felt too drastic all the time, the messaging worked. The four leaders' debates between Ardern and Judith Collins served mostly to demonstrate the many similarities between the two parties.

When a capital gains tax was raised, Collins said she didn't think it was a good idea and would not implement it, while Ardern said she did think it was a good idea but also would not implement it. Where the leaders differed was in their mannerisms. Ardern's capacity to communicate calmly and clearly was on full display throughout the debates. Collins, however, adopted a more adversarial approach, repeatedly referring to Ardern as 'Miss Ardern' or 'dear'. It was old politics versus new politics, and while Collins may have created some entertaining viewing, it was new politics that ultimately won out.

LABOUR WON. ON THEIR OWN. For the first time in the history of mixed-member proportional representation in New Zealand, a single party gained enough votes to govern alone. In the hours leading up to polls closing at 7 pm, predictions were all over the place. Could ACT really jump from 0.5 per cent of the party vote in 2017 to almost 8 per cent in 2020? Would Deputy Prime Minister Winston Peters and New Zealand First be out of parliament entirely? Could the Greens manage to get over the 5 per cent threshold, even with Labour doing so well?

The answer was yes to all of the above.

Labour won 50 per cent of party votes and the results were showing as much at 7.16 pm. National won only 25.6 per cent, the Greens 7.9 per cent, ACT 7.6 per cent, and New Zealand First 2.6 per cent.

It was expected that National would lose party votes a little to the left (Labour) and a little to the right (ACT), but it was also predicted that Labour would gain votes from both sides too (Greens to the left, National to the right). Astonishingly, the Greens did better than they had in 2017, signalling a shift of the entire voting population to the left.

Labour won a staggering number of seats in parliament, but the biggest winner of the night was the Greens' Chlöe Swarbrick. Swarbrick, twenty-six, a former fashion designer turned political trailblazer, was an ambitious list MP for the Greens who decided to run in Auckland Central, Ardern's old electorate, despite it historically being a two-horse race between the major parties. Due to Nikki Kaye's abrupt departure, both Labour and National candidates were relatively unknown, so in stepped Swarbrick, representing a party that had only won one electorate seat in its history (in 1999). It was a risky move, with Labour's candidate, Helen White, repeatedly asking Swarbrick to withdraw from the race so as not to split the left vote. Instead, after an intense grassroots campaign, Swarbrick split both sides of the vote and made history, winning Auckland Central by 1068 votes.

Like Ardern, Swarbrick looked to be a future party leader. And like Ardern, Swarbrick insisted she had no desire for such a position. But what set Swarbrick apart was her willingness to criticise those on the same side of the political aisle as her, particularly Ardern.

Two weeks after Labour's landslide victory, liberal voters were once again disappointed by what they saw as a lack of political conviction from Ardern. The first time was when she failed to use political capital to implement a capital gains tax. This time it was because of weed. New Zealanders cast four votes in the 2020 election. One electorate vote, one party vote, and two referendum votes: one for legalising cannabis and one for legalising euthanasia. The campaigns for the referendums had been years in the making, with David Seymour leading the push for legalising assisted dying, and Chlöe Swarbrick fronting the yes campaign for the legalisation of recreational cannabis.

The cannabis referendum was a drug issue but also a race issue. A report by Ardern's chief science adviser, Juliet Gerrard, showed that Māori were three times more likely to be arrested and convicted of a cannabis-related crime than non-Māori, were almost twice as likely to go to court for a first offence and nearly seven times more likely to be charged.

After years of being coy when asked about her history with (or without) drugs, Ardern confirmed during a leaders' debate that she had used marijuana. It wasn't much of a revelation – by that point it would have been weirder if she'd said she'd never smoked weed – but it was a clear answer at least. Except it was the only answer she was willing to give on the subject. A number of MPs had been vocal about their stance in the cannabis referendum, including former Labour leader and then justice minister Andrew Little, who publicly stated he'd be voting yes. Despite repeated prompts from reporters, MPs and debate moderators – and although she had often said she didn't think people should be criminalised and imprisoned for possession of marijuana – Ardern refused to reveal which way she'd be voting in the referendum. Her reasoning was that as prime minister it was only her responsibility to facilitate the referendum and give the public a choice, not to persuade them to vote a particular way. 'My vote is as good as my neighbour's vote,' insisted Ardern.

As election day neared, the euthanasia referendum (which Ardern had publicly expressed her support for) looked like it would pass comfortably. The cannabis referendum, however, remained close. Public backing from the most trusted and supported prime minister ever would certainly have helped the yes campaign, but Ardern refused to budge.

Preliminary results were announced a fortnight after Labour's historic win, showing the euthanasia bill would pass but the cannabis legislation was dead in the water, with 53 per cent voting against it. That same day, Ardern revealed that she had voted yes in the cannabis referendum. Supporters of the yes campaign were furious. Then Justice Minister Little confirmed that the government would not look to implement drug reform in their next term. After all votes were counted, the cannabis referendum did not pass. The votes against it totalled 50.7 per cent.

Swarbrick didn't hold back when asked what she thought of Ardern's late vote revelation. 'I'm in the Greens because I have the courage of my convictions,' she said.

Does Ardern have the courage of her convictions? It's a question many have asked since 2017 and continue to ask as she enters her second term. With her party now governing alone, without Winston Peters as handbrake, Ardern has the power to enact policies that reflect her values. But will she do so? Years of championing property taxes became a pledge to not tax capital gains so long as she is in office. A strong stance against the criminalisation of cannabis became the sidelining of drug reform in that area. These are convictions without follow-through that have disappointed some of those who believed Ardern's promise of radical transformation.

But New Zealand has seen significant transformation in other areas. When Ardern announced her cabinet in October 2020, it looked unlike any previous one. It actually looked like New Zealand. Half of Labour's ministers were people of colour and half were Pākehā. Nanaia Mahuta, the first MP to display a moko kauae (sacred Māori face tattoo) in parliament, was appointed as New Zealand's first female foreign minister. And Labour's eight plus the

Greens' four LGBTQIA+ MPs made New Zealand the most rainbow parliament in the world. Ardern had built a team around her that accurately represented the wider community, and those ministers would fight for the communities they represented. Compared to the National Party (all but three of its thirty-three MPs were Pākehā), Labour were looking more and more like the party of the future.

It's easy to compare New Zealand to countries overseas and feel that the small nation at the bottom of the world has it figured out. Ardern continues to be a beacon of hope for young people wishing for a better future. Her empathy and kindness have inspired millions, even while her cautious approach on domestic matters has led to disappointment among local supporters. Once most remarkable for being pregnant while in office, her parenting is now a sidenote to her many other achievements. But Ardern's legacy still lies ahead of her – how she is remembered will be heavily determined by the actions of her government in her second term, with Ardern wielding huge power in a small country.

What she does with that power is up to her.

Speeches

New Zealand National Statement to the United Nations General Assembly, 28 September 2018

E ngā mana nui o ngā whenua o te ao
  Tēnā koutou katoa
  Nei rā te reo mihi maioha o Aotearoa
  Tēnā tātau i ngā kaupapa kōrero
  Ka arahina e tātau
  Me te ngakau pono
  Me te kotahitanga o te tangata
Madam President,
Mr Secretary-General,
Friends in the global community.

My opening remarks were in Te Reo Māori, the language of the indigenous people of Aotearoa New Zealand. As is tradition, I acknowledged those who are here, why we are here, and the importance of our work.

It seems a fitting place to start. I'm struck as a leader attending my first United Nations General Assembly by the power and potential that resides here. But in New Zealand, we have always been acutely aware of that.

We are a remote nation at the bottom of the South Pacific. Our nearest neighbours take three hours to reach by plane, and anywhere that takes less than twelve hours is considered close. I have no doubt though, that our geographic isolation has contributed to our values.

We are a self-deprecating people. We're not ones for status. We'll celebrate the local person who volunteers at their sports club as much as we will the successful entrepreneur. Our empathy and strong sense of justice is matched only by our pragmatism. We are, after all, a country made up of two main islands – one simply named North and the other, South. For all of that, our isolation has not made us insular. In fact, our engagement with the world has helped shape who we are.

I am a child of the '80s. A period in New Zealand's history where we didn't just observe international events, we challenged them. Whether it was apartheid in South Africa, or nuclear testing in the Pacific, I grew up learning about my country and who we were, by the way that we reacted to international events. Whether it was taking to the streets or changing our laws, we have seen ourselves as members of a community, and one that we have a duty to use our voice within.

I am an incredibly proud New Zealander, but much of that pride has come from being a strong and active member of our international community, not in spite of it. And at the heart of that international community, has been this place.

Emerging from a catastrophic war, we have collectively established through convention, charters and rules a set of international norms and human rights. All of these are an acknowledgement that we are not isolated, governments do have obligations to their people and each other, and that our actions have a global effect.

In 1945, New Zealand Prime Minister Peter Fraser said that the UN Charter offered perhaps a last opportunity to work in unison to realise the hope in the hearts of all of us, for a peace that would be real, lasting, and worthy of human dignity. But none of these founding principles should be consigned to the history books. In fact, given the challenges we face today, and how truly global they are in their nature and impact, the need for collective action and multilateralism has never been clearer. And yet, for all of that, the debate and dialogue we hear globally is not centred on the relevance and importance of our international institutions. Instead, we find ourselves having to defend their very existence.

That surely leaves us all with the question, how did we get here, and how do we get out?

If anything unites us politically in this place right now it is this – globalisation has had a massive impact on our nations and the people we serve. While that impact has been positive for many, for others it has not. The transitions our economies have made have often been jarring, and the consequences harsh. And so amongst unprecedented global economic growth, we have still seen a growing sense of isolation, dislocation, and a sense of insecurity and the erosion of hope.

As politicians and governments, we all have choices in how we respond to these challenges. We can use the environment to blame nameless, faceless 'other', to feed the sense of insecurity, to retreat into greater levels of isolationism. Or we can acknowledge the problems we have and seek to fix them.

Generational change

In New Zealand, going it alone is not an option. Aside from our history, we are also a trading nation. And proudly so. But even without those founding principles, there are not just questions of nationhood to consider. There are generational demands upon us too.

It should hardly come as a surprise that we have seen a global trend of young people showing dissatisfaction with our political systems, and calling on us to do things differently – why wouldn't they when they themselves have had to adapt so rapidly to a changing world?

Within a few short decades we now have a generation who will grow up more connected than ever before. Digital transformation will determine whether the jobs they are training for will even exist in two decades. In education or the job market, they won't just compete with their neighbour, but their neighbouring country. This generation is a borderless one – at least in a virtual sense. One that increasingly see themselves as global citizens. And as their reality changes, they expect ours to as well – that we'll see and understand our collective impact, and that we'll change the way we use our power.

And if we're looking for an example of where the next generation is calling on us to make that change, we need look no further than climate change.

Global challenges

Two weeks ago, Pacific Island leaders gathered together at the Pacific Islands Forum. It was at this meeting, on the small island nation of Nauru, that climate change was declared the single biggest threat to the security of the Pacific. Please, just think about this for a moment. Of all of the challenges we debate and discuss, rising sea levels present the single biggest threat to our region. For those who live in the South Pacific, the impacts of climate change are not academic, or even arguable. They are watching the sea levels rise, the extreme weather events increase, and the impact on their water supply and food crops. We can talk all we like about the science and what it means, what temperature rises we need to limit in order to survive, but there is a grinding reality in hearing someone from a Pacific island talk about where the sea was when they were a child, and potential loss of their entire village as an adult.

Our action in the wake of this global challenge remains optional. But the impact of inaction does not. Nations like Tuvalu, the Marshall Islands, or Kiribati – small countries who've contributed the least to global climate change – are and will suffer the full force of a warming planet.

If my Pacific neighbours do not have the option of opting out of the effects of climate change, why should we be able to opt out of taking action to stop it? Any disintegration of multilateralism – any undermining of climate related targets and agreements – aren't interesting footnotes in geopolitical history. They are catastrophic.

In New Zealand we are determined to play our part. We will not issue any further offshore oil and gas exploration permits. We have set a goal of 100 per cent renewable energy generation by 2035, established a green infrastructure fund to encourage innovation, and rolled out an initiative to plant one billion trees over the next ten years.

These plans are unashamedly ambitious. The threat climate change poses demands it. But we only represent less than 0.2 per cent of global emissions. That's why, as a global community, not since the inception of the United Nations has there been a greater example of the importance of collective action and multilateralism, than climate change. It should be a rallying cry to all of us.

And yet there is a hesitance we can ill afford. A calculation of personal cost, of self-interest. But this is not the only challenge where domestic self-interest is the first response, and where an international or collective approach has been diluted at best, or rejected at worst.

Rebuilding multilateralism

But it would be both unfair and naive to argue that retreating to our own borders and interests has meant turning our backs on a perfect system. The international institutions we have committed ourselves to have not been perfect. But they can be fixed.

And that is why the challenge I wish to issue today is this – together, we must rebuild and recommit to multilateralism. We must redouble our efforts to work as a global community. We must rediscover our shared belief in the value, rather than the harm, of connectedness. We must demonstrate that collective international action not only works, but that it is in all of our best interests.

We must show the next generation that we are listening, and that we have heard them.

Connectedness

But if we're truly going to take on a reform agenda, we need to acknowledge the fallings that led us to this crossroad.

International trade for instance, has helped bring millions of people out of poverty around the world. But some have felt their standard of living slide. In New Zealand, we ourselves have seen the hesitancy around trade agreements amongst our own population.

The correct response to this is not to repeat mistakes of the past and be seduced by the false promises of protectionism. Rather, we must all work to ensure that the benefits of trade are distributed fairly across our societies. We can't rely on international institutions to do this. In the same way as we cannot blame them if they haven't delivered these benefits. It is incumbent on us to build productive, sustainable, inclusive economies, and demonstrate to our peoples that when done right, international economic integration can make us all better off.

And if we want to ensure anyone is better off, surely it should be the most vulnerable.

In New Zealand we have set ourselves an ambitious goal. We want to be the best place in the world to be a child. It's hardly the stuff of hard and fast measures – after all, how do you measure play, a feeling of security, happiness? But we can measure material deprivation, and we can measure poverty, and so we will. And not only that, we are making it law that we report on those numbers every single year alongside our budgets. What better way to hold ourselves to account, and what better group to do that for than children?

But if we are focused on nurturing that next generation, we have to equally worry about what it is we are handing down to them too – including our environment. In the Māori language there is a word that captures the importance of that role – *Kaitiakitanga*.

It means guardianship. The idea that we have been entrusted with our environment, and we have a duty of care. For us, that has meant taking action to address degradation, like setting standards to make our rivers swimmable, reducing waste and phasing out single-use plastic bags, right through to eradicating predators and protecting our biodiversity.

The race to grow our economies and increase wealth makes us all the poorer if it comes at the cost of our environment. In New Zealand, we are determined to prove that it doesn't have to be this way. But these are all actions and initiatives that we can take domestically that ease the blame and pressure on our international institutions.

That doesn't mean they don't need fixing.

Reforming the UN

As the heart of the multilateral system, the United Nations must lead the way. We strongly support the Secretary-General's reform efforts to make the UN more responsive and effective, modernised so that it is capable of dealing with today's challenges. We encourage him to be ambitious. And we stand with him in that ambition. But ultimately it is up to us – the Member States – to drive change at the UN.

This includes reforming the Security Council. If we want the Council to fulfil its purpose of maintaining international peace and security, its practices need to be updated so it is not hamstrung by the use of the veto. New thinking will also be needed if we are to achieve the vision encapsulated in the Sustainable Development Goals.

In New Zealand, we have sought to embed the principles behind the SDGs in a new living standards framework that is guiding policy making, and the management of our resources. And we remain committed to supporting the rollout of the SDGs alongside international partners through a significant increase in our Official Development Assistance budget.

Universal values

But revitalising our international rules-based system isn't just about the mechanics of how we work together. It also means renewing our commitment to our values. The UN Charter recalls that the Organisation was formed to save succeeding generations from the scourge of war, which through two World Wars had brought untold sorrow to humanity. If we forget this history and the principles which drove the creation of the UN we will be doomed to repeat the mistakes of the past.

In an increasingly uncertain world it is more important than ever that we remember the core values on which the UN was built. That all people are equal. That everyone is entitled to have their dignity and human rights respected. That we must strive to promote social progress and better standards of life in larger freedom. And we must consistently hold ourselves to account on each.

Amongst renewing this commitment though, we have to acknowledge where accountability must continue – and that is especially the case when it comes to equality. So many gains have been made, each worthy of celebration. In New Zealand we have just marked the 125th year since women were granted the right to vote. We were the first in the world to do so. As a girl I never ever grew up believing that my gender would stand in the way of me achieving whatever I wanted to in life.

I am, after all, not the first, but the third female Prime Minister of New Zealand.

But for all of that, we still have a gender pay gap, an over representation of women in low-paid work, and domestic violence. And we are not alone. It seems surprising that in this modern age we have to recommit ourselves to gender equality, but we do. And I for one will never celebrate the gains we have made for women domestically while internationally other women and girls experience a lack of the most basic opportunities and dignity.

Me Too must become We Too.

We are all in this together.

Conclusion

I accept that the list of demands on all of us is long. Be it domestic, or international, we are operating in challenging times. We face what we call in New Zealand 'wicked problems'. Ones that are intertwined and interrelated. Perhaps then it is time to step back from the chaos and ask what we want. It is in that space that we'll find simplicity. The simplicity of peace, of prosperity, of fairness.

If I could distil it down into one concept that we are pursuing in New Zealand it is simple and it is this. Kindness.

In the face of isolationism, protectionism, racism – the simple concept of looking outwardly and beyond ourselves, of kindness and collectivism, might just be as good a starting point as any. So let's start here with the institutions that have served us well in times of need, and will do so again.

In the meantime, I can assure all of you, New Zealand remains committed to continue to do our part to building and sustaining international peace and security. To promoting and defending an open, inclusive, and rules-based international order based on universal values.

To being pragmatic, empathetic, strong and kind.

The next generation after all, deserves no less.

Tena koutou, tena koutou, tena tatou katoa.

Statement on Christchurch Mosque terror attack, 19 March 2019

Al salam Alaikum. Peace be upon you. And peace be upon all of us.

The 15th of March will now forever be a day etched in our collective memories. On a quiet Friday afternoon a man stormed into a place of peaceful worship and took away the lives of fifty people.

That quiet Friday afternoon has become our darkest of days.

But for the families, it was more than that. It was the day that the simple act of prayer – of practising their Muslim faith and religion – led to the loss of their loved ones' lives.

Those loved ones, were brothers, daughters, fathers and children.

They were New Zealanders. They are us.

And because they are us, we, as a nation, we mourn them. We feel a huge duty of care to them. And we have so much we feel the need to say and to do.

One of the roles I never anticipated having, and hoped never to have, is to voice the grief of a nation. At this time, it has been second only to securing the care of those affected, and the safety of everyone.

And in this role, I wanted to speak directly to the families. We cannot know your grief, but we can walk with you at every stage. We can, and we will, surround you with aroha, manaakitanga and all that makes us, us. Our hearts are heavy but our spirit is strong.

Six minutes after a 111 call was placed alerting the police to the shootings at Al-Noor mosque, police were on the scene.

The arrest itself was nothing short of an act of bravery. Two country police officers rammed the vehicle from which the offender was still shooting. They pulled open his car door, when there were explosives inside, and pulled him out.

I know we all wish to acknowledge that their acts put the safety of New Zealanders above their own, and we thank them. But they were not the only ones who showed extraordinary courage.

Naeem Rashid, originally from Pakistan, died after rushing at the terrorist and trying to wrestle the gun from him. He lost his life trying to save those who were worshipping alongside him.

Abdul Aziz, originally from Afghanistan, confronted and faced down the armed terrorist after grabbing the nearest thing to hand – a simple eftpos machine. He risked his life and no doubt saved many with his selfless bravery.

There will be countless stories, some of which we may never know, but to each, we acknowledge you in this place, in this House.

For many of us the first sign of the scale of this terrorist attack was the images of ambulance staff transporting victims to Christchurch hospital. To the first responders, the ambulance staff and the health professionals who have assisted – and who continue to assist those who have been injured – please accept the heartfelt thanks of us all. I saw first-hand your care and your professionalism in the face of extraordinary challenges. We are proud of your work, and incredibly grateful for it.

I'd like to talk about some of the immediate measures currently in place especially to ensure the safety of our Muslim community, and more broadly the safety of everyone.

As a nation, we do remain on high alert. While there isn't a specific threat at present, we are maintaining vigilance. Unfortunately, we have seen in countries that know the horrors of terrorism more than us, there is a pattern of increased tension and actions over the weeks that follow that means we do need to ensure that vigilance is maintained.

There is an additional and ongoing security presence in Christchurch, and as the police have indicated, there will continue to be a police presence at mosques around the country while their doors are open. When they are closed, police will be in the vicinity.

There is a huge focus on ensuring the needs of families are met. That has to be our priority. A community welfare centre has been set up near the hospital in Christchurch to make sure people know how to access support.

Visas for family members overseas are being prioritised so that they can attend funerals. Funeral costs are covered, and we have moved quickly to ensure that this includes repatriation costs for any family members who would like to move their loved ones away from New Zealand.

We are working to provide mental health and social support. The 1737 number yesterday received roughly 600 texts or phone calls. They are on average lasting around forty minutes, and I encourage anyone in need to reach out and use these services. They are there for you.

Our language service has also provided support from more than 5000 contacts, ensuring whether you are ACC or MSD, you are able to pass on the support that is needed, in the language that is needed. To all those working within this service, we say thank you.

Our security and intelligence services are receiving a range of additional information. As has been the case in the past, these are being taken extremely seriously, and they are being followed up.

I know though that there have rightly been questions around how this could have happened here. In a place that prides itself on being open, peaceful, diverse. And there is anger that it has happened here.

There are many questions that need to be answered, and the assurance that I give you is that they will be.

Yesterday cabinet agreed that an inquiry, one that looks into the events that led up to the attack on 15 March, will occur. We will examine what we did know, could have known, or should have known. We cannot allow this to happen again.

Part of ensuring the safety of New Zealanders must include a frank examination of our gun laws. As I have already said our gun laws will change. Cabinet met yesterday and made in-principle decisions, seventy-two hours after the attack.

Before we meet again next Monday, these decisions will be announced.

There is one person at the centre of this act of terror against our Muslim community in New Zealand. A 28-year-old man – an Australian citizen – has been charged with one count of murder. Other charges will follow. He will face the full force of the law in New Zealand. The families of the fallen will have justice.

He sought many things from his act of terror, but one was notoriety.

And that is why you will never hear me mention his name. He is a terrorist. He is a criminal. He is an extremist.

But he will, when I speak, be nameless.

And to others I implore you: speak the names of those who were lost, rather than the name of the man who took them. He may have sought notoriety, but we in New Zealand will give him nothing. Not even his name.

We will also look at the role social media played and what steps we can take, including on the international stage, and in unison with our partners. There is no question that ideas and language of division and hate have existed for decades, but their form of distribution, the tools of organisation, they are new.

We cannot simply sit back and accept that these platforms just exist and that what is said on them is not the responsibility of the place where they are published. They are the publisher. Not just the postman. There cannot be a case of all profit no responsibility. This of course doesn't take away the responsibility we too must show as a nation, to confront racism, violence and extremism. I don't have all of the answers now, but we must collectively find them. And we must act.

We are deeply grateful for all messages of sympathy, support and solidarity that we are receiving from our friends all around the world. And we are grateful to the global Muslim community who have stood with us, and we stand with them.

I acknowledge that we too also stand with Christchurch, in a devastating blow that this has been to their recovery. I acknowledge every member of this House that has stood alongside their Muslim community but especially those in Canterbury as we acknowledge this double grief.

As I conclude I acknowledge there are many stories that will have struck all of us since the 15th of March.

One I wish to mention, is that of Hati Mohemmed Daoud Nabi.

He was the 71-year-old man who opened the door at the Al-Noor mosque and uttered the words 'Hello brother, welcome'. His final words.

Of course he had no idea of the hate that sat behind the door, but his welcome tells us so much – that he was a member of a faith that welcomed all its members, that showed openness, and care.

I have said many times, we are a nation of 200 ethnicities, 160 languages. We open our doors to others and say welcome. And the only thing that must change after the events of Friday is that this same door must close on all of those who espouse hate and fear.

Yes, the person who committed these acts was not from here. He was not raised here. He did not find his ideology here, but that is not to say that those very same views do not live here.

I know that as a nation, we wish to provide every comfort we can to our Muslim community in this darkest of times. And we are. The mountain of flowers around the country that lie at the doors of mosques, the spontaneous song outside the gates. These are ways of expressing an outpouring of love and empathy. But we wish to do more.

We wish for every member of our communities to also feel safe.

Safety means being free from the fear of violence.

But it also means being free from the fear of those sentiments of racism and hate, that create a place where violence can flourish.

And every single one of us has the power to change that.

On Friday it will be a week since the attack. Members of the Muslim community will gather for worship on that day.

Let us acknowledge their grief as they do.
Let's support them as they gather again for worship.
We are one, they are us.
Tātau tātau
Al salam Alaikum
Weh Rahmat Allah
Weh Barakaatuh.

Sources

Prologue: 19 October 2017
Tracy Watkins, "'I don't want to be prime minister" – Jacinda Ardern', *Stuff*, 28 November 2015.

1. From Murupara to Morrinsville
'Debating team talks its way to North Island win', *Waikato Times*, 1 October 1996.
'Jacinda Ardern on her role model mum', *Now to Love*, 20 October 2017.
'Jacinda Ardern, the pregnant prime minister of New Zealand, on her work/life balance and meeting Barack Obama', *The Sunday Times*, 8 April 2018.
Jacinda Ardern, Maiden statement, *Hansard*, vol. 651, 2008, p. 753.
Jacinda Ardern, 'Wellbeing a cure for inequality', Speech, 25 September 2019.
Kelly Bertrand, 'Jacinda Ardern's country childhood', *New Zealand Woman's Weekly*, 30 June 2014.
Michelle Duff, *Jacinda Ardern: The Story Behind an Extraordinary Leader*, Allen & Unwin, Crows Nest, 2019.
Gregor Fountain, 'An extraordinary job', PPTA website, 1 April 2019.

Dr Jarrod Gilbert, 'Life, kids and being Jacinda', *The New Zealand Herald*, 19 January 2018.

Dale Husband, 'Jacinda: Lofty goals and small-town values', *E-Tangata*, 26 August 2017.

David Lange, Oxford University debate on nuclear weapons, 1 March 1985.

Mark Sainsbury, 'Jacinda Ardern: Running on instinct', *Noted*, 16 September 2017.

Katrina Tanirau, 'Labour leader Jacinda Ardern hits hometown in campaign trail', *Stuff*, 10 August 2017.

2. Leaving the Church

'Ask me anything with Jacinda Ardern!', Reddit, 23 March 2008.

Dr Jarrod Gilbert, 'Life, kids and being Jacinda', *The New Zealand Herald*, 19 January 2018.

Amanda Hooton, '48 hours with Jacinda: Warm, earnest, accessible – is our PM too good to be true?', *Stuff*, 31 March 2018.

Kim Knight, 'The politics of life: The truth about Jacinda Ardern', *The New Zealand Herald*, 29 January 2017.

Nadia Kohmani, 'David Cameron, a pig's head and a secret society at Oxford University – explained', *The Guardian*, 21 September 2015.

Kate McCann, 'Theresa May admits "running through fields of wheat" is the naughtiest thing she ever did', *The Telegraph* (UK), 5 June 2017.

Alex McKinnon, 'Australia's prime minister has a pants-shitting problem', *The Outline*, 22 May 2019.

Tad Walch, 'President Nelson meets New Zealand prime minister Jacinda Ardern, says church will donate to mosque', *Deseret News*, 19 May 2019.

3. The Apprenticeship

'The back bench baby MPs', *The New Zealand Herald*, 8 November 2008.

Natalie Akoorie, 'Youngest MP keen to get down to work', *Stuff*, 11 November 2008.

Jacinda Ardern, Maiden statement, *Hansard*, Vol. 651, 2008.

Don Brasch, 'Nationhood', Speech, Orewa Rotary Club, 27 January 2004.

Tim Donoghue, 'Labour woos families commissioner as MP', *The Dominion Post*, 2 April 2008.

Adam Dudding, 'Jacinda Ardern: I didn't want to work for Tony Blair', *Stuff*, 27 August 2017.

Brian Edwards, *Helen Clark: Portrait of a Prime Minister*, Politico's Publishing, London, 2002.

James Ihaka, 'Eyes on tussle in bellwether seat', *The New Zealand Herald*, 13 October 2008.

Colin James, 'A change of political generations', colinjames.co.nz, 7 October 2008.

Anne Mellbye, 'A brief history of the third way', *The Guardian*, 10 February 2003.

Paula Oliver, 'Parties chasing votes of expat Kiwis', *The New Zealand Herald*, 7 June 2008.

John Rougham, 'A word with Kate Sutton', *The New Zealand Herald*, 22 October 2008.

4. *A Rival*

'As it happened: New Zealand election 2014', *The New Zealand Herald*, 20 September 2014.

'Meeting Nikki Kaye: Young but a "tough cookie"', *The New Zealand Herald*, 16 February 2013.

'Pitch perfect: Winning strategies for women candidates', Barbara Lee Family Foundation, 8 November 2012, www.barbaraleefoundation.org/wp-content/uploads/BLFF-Lake-Pitch-Perfect-Wining-Strategies-for-Women-Candidates-11.08.12.pdf.

'Who knew tax reform was such a turn-on?' *The Sunday Star-Times*, 14 February 2010.

Jacinda Ardern, 'Stardust & substance', Auckland Writers Festival, 19 May 2019, vimeo.com/337427477.

Guyon Espiner, 'Jacinda Ardern: One to watch', *Noted*, 20 July 2012.

Patrick Gower, 'Young gun targets city seat', *The New Zealand Herald*, 23 November 2009.

Jonathan Milne, 'High noon for old blood', *The New Zealand Herald*, 1 November 2008.

Jane Phare, 'Battle looming in Auckland Central', *The New Zealand Herald*, 4 May 2008.

TVNZ, 'Political young guns on Breakfast', Clips, *Breakfast*, 2009–2012.

Simon Wilson, 'My dinner with Nikki & Jacinda', *Metro* (NZ), Issue 358, November 2011.

Audrey Young, 'Blue-green ambitions', *The New Zealand Herald*, 26 March 2010.

5.   *The Rise Begins*

'Bruiser Bennett and the beneficiaries', *Stuff*, 27 August 2009.

'Clarke Gayford reveals his first date with Prime Minister Jacinda Ardern', *New Zealand Woman's Weekly*, 25 September 2018.

'David Shearer's dead snapper stunt', *Stuff*, 20 August 2013.

'Is romance blossoming for MP?' *The New Zealand Herald*, 15 September 2014.

'Labour leader David Shearer steps down', *The New Zealand Herald*, 22 August 2013.

'The Michelle Hewitson interview: Jacinda Ardern', *The New Zealand Herald*, 26 April 2014.

'Wintec Press Club: Jacinda Ardern edition', *Quote Unquote* (blog), 26 May 2017.

Jacinda Ardern, 'Stardust & substance', Auckland Writers Festival, 19 May 2019, vimeo.com/337427477.

Emma Clifton, 'Labour's Jacinda Ardern reveals why she doesn't want to be prime minister', *Next*, 15 June 2017.

Jane Clifton, 'Annette King – and Jacinda Ardern – deserved better than this', *Noted*, 1 March 2017.

Simon Collins, 'David Cunliffe: I'm sorry for being a man', *The New Zealand Herald*, 4 July 2014.

Simon Day, 'Out with the old, in with the new: Robertson', *Waikato Times*, 20 October 2014.

John Key, Resignation speech, 5 December 2016.

Andrew Little, Facebook post, 1 March 2017.

Jo Moir, 'Ardern climbs Labour ladder', *Stuff*, 8 October 2012.

Fran O'Sullivan, 'Jacinda Ardern needs to put in the hard yards', *The New Zealand Herald*, 4 March 2017.

Vernon Small, 'Annette King's move from defiance to acceptance boosts Labour's chances in September', *Stuff*, 1 March 2017.

Julia Llewellyn Smith, 'Meet New Zealand's "First Bloke"; When the country's PM, Jacinda Ardern, gives birth next month, her partner Clarke will be taking on stay-at-home-dad duties', *The Daily Telegraph* (UK), 1 May 2018.

Claire Trevett, 'Ardern romps home in boring by-election', *The New Zealand Herald*, 25 February 2017.

Claire Trevett, 'Labour MP Jacinda Ardern wants to stand in David Shearer's Mt Albert electorate', *The New Zealand Herald*, 14 December 2016.

Tracy Watkins, '"I don't want to be prime minister" – Jacinda Ardern', *Stuff*, 28 November 2015.

6.   *The Press Conference*

'Andrew Little's full statement on resignation', *The New Zealand Herald*, 1 August 2017.

AAP, 'Jacinda Ardern rejected Labour leadership "seven times"', *The New Zealand Herald*, 27 September 2017.

Eugene Bingham and Paula Penfold, 'A *Stuff* circuit interview: The demise and rise of Andrew Little', *Stuff*, December 2017.

Mei Heron (@meiheron), Twitter post, 1 August 2017.

Toby Manhire, 'Poll rewards Turei's welfare bombshell but Labour dives deeper into the abyss', *The Spinoff*, 30 July 2017.

Claire Trevett, 'Leaders unplugged: Labour Party Jacinda Ardern', *The New Zealand Herald*, 12 August 2017.

7.   *The First 72 Hours*

'Greens co-leader Metiria Turei's benefit history investigated', *RNZ*, 26 July 2017.

'Paddy Gower receives gift from Gerry Brownlee', *The New Zealand Herald*, 7 August 2017.

'Should Metiria Turei stand down as co-leader of the Greens?', *The AM Show*, MediaWork New Zealand, Auckland, 3 August 2017.

'Timeline: Green Party co-leader Metiria Turei's downfall', *RNZ*, 9 August 2017.

Henry Cooke, 'Recap: Labour unveils election campaign slogan, as it says Turei would never have made it with them', *Stuff*, 4 August 2017.

Henry Cooke, 'When Jacinda Ardern knifed Metiria Turei she changed the election for good', *Stuff*, 21 September 2017.

Mei Heron, 'Greens' Turei reveals struggles at family policy launch', *RNZ*, 16 July 2017.

Bernard Hickey, 'Labour and Green parties sign first ever Memorandum of Understanding to work together to change government', *interest.co.nz*, 31 May 2016.

Stacey Kirk, 'Metiria Turei's electoral admission "not good" – Labour', *Stuff*, 4 August 2017.

Jenna Lynch, 'More questions raised about Metiria Turei's living situation', *Newshub*, 3 August 2017.

Toby Manhire, 'Poll rewards Turei's welfare bombshell but Labour dives deeper into the abyss', *The Spinoff*, 30 July 2017.

Tracy Watkins, 'Jacinda Ardern has been Labour leader for 24 hours – so what's changed?' *Stuff*, 2 August 2017.

Tracy Watkins, 'Jacinda Ardern shows her steel in week one', *Stuff*, 5 August 2017.

8. The Campaign

'Ardern attends grandmother's funeral', *Otago Daily Times*, 22 September 2017.

'Barnaby Joyce to face by-election after High Court ruling; Roberts, Nash also booted out of parliament', *ABC News*, 30 September 2017.

'Broadsides: Should NZ have a capital gains tax?', *The New Zealand Herald*, 20 July 2011.

'Watch the full Newshub Leaders Debate', *Newshub*, 4 September 2017.

Jacinda Ardern, Announcement at Hillmorton High, Christchurch, 8 September 2017.

Jacinda Ardern, Facebook Live Q&A, 3 August 2017.

Jacinda Ardern, Facebook Live Q&A, 9 August 2017.

Jacinda Ardern, 'Stardust & substance', Auckland Writers Festival, 19 May 2019, vimeo.com/337427477.

Jacinda Ardern (@jacindaardern), Twitter post, 15 August 2017.

Julie Bishop, Press conference, Parliament House, Canberra, 16 August 2017.

Steve Braunias, 'On the campaign trail with Jacinda Ardern', *The New Zealand Herald*, 9 September 2017.

Lloyd Burr, 'Newshub-Reid Research poll: NZ First overtakes Greens as third biggest party', *Newshub*, 21 January 2020.

Michael Daly, 'Steven Joyce sticks to $11.7 billion hole in government budget', *Stuff*, 23 November 2017.

Stephen Levine (ed.), *Stardust and Substance: The New Zealand General Election of 2017*, Victoria University Press, Wellington, 2018.

Toby Manhire, 'The final poll, and one that befits a pulsating campaign', *The Spinoff*, 21 September 2017.

Toby Manhire, 'Labour soaks up the Town Hall rapture as Ardern goes nuclear on climate', *The Spinoff*, 20 August 2017.

Toby Manhire, 'Of tax U-turns, captain's calls and clusterfucks', *The Spinoff*, 14 September 2017.

Eleanor Ainge Roy, 'New Zealand election: Jacinda Ardern vows to decriminalise abortion', *The Guardian*, 5 September 2017.

Andrew Taylor, 'Jacinda Ardern as prime minister makes things awkward for Australian foreign minister', *Stuff*, 20 September 2017.

Tracy Watkins, 'King gives parting blessing for Ardern', *The Press*, 11 August 2017.

9. Election Night

'Watch: "Next question!" – belligerent Winston Peters has press pack in stitches after shutting down Aussie reporter', *1 News*, 27 September.

'"We could and should be doing far better" – NZ First chooses Labour', *RNZ*, YouTube video, 19 October 2017.

'Who's who in parliament?', New Zealand Parliament/Pāremata Aotearoa, 8 February 2018.

Anna Bracewell-Worrall, 'Jacinda Ardern full speech: Let's keep doing this', *Newshub*, 23 September 2017.

Madeleine Chapman, 'Winston Peters is the hot girl on campus: A sexy guide to MMP relationships', *The Spinoff*, 7 October 2017.

Henry Cooke, 'A brief history of Winston Raymond Peters', *Stuff*, 21 June 2018.

Brad Flahive, 'Jacinda thanks the voters before tucking into a sausage', *Stuff*, 23 September 2017.

John Harvey and Brent Edwards, *Annette King: The Authorised Biography*, Upstart Press, Auckland, 2019.

Katie Kenny, 'Live: The day after the election', *Stuff*, 24 September 2017.

Toby Manhire, '7.17pm: *The Spinoff*'s rash call of the election result based on 5% of vote counted', *The Spinoff*, 23 September 2017.

Toby Manhire, '11.00pm: Bill English wins. Winston Peter loses. And Winston Peters wins', *The Spinoff*, 23 September 2017.

10. The Diplomat

'Conversations: Pania Newton', *E-Tangata*, 5 May 2019.

'Jacinda Ardern meets with Malcolm Turnbull, rebuffs Manus Island offer', *The New Zealand Herald*, 5 November 2017.

'"This will be a government of change" Jacinda Ardern tells caucus', *The New Zealand Herald*, 20 October 2017.

'Trump thought Jacinda Ardern was Justin Trudeau's wife – Tom Sainsbury', *Newshub*, 19 November 2017.

'"A wonderful new neighbourhood": Fletcher Residential buys "sacred" Māori land at Ihumatao in south Auckland', *Stuff*, 28 December 2016.

Jacinda Ardern, 'Prime Minister's Waitangi powhiri speech', Beehive.govt.nz, 5 February 2018.

Maria Bargh and Andrew Geddes, 'What now for the Māori seats?' *The Spinoff*, 15 August 2018.

Ryan Bridge, 'Jacinda Ardern's 5 day visit to Waitangi', *Your Sunday*, RadioLIVE, 28 January 2018, www.magic.co.nz/home/archivedtalk/audio/2018/01/your-sunday-in-case-you-missed-it.html.

Mikaela Collins, 'Cabinet ministers to cook food for public at Prime Minister's Waitangi Day Breakfast', *The New Zealand Herald*, 24 January 2018.

Peter de Graaf, 'Prime Minister Jacinda Ardern breaks new ground at Waitangi', *The New Zealand Herald*, 3 February 2018.

Wena Harawira, 'Sacrifices but no reward', *E-Tangata*, 3 October 2015.

Leonie Hayden, 'Let's not forget that Māori women had the vote long before Europeans arrived', *The Spinoff*, 29 September 2018.

Leonie Hayden (@sharkpatu), Twitter post, 6 February 2018.

Veranoa Hetet, 'They're not all korowai: A master weaver on how to identify Māori garments', *The Spinoff*, 26 April 2018.

Annabelle Lee, 'Why Jacinda Ardern's decision to spend five days at Waitangi is a really big deal', *The Spinoff*, 24 January 2018.

Peter Meihana, 'Teaching NZ history could be the most important nation-building project of a generation', *Stuff*, 20 September 2019.

Ministry for Culture and Heritage, 'Waitangi Day', New Zealand History (website), last modified 5 August 2014, nzhistory.govt.nz/politics/treaty/waitangi-day/waitangi-day-1990s.

Jo Moir, 'The prime minister's five days at Waitangi has gone off with a barely a protest', *Stuff*, 6 February 2018.

New Zealand Labour Party, 'Taihoa at Ihumaao says Labour', *Scoop*, 27 August 2015.

Parliamentary Library, 'The origins of the Māori seats', Parliamentary Library Research Paper, 9 November 2003.

Richard Prebble, 'Jacinda Ardern will regret this coalition of losers', *The New Zealand Herald*, 20 October 2017.

Eleanor Ainge Roy, 'Jacinda Ardern to meet Donald Trump for first formal meeting', *The Guardian*, 17 September 2019.

Eleanor Ainge Roy, 'Jacinda Ardern wears Māori cloak to Buckingham Palace', *The Guardian*, 20 April 2018.

Shane Te Pou, 'Māori don't need Chris Hipkins to tell us what's best for our mokopuna', *The Spinoff*, 27 August 2018.

11. *Working Motherhood*

'Flowers for Prime Minister Jacinda Ardern from Saudi Arabia "too big" for hospital room', *The New Zealand Herald*, 23 June 2018.

'Here comes the baby: Prime Minister Jacinda Ardern in labour, at Auckland Hospital with partner Clarke Gayford', *The New Zealand Herald*, 21 June 2018.

'Jacinda Ardern's reaction to seeing Neve at the UN and why it's significant she's there', *Stuff*, 26 September 2018.

'Jacinda's baby: Kiwi midwife explains how long we'll have to wait', *The New Zealand Herald*, 21 June 2018.

'Live blog: Jacinda Ardern and Clarke Gayford create entirely new human', *The Spinoff*, 24 June 2018.

'Prime Minister Jacinda Ardern gives birth to baby girl, with Clarke Gayford alongside, at Auckland Hospital', *The New Zealand Herald*, 22 June 2018.

'Special delivery: The route Prime Minister Jacinda Ardern took to hospital', *The New Zealand Herald*, 21 June 2018.

Charles Anderson, 'Jacinda Ardern #babywatch sends New Zealand media gaga', *The Guardian*, 21 June 2018.

Charles Anderson, 'New Zealand PM Jacinda Ardern goes into hospital to give birth', *The Guardian*, 21 June 2018.

Charles Anderson, 'New Zealand's Jacinda Ardern welcomes baby girl "to our village"', *The Guardian*, 21 June 2018.

Jacinda Ardern, 'Welcome to our village wee one', Instagram post, 21 June 2018, www.instagram.com/p/BkRrm87F8Cb.

Madeleine Chapman, 'Waiting for Neve Te Aroha: Inside the media room at Auckland Hospital', *The Spinoff*, 25 June 2018.

Emma Clifton, 'Jacinda Ardern: Our new life with Neve', *Now to Love*, 30 January 2019.

Helena de Bertodano, 'The Magazine Interview: Jacinda Ardern, the pregnant prime minister of New Zealand, on her work/life balance and meeting Barack Obama', *The Times* (UK), 8 April 2018.

Clark Gayford (@NZClarke), 'Because everyone on twitter's been asking', Twitter post, 25 September 2018, twitter.com/NZClarke/status/1044252770268672000.

Leith Huffadine, 'Google plays tribute to PM Jacinda Ardern's baby', *Stuff*, 22 June 2018.

Emma Hurley, 'Timelines: How Prime Minister Jacinda Ardern's pregnancy unfolded', *Newshub*, 21 June 2018.

M. Ilyas Khan, 'Ardern and Bhutto: Two different pregnancies in power', *BBC News*, 21 June 2018.

Kim Knight, 'Exclusive: Labour's Jacinda Ardern and partner Clarke Gayford', *The New Zealand Herald*, 19 August 2017.

Amy Maas, 'Confession: "I killed Prime Minister Jacinda Ardern's cat, Paddles"', *Stuff*, 10 July 2019.

Sarah McMullan, 'The perfect playlist to welcome Jacinda Ardern's baby', *Stuff*, 21 June 2018.

Eleanor Ainge Roy, 'Babies in the Beehive: The man behind New Zealand's child-friendly parliament', *The Guardian*, 31 August 2019.

12. Helen and Jacinda

'Abortion law reform just leapt its first hurdle. Here's what the MPs said,' *The Spinoff*, 9 August 2019.

'Labour president Nigel Haworth resigns as Jacinda Ardern issues apology', *The Spinoff*, 11 September 2019.

'NZ Politics daily: Jacinda Ardern and the "pretty little thing" debate', *NBR*, 3 September 2015.

'Storm erupts over Gareth Morgan's "lipstick on a pig" tweet', *The New Zealand Herald*, 21 August 2017.

'Winston Peters calls Labour turmoil a "disgraceful orgy of speculation"', *Newstalk ZB*, 16 September 2019.

Jacinda Ardern, 'Breaking silence', *Metro* (NZ), Issue 398, November 2015.

Hilary Barry (@Hilary_Barry), 'Panelist describes @jacindaardern's skill in politics', Twitter post, 26 August 2015, twitter.com/Hilary_Barry/status/636273505554665472.

Anna Bracewell-Worrall, 'Jacinda Ardern: It is "totally unacceptable" to ask women about baby plans', *Newshub*, 2 July 2017.

Alex Casey, 'A Labour volunteer alleged a violent sexual assault by a Labour staffer. This is her story', *The Spinoff*, 9 September 2019.

Brian Edwards, *Helen Clark: Portrait of a Prime Minister*, Politico's Publishing, London, 2002.

Matthew Hooton, 'Pretty bloody stupid', *Metro* (NZ), Issue 397, October 2015.

Alison Mau, 'Alison Mau: Labour sex assault group's masterful moves – and what they want', *Stuff*, 15 September 2019.

Gareth Morgan (@garethmorgannz), 'Sure but it's pathetic isn't it?', Twitter post, 20 August 2017, twitter.com/garethmorgannz/status/899178564989329409.

New Zealand Labour Party, '#LIVE Post-Cabinet press conference 16 September', Facebook post, 15 September 2019, www.facebook.com/NZLabourParty/videos/2459299004328695.

Tova O'Brien, 'Complainant "shocked" at new Labour representative after Nigel Hawthorn's resignation', *Newshub*, 12 September 2019.

Jane Patterson, 'Sexual assault allegations against ex-Labour staffer "not established"', *RNZ*, 18 December 2019.

Zane Small, 'PM Jacinda Ardern gives "timeline" of events around
    Labour sexual assault claims', *Newshub*, 12 September 2019.
Andrea Vance, 'Staffer at centre of Labour abuse claims has resigned',
    Stuff, 12 September 2019.

13. *Christchurch, 15 March 2019*

'Christchurch mosque shootings: Police reveal how they caught the
    alleged gunman', *The New Zealand Herald*, 18 March 2019.
'Christchurch shootings: Stories of heroism emerge from attacks',
    BBC News, 17 March 2019.
'Christchurch shootings: Vigils around NZ – live updates', *Stuff*,
    18 March 2019.
'The end of our innocence', *Stuff*, 15 March 2019.
'"I don't know how many people died" – witnesses of Christchurch
    mosque shooting', *1 News*, 15 March 2019.
Natalie Akoorie, 'Live: Christchurch mosque shootings: Friday's
    national day of reflection – the call to prayer, mosques open
    doors', *The New Zealand Herald*, 22 March 2019.
Jacinda Ardern, '#LIVE update on Christchurch', Facebook
    post, 14 March 2019, www.facebook.com/jacindaardern/
    videos/311920353011570.
Jacinda Ardern, '#LIVE press conference', Facebook post,
    15 March 2019, www.facebook.com/jacindaardern/
    videos/853025415038912.
Jacinda Ardern, 'Nationwide reflection for victims of Christchurch
    terror attack announced', Beehive.govt.nz, 21 March 2019.
Jacinda Ardern, Statement on Christchurch mass shooting, 3.30pm,
    16 March 2019.
Jacinda Ardern and Stuart Nash, 'New Zealand bans military
    style semi-automatics and assault rifles', Beehive.govt.nz,
    21 March 2019.
Kurt Bayer, 'Firearms register announced as part of Government's
    second tranche of gun law reforms', *The New Zealand Herald*,
    14 March 2019.
Mohammed bin Rashid Al Maktoum (@HHShkMohd),
    'New Zealand today fell silent in honor of the mosque
    attack's martyrs', Twitter post, twitter.com/HHShkMohd/
    status/1109124817888915461.

John Campbell (@JohnJCampbell), 'Jay Waaka, one of the road crew', Twitter post, 18 March 2019, twitter.com/JohnJCampbell/status/1107348003025637377.

Madeleine Chapman, 'Jacinda Ardern, after Christchurch', *The Spinoff*, 22 March 2019.

Gamal Fouda, '"Hate will be undone, and love will redeem us": Imam Fouda, a week on', *The Spinoff*, 22 March 2019.

The Guardian, 'Thousands gather in Christchurch to mark one week on from deadly Mosque shootings – watch live', YouTube video, 21 March 2019, www.youtube.com/watch?v=MrOPS8XIt0Y.

Shaiq Hussain and Pamela Constable, 'Pakistan vows to honour "martyr" who tried to stop Christchurch mosque gunman', *Stuff*, 18 March 2019.

Nikki Macdonald, 'Alleged shooter approached Linwood mosque from wrong side, giving those inside time to hide, survivor says', *Stuff*, 18 March 2019.

Toby Manhire, 'Jacinda Ardern: "Very little of what I have done has been deliberate. It's intuitive"', *The Guardian*, 6 April 2019.

Thomas Mead, '"I don't hate him, I love him": Widower forgives Christchurch gunman who killed his wife', *Newshub*, 17 March 2019.

Newshub, 'New Zealand Prime Minister's meeting with Christchurch Muslim community', YouTube video, 21 March 2019, www.youtube.com/watch?v=L9OdUnyHCdg.

Kate Newton, 'New Zealand's darkest day: A timelines of the Christchurch terror attacks', *RNZ*, 21 March 2019.

The New Zealand Herald, 'Jacinda Ardern visits Cashmere High School in Christchurch', Facebook post, 19 March 2019, www.facebook.com/nzherald.co.nz/videos/638626069914560.

Mick O'Reilly and Logan Fish, 'Abdul Aziz Wahabzadah, a hero from Christchurch attacks recounts the day', *Gulf News*, 13 June 2019.

Adele Redmond, Dominic Harris, Oliver Lewis and Harrison Christian, 'Heroic worshippers tried to stop terror attacks at Christchurch mosques', *Stuff*, 16 March 2019.

Matthew Theunissen, 'Abdul Aziz: Saved lives by running at gunman in Mosque', *RNZ*, 17 March 2019.

Lynley Ward, "'I'm so grateful I was part of this kind gesture": Naima Abdi on the hug with Jacinda Ardern that made history', *Now to Love*, 9 April 2019.

14. *Highs and Lows*

'\$320m package to tackle family and sexual violence "a good foundation"', *RNZ*, 20 May 2019.

'The Christchurch Call: Full text' *The Spinoff*, 16 May 2019.

'Editorial: Kiwi build solid base for future at last', *The New Zealand Herald*, 21 November 2012.

'Election 2014: Labour promises 100,000 more affordable homes', *The New Zealand Herald*, 27 August 2014.

'Fiona Ross appointed Director, Family Violence and Sexual Violence Joint Venture', New Zealand Family Violence Clearinghouse, 3 April 2019, nzfvc.org.nz/news/ fiona-ross-appointed-director-family-violence-and-sexual-violence-joint-venture.

'Median price – REINZ', Interest.co.nz, no date, www.interest. co.nz/charts/real-estate/median-price-reinz.

'New Zealand to head five-country climate trade agreement talks – Jacinda Ardern', *RNZ*, 26 September 2019.

'PM: Labour's KiwiBuild housing policy "dishonest"', *The New Zealand Herald*, 25 January 2013.

'Two vents on the Wellbeing Budget', *RNZ*, 31 May 2019.

'What exactly is a wellbeing budget?', *RNZ*, 3 May 2019.

'World's greatest leaders', *Fortune*, 19 April 2019.

Jacinda Ardern, 'New Zealand and France seek to end use of social media for acts of terrorism', press release, 24 April 2019.

Jacinda Ardern, New Zealand National Statement to United Nations General Assembly, 28 September 2018.

John Anthony, 'NZ First put an end to capital gains tax, Shane Jones claims in post-Budget speech', *Stuff*, 31 May 2019.

Kurt Bayer, 'Christchurch teen arrested for objectionable material after mosque attacks', *The New Zealand Herald*, 29 March 2019.

Madeleine Chapman, 'A special episode of The Block NZ: Kiwibuild edition', *The Spinoff*, 2 September 2018.

Henry Cooke, 'Capital gains tax: Jacinda Ardern took a lifeboat off a ship she could have saved', *Stuff*, 21 April 2019.

Henry Cooke, 'Government must be bold enough to bring
in capital gains tax, Green leader James Shaw says', *Stuff*,
12 February 2019.

Henry Cooke, 'How KiwiBuild fell down, and whether anything
can be saved from the wreckage', *Stuff*, 21 June 2019.

Henry Cooke, 'Refugee quota lifting to 1500 by 2020', *Stuff*,
19 September 2018.

Michael Daly, 'Winston Peters casts doubt on rise in refugee quota',
Stuff, 4 September 2018.

Guyon Espiner, 'Jacinda Ardern: One to watch', *Noted*, 20 July 2012.

Anne Gibson, 'Phil Twyford reveals $2b KiwiBuild housing
scheme', *The New Zealand Herald*, 25 October 2017.

Charlotte Graham-McLay, 'New Zealand's Next Liberal Milestone:
A Budget Guided by "Well-Being"', *The New York Times*,
22 May 2019.

Calum Henderson, 'History in pictures – the 2016 Waitangi Dildo
Incident', *The Spinoff*, 5 February 2016.

Helena Horton, '"No one marched when I was elected": New
Zealand Prime Minister's biting response to Donald Trump', *The
Telegraph* (UK), 16 November 2017.

Nicholas Jones, 'Housing constrained by lack of builders, lending:
Treasury', *The New Zealand Herald*, 14 December 2017.

The Late Show with Stephen Colbert, CBS, 27 September 2018.

Amelia Lester, 'New Zealand's prime minister, Jacinda Ardern,
is young, forward-looking, and unabashedly liberal – call her
the anti-Trump', *Vogue* (USA), 14 February 2018. Madeleine
Chapman, 'A step-by-step guide to writing a Jacinda Ardern profile', *The Spinoff*, 15 February 2018.

Jan Logie, 'New steps in improving our response to family violence',
beehive.govt.nz, 25 March 2019.

Tony Manhire, 'John Oliver's weird fixation on New Zealand: The
complete works (so far)', *The Spinoff*, 19 February 2019.

Craig McCulloch, 'Christchurch Call: Tech companies overhaul
organisation to stop terrorists online', *RNZ*, 24 September 2019.

Ministry of Foreign Affairs and Trade, The Christchurch Call (website), no date, www.christchurchcall.com.

Laine Moger, 'Mental health services gets $6M funding boost, prime
minister announces', *Stuff*, 8 September 2019.

Jo Moir, 'Help for first home buyers as war for votes heats up', *Stuff*, 10 September 2017.

Winston Peters (@winstonpeters), 'No capital gains tax', Twitter post, 17 April 2019, twitter.com/winstonpeters/status/1118343994038050816.

Anjum Rahman, 'We warned you, we begged, we pleaded and now we demand accountability', *The Spinoff*, 17 March 2019.

Eleanor Ainge Roy, 'New Zealand's world-first "wellbeing" budget to focus on poverty and mental health', *The Guardian*, 14 May 2019.

Brian Rudman, 'Labour needs to build on its housing policy', *The New Zealand Herald*, 30 January 2013.

Sam Sachdeva, 'Ardern on Trump, and adjusting to life at the top', *Newsroom*, 16 November 2017.

James Shaw (@jamespeshaw), 'Disappointed!!!', Twitter post, 17 April 2019, twitter.com/jamespeshaw/status/1118358549996998657.

Vernon Small, 'The government's handling of housing crisis giving Labour something to celebrate', *Stuff*, 7 July 2016.

Cass R. Sunstein, 'New Zealand's "well-being" budget is worth copying', *Bloomberg*, 7 June 2019.

Tax Working Group, *Future of Tax: Final Report Volume 1 – Recommendations*, Tax Working Group, Wellington, 2019.

Tax Working Group, 'What is the Tax Working Group?', Tax Working Group (website), no date, taxworkinggroup.govt.nz/what-is-the-tax-working-group.

Rino Tirikatene, 'What does a Wellbeing Budget in action look like?', *Stuff*, 13 June 2019.

Laura Walters and Jo Moir, 'Government's three strikes repeal killed by NZ First', *Stuff*, 11 June 2018.

Lally Weymouth, 'Jacinda Ardern on how to respond to gun violence', *Stuff*, 13 September 2019.

Olivia Wills, 'The Wellbeing Budget and what it means for mental health', *The Spinoff*, 31 May 2019.

Kim Willsher, 'Leaders and tech firms pledge to tackle extremist violence online', *The Guardian*, 16 May 2019.

Audrey Young, 'Jacinda Ardern on her international profile ... it's not about me, it's about New Zealand', *The New Zealand Herald*, 14 September 2019.

15. A New Kind of Leader

'Fiona Ross appointed Director, Family Violence and Sexual Violence Joint Venture', New Zealand Family Violence Clearinghouse, 3 April 2019, nzfvc.org.nz/news/fiona-ross-appointed-director-family-violence-and-sexual-violence-joint-venture.

'Labour's Jacinda Ardern reveals why politics feels so personal', *Now to Love*, 31 July 2017.

Anna Bracewell-Worrall, 'Revealed: The MPs who have smoked marijuana', *Newshub*, 7 May 2019.

Helena de Bertodano, 'The Magazine Interview: Jacinda Ardern, the pregnant prime minister of New Zealand, on her work/life balance and meeting Barack Obama', *The Times* (UK), 8 April 2018.

Michael Field, 'More than neighbours', *Stuff*, 8 August 2010.

Colin James, 'The last Labour prime minister: The first New Zealand Prime Minister', colinjames.co.nz, 3 November 2012.

Ministry for Culture and Heritage, 'Labour government cancels Springbok rugby tour', New Zealand History (website), last modified 9 December 2016, nzhistory.govt.nz/page/labour-government-postpones-springbok-tour.

James Mitchell, 'Immigration and national identity in 1970s New Zealand', PhD thesis, University of Otago, 2003.

Acknowledgements

I'm grateful to Sophy Williams, Kirstie Innes-Will and everyone at Nero for driving this project and pushing it to the finish.

I'm grateful to the dozens of politicians, reporters, staffers and friends of Jacinda who spoke to me. Thank you for building the foundations of this book.

I'm grateful to the dozens more who weren't officially interviewed but who gleefully shared unsubstantiated rumours: thank you for the entertainment.

I'm grateful and I'm sorry to every journalist who immediately searched for their name in the index but only found it in the source list.

I'm grateful to Polly Pope and Phil Pinner, *The Spinoff* and Simon Chesterman for providing spaces for me to write and never questioning my work and sleep habits.

I'm grateful to Christel Chapman and Leonie Hayden for reading early chapters and giving invaluable feedback.

I'm grateful to Toby Manhire for reading early chapters and spending the past four years patiently explaining basic political concepts to me.

I'm grateful to Duncan Greive for opening so many doors, including the very first one in my writing career.

I'm grateful to Amber Easby for lending me her mind whenever I lose mine.

I'm grateful to Ashleigh Bogle, Alex Casey and Tina Tiller for always knowing when to laugh at my pain and when to provide relief.

I'm grateful to my extended family for being the massive support network that every writer dreams of.

I'm grateful to my siblings for always encouraging me to do the things that scare me.

And as always, I'm grateful to my parents for everything else.

Index

About the Author

Madeleine Chapman is a New Zealand writer of Sāmoan, Chinese and Tuvaluan descent. She is the co-author of Steven Adams' bestselling autobiography *My Life, My Fight* (Penguin Random House NZ) and was a senior writer at *The Spinoff* until 2020. Chapman was named the 2018 Young Business Journalist of the Year and the 2019 Humour Opinion Writer of the Year. She lives in Porirua with her parents.